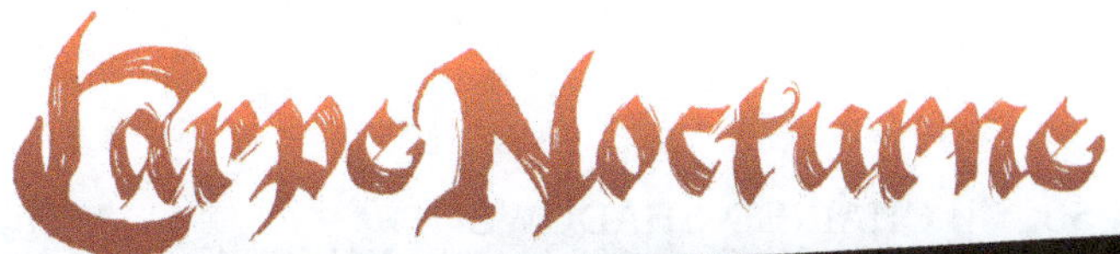

OTHER THAN THE NORM

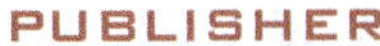

VOLUME XII
SPRING 2017

PUBLISHER
Visual Adjectives

EDITOR-IN-CHIEF
Paula Andrews Powles

MANAGING EDITOR
Michael Jack

ASSISTANT MANAGING EDITOR
Zahara's Tangled Web

CONTRIBUTORS
Alexis Marshall
Asylum Attendant
Bryan Akerley
Chirality
Cosmic
Dawn Wood
Digital Racket
Fairlyinnocent
Hyde Falkenstine
Isolde de Mortimer
James Donnelly
Jesse Orr
Jezibell Anat
John David Howard
Joseph Zuchowski
Kathleen Sharkey
Misty Pendragon
Nicola Thompson
Noel Rivera
Samm Sanity
Sergio Manghina
Sonnett57
Trixxi Divine
XXX Zombieboy XXX
Zahara's Tangled Web
Zannie Campbell

Subscribe

Never miss an issue.
Have Carpe Nocturne Magazine delivered directly
to your front door or office four times a year.
subscribe@carpenocturne.net

Carpe Nocturne Magazine is available in
Digital and Print editions!
Available in print at Amazon.com, BarnesandNoble.com
and other retailers.

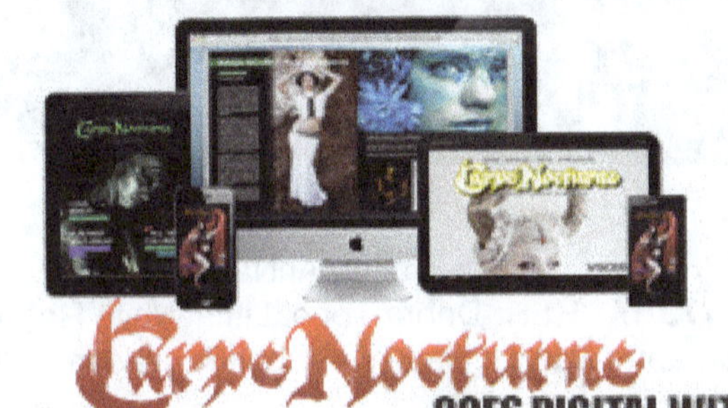

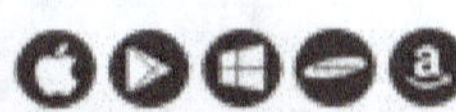
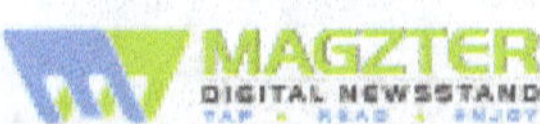

*Carpe Nocturne Magazine Volume XII · Spring 2017
is a publication of Visual Adjectives, LLC
and published four times a year.
All reviews and coverage expressed in this publication
are the opinions of the writer and/or those being interviewed
and may not be shared by Visual Adjectives.
Copyright © 2017 by Visual Adjectives, LLC.
All rights reserved.
14280 Military Trail, #7501, Delray Beach, FL 33482, USA.
No work may be copied or reproduced without
the express permission of the editor or publisher.*

Correspondences should be addressed to:

*CARPE NOCTURNE MAGAZINE
14280 Military Trail, #7501
Delray Beach, FL 33482 USA*

*E-mail: editor@carpenocturnemagazine.com
www.carpenocturnemagazine.com
p: 561-809-3834 f: 904-701-6272*

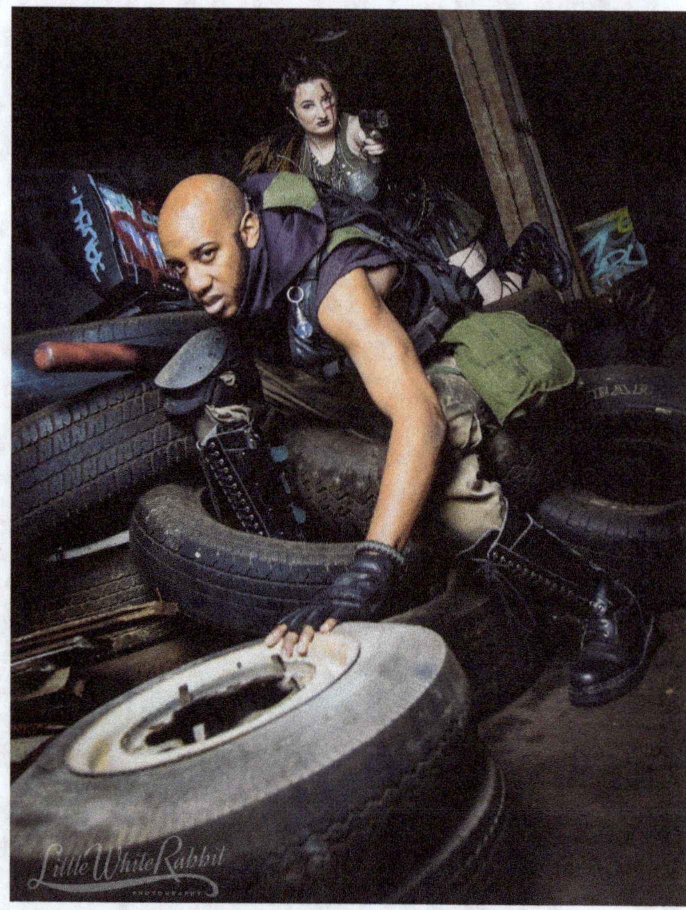

On the Cover
MODEL: Tony Ballard-Smoot, AnNalise Rose
PHOTOGRAPHER: Debra Tope, Little White Rabbit
Photography, www.LittleWhiteRabbitPhoto.com
PAGE: 35

COLUMNS
9 | THE ALCHEMISTS' CLOSET
Bee Stings and Bug Bites

13 | BLOODY MARVELOUS
Bloody Hell Spock!

43 | DARK CORNERS
*From the Darkest Corners of Our Imaginations,
Soar the Most Beautiful Creations*

79 | SEATTLE SOUNDS
Sköld Seattle Show 2016

44 | FICTIONAL ANECDOTES
Unknown Cargo

52 | TORN CURTAIN
The Lost Moment

56 | LOST FAVORITES
*Spacehunter: Adventures in the Forbidden
Zone*

50 | CHAINED SHADOWS
A Gathering of Things in Noir Style

53 | DEARLY DEPARTED
Chuck Berry | George Michael

49 | AWESOME TRACKS
Dickie Goodman

58 | SOUNDS OF THE LIVING DEAD
Music Reviews

54 | HOW NOT TO GET EATEN
zzzzzzzzzzSLEEPzzzzzzzzzz

47 | GOTHIC BREWER'S GUIDE
Because Black is a Thirsty Color

42 | THE VOICE OF THE NEW DARK CULTURE
Dating 101

ART
4 | LAURA ZAKROFF
Casting and Artistic Spell

ENTERTAINMENT
10 | GOTHIC COUNTRY
Ghost and Guns

12 | THE DIRTY SHOW
Raunchy and Naughty Splendor

FASHION
26 | CORSETS

28 | CYBERDOG
Futuristic Club Wear

20 | MINIMALISM AND MAKEUP

14 | RAZORCANDI
A Decade of Dark Beauty

21 | PAWSTAR

31 | VISCERAL ATTRACTIONS
Photography

FILM & LITERATURE
68 | SPLIT
Mad-Villainy

76 | 10 MOST DISTURBING FILMS

57 | NIGHTMARE WORLD
Volumes. 1 - 3

72 | KURT AMACKER
An Afternoon Interview

LIFE & STYLE
70 | BELLY DANCE GOALS

MUSIC
60 | VIKTORIA MODESTA
World's First Bionic Pop Star

59 | XE-NONE

63 | MICHALE GRAVES

65 | MIDNIGHT SYNDICATE

75 | BOTDF
The End of Blood on the Dance Floor

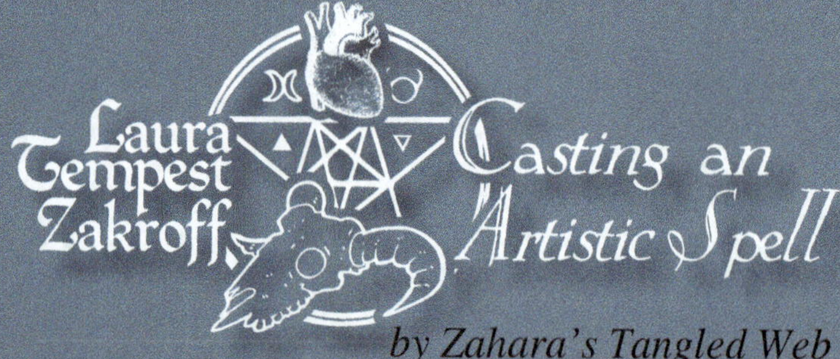

by Zahara's Tangled Web

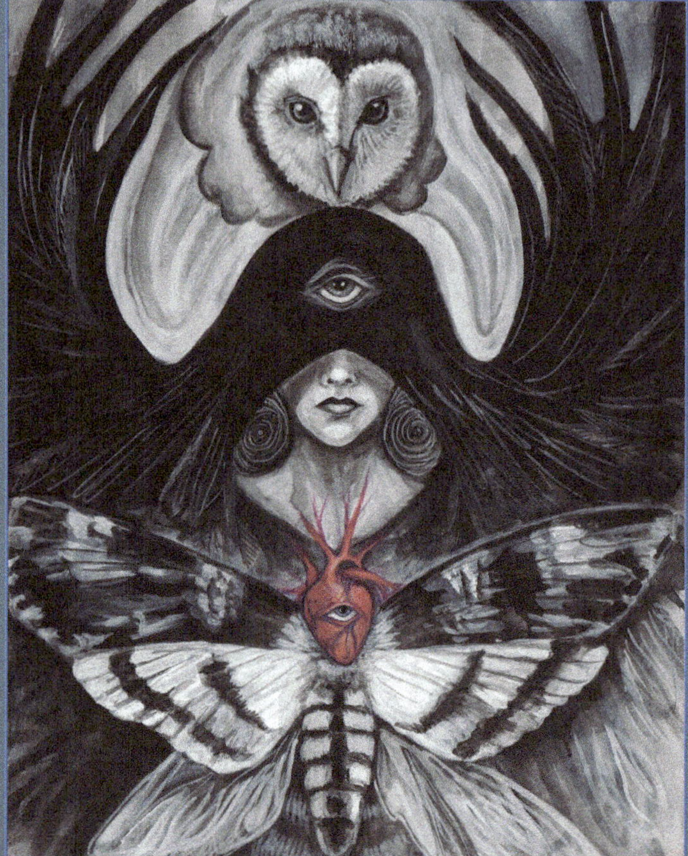

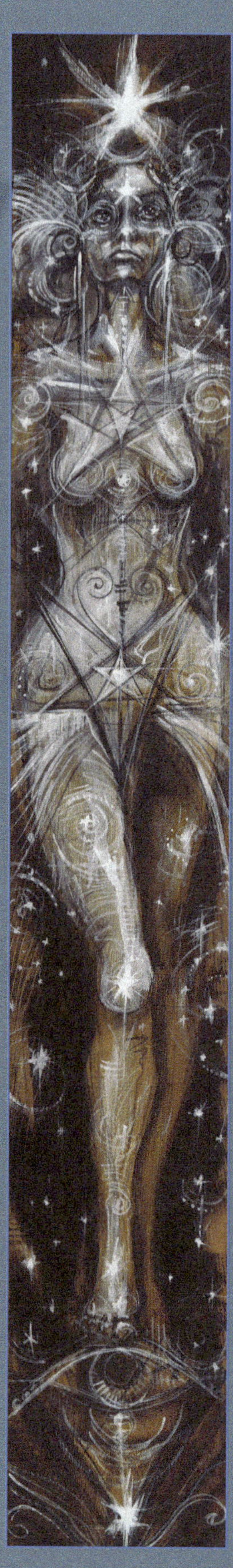

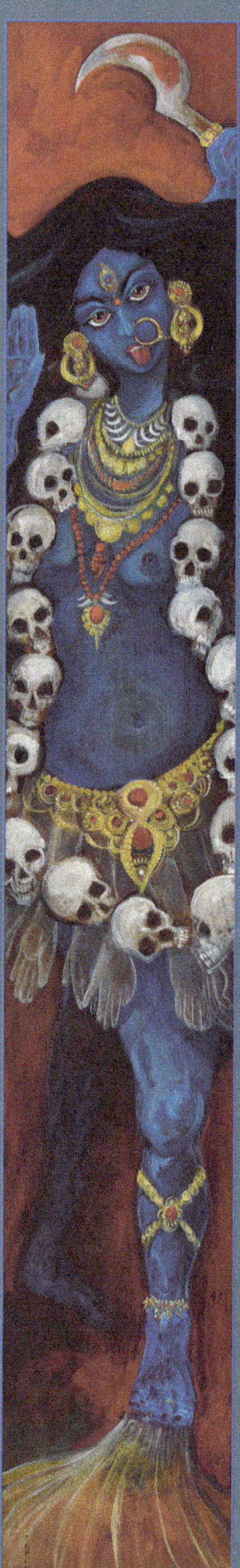

Scrolling through Facebook late one night in December, I noticed a post from Laura Tempest Zakroff (www.owlkeyme.com), describing her journey as an artist over the course of 2016. She was reflecting on how she spends her time and where her focus has shifted. Laura has a wide range of creative pursuits and manages to be successful in multiple arenas. She is known as a belly dancer, painter, writer, and much more… a true Renaissance woman. Residing with her musician husband in Seattle, Washington, Laura finds quite a bit of inspiration in the lush nature that surrounds her.

Laura earned her Bachelor of Fine Arts from the Rhode Island School of Design, and gained additional training from the Governor's School for the Arts (SC) and the Fleisher Art Memorial (PA). She's received awards and honors worldwide, and her work has appeared in several publications.

I first met Laura (known as Tempest in the belly dance world) in Louisville, KY over a decade ago. At the time, I only knew her as one of the vampy belly dancers on the "Gothic Bellydance" DVD. Over the years, I've enjoyed watching her evolve as a painter and reading her insightful belly dance blog posts at http://darklydramatic.blogspot.com. Gazing at some of her more recent paintings, it's clear Laura has a lot to say, whether it's using words or brush strokes.

Laura frequently paints whatever comes to her, weaving symbols and esoteric imagery into her paintings and designs. She describes her sketching/drawing style as very loose, with "forms created by building up many lines versus neat and precise - which inherently gives the art a sense of movement. My painting style balances detail and energetic strokes to create a sense of mystery and myth - often with layers of rich color." The subject matter is about myth, visions, stories, and dreams, as well as nature and organic shapes. It's easy to find the feminine divine in many of her paintings, sometimes leaving one feeling as though they've peered through a smoky veil connecting this world with other realms.

"I tend to work fairly fast - and I'm often working on several pieces at once. At least, in the sense that as one piece dries, I'm working on another panel. Timing though depends on the size of the painting, and how easily it comes along." Laura can finish some of her work in a single day, while others take longer. She's similar to other artists I've met over the years, in that some of her paintings get started, and are then put aside for a time (months or even years). "But most get finished within a day or two of when I start on them." This leads to a tremendous body of work, which is available online and in her festival booth at various conventions across the US.

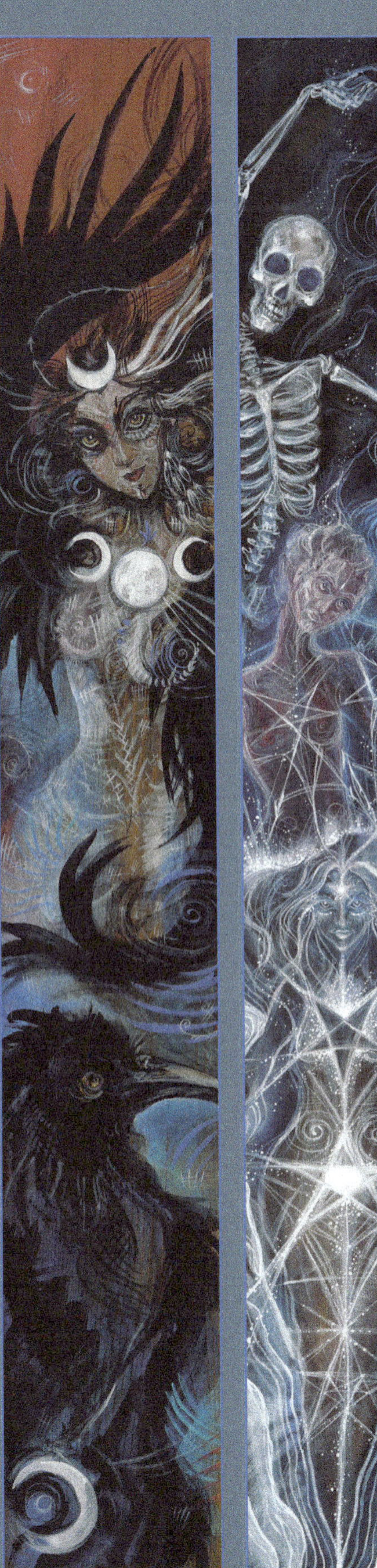

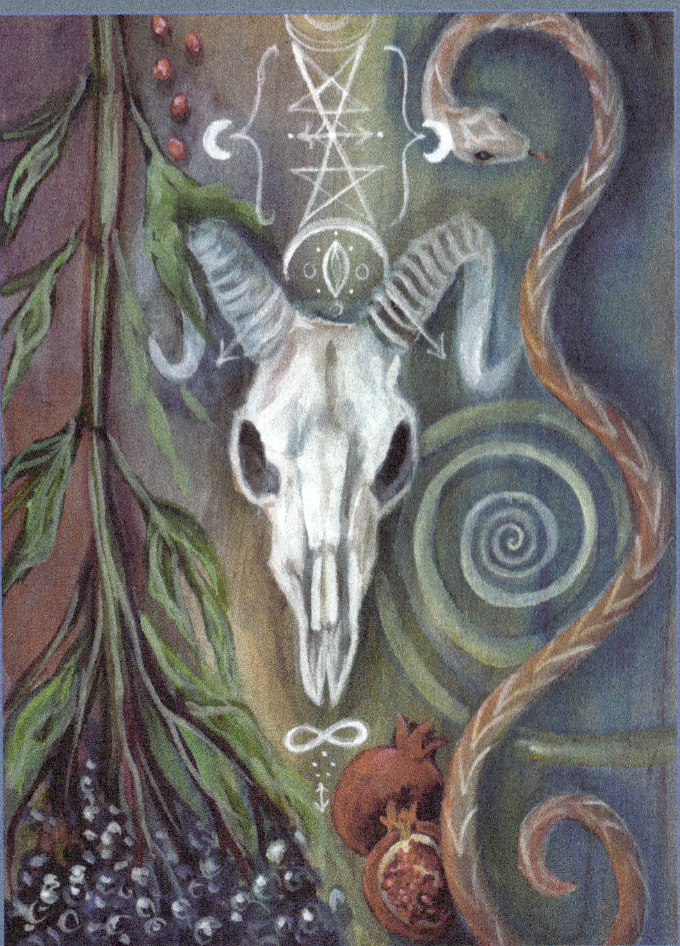

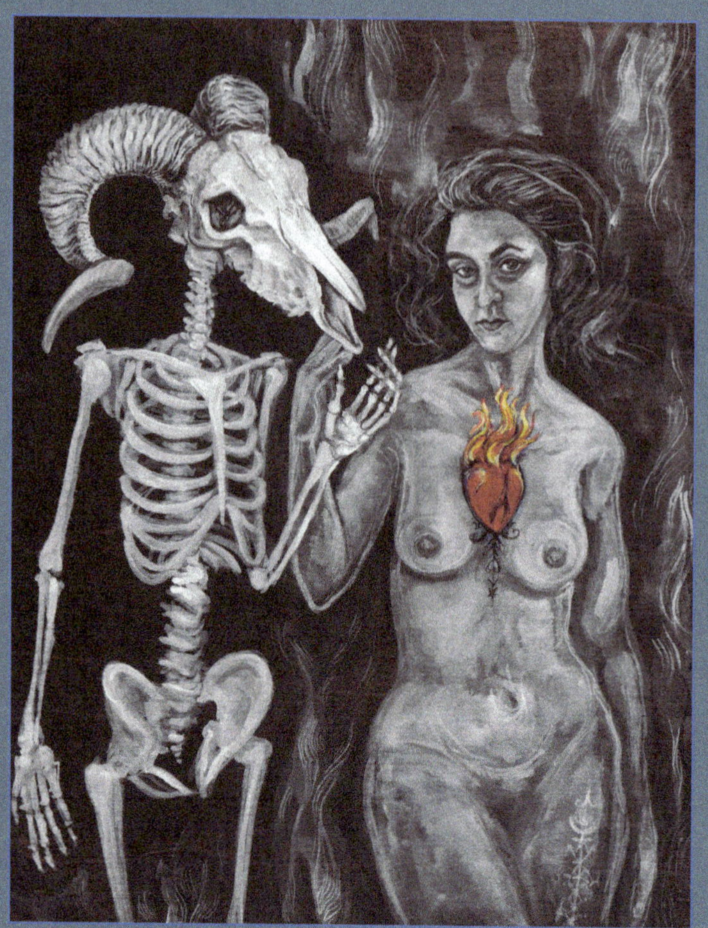

of the titles/themes I had set." This pre-determined plan for paintings may have stressed or discouraged other artists, but Laura's approach worked perfectly. The images in the Iconomage series are vibrant and exquisite, from the poised elegance of "Athena-Minerva" to the smoldering hearth fires of "Hecate".

Laura is adept at using social media to consult with her fans when she has a spark of inspiration for something new. One recent project was a set of holiday cards featuring La Befana and a Yule Goat. The sketches captured Laura's whimsical side and proved to be a hit with her contacts. "Last year was crazy with how well both designs were received! I will probably offer those designs again, and possibly some new ones for 2017." Future cards and calendars will be announced through her website.

Asking Laura to choose favorite pieces of her art is like asking a parent to name their favorite child, but I was curious to see which ones resonate most with her. There's no shortage of output, from sketches and paintings to coloring books. "An artist's favorites are usually the most recent work, and that's true for me. The Witch Essence series (http://owlkeyme.com/new-work.html) is a new body of work that's mainly monochromatic with tiny bursts of color. It's heavily influenced by visions and dreams I have had, and the question - What is a Witch?"

Another favorite would be her second book "Sigil Witchery: A Modern Traditional Witch's Guide to Sigil Magick", which should be released from Llewellyn in January 2018. She just finished the first draft, and she's very excited about the upcoming book release and sharing her experiences with a broader audience. "It's my take on sigil magick,

Although she enjoys doing commissions, Laura doesn't have much spare time to do them. In addition to painting and writing books (which we'll discuss soon), she also vends at several events each year and travels with her husband in his Nathaniel Johnstone Band tours, where she plays keyboards and percussion, as well as belly dances in the shows. Her Patreon site (https://www.patreon.com/owlkeyme) allows her to keep in touch with her fans, and those who donate at the $5 and above level can request a custom sigil, which she especially enjoys creating. Customers can also directly contract her through the magodjinn.com website for sigils. "It typically takes a couple of weeks or so for small work, and upwards of 4-8 weeks for larger, depending on my schedule."

Some of my favorite Zakroff paintings are from the Iconomage series (www.owlkeyme.com/iconomage.html). These panels are very popular, featuring images of Persephone, Kali Ma, etc. This particular body of work was created for the prestigious 2015 DragonCon art show. She was thrilled to be selected for the showcase, which presented some interesting challenges in timing. "They required the titles, info, and pricing of all of the artwork about 2.5 months in advance - and very little changes can be made to the list. Being that I create art very quickly and frequently, and was in the middle of a busy festival season, I didn't see how I was going to hold on to a large body of work that long. So I thought about it, and realized I had this great stack of cedar panels a friend had gifted me. I measured out the exhibition space, figured out how many panels I could fit (3', 2', 1' tall), and then I brainstormed titles. I assigned them to the various sizes, then a few weeks before the event, I made the artwork, basing it off

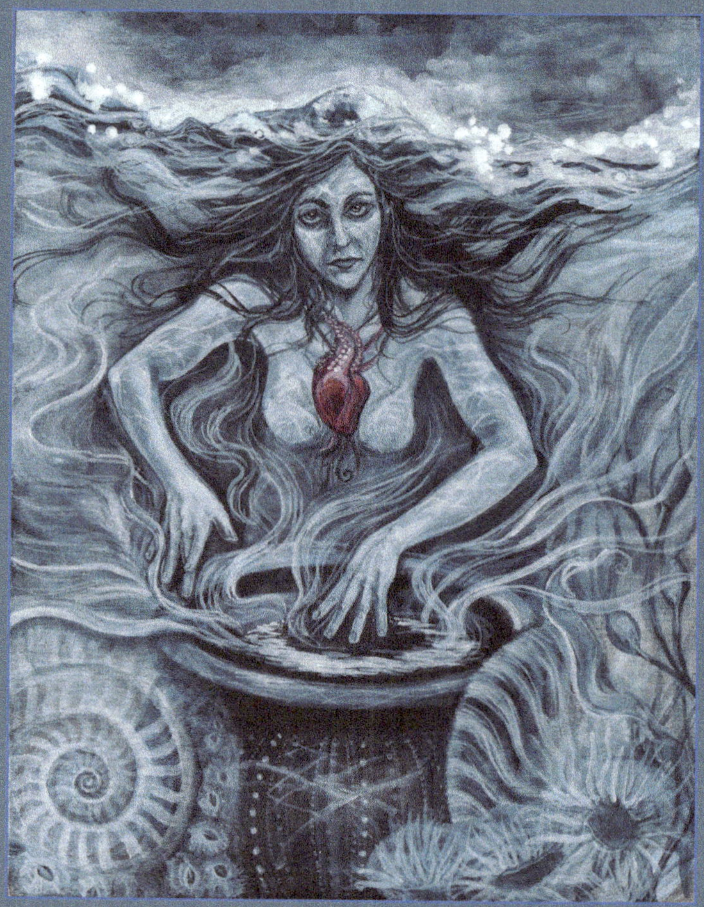

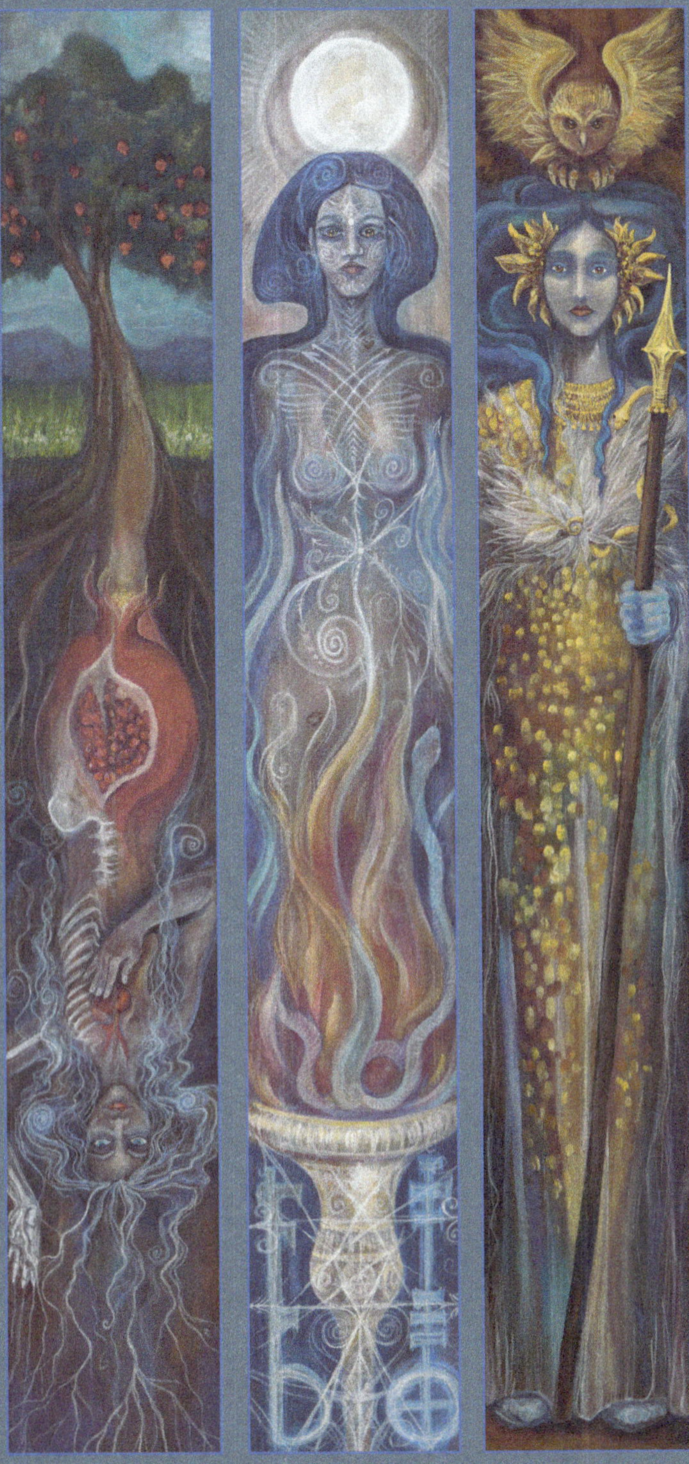

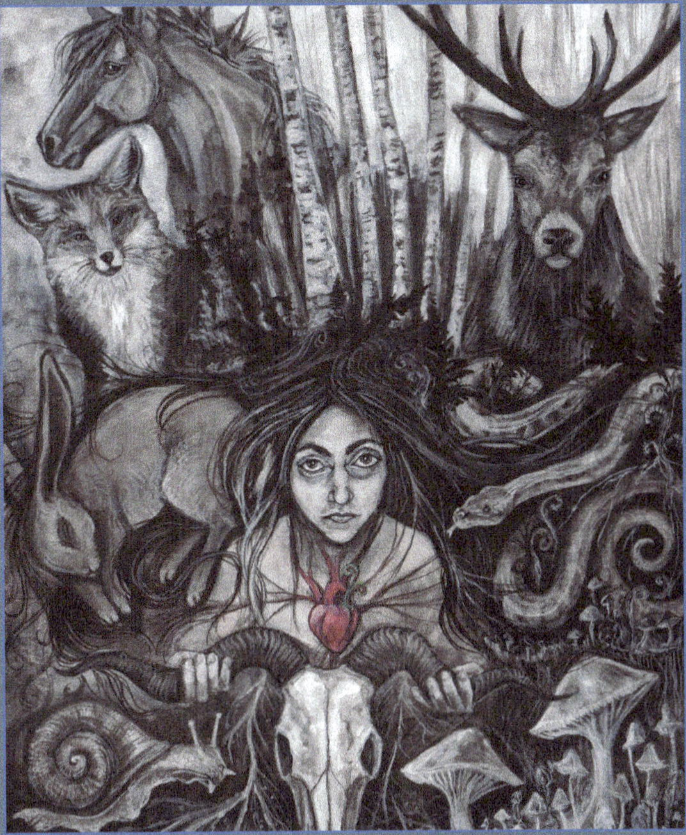

means Laura will be busy doing book signings and tours this summer. In addition to being carried online through Amazon, "The Witch's Cauldron" will be available in bookstores and occult shops nationwide.

Laura had a very busy 2016, so what would she most like to accomplish this year? "Besides taking down the patriarchy? My goal is to keep making artwork, to keep growing as an artist and to get my work out there to more people - in all of its forms." She'll be vending at several events, including PantheaCon (San Jose, CA), Convocation (Detroit, MI), Paganicon (Minneapolis, MN), and Norwescon (Seattle, WA). Additional events will be announced on her website.

What the future holds for her is anybody's guess. Laura seems very comfortable gazing back into the past just long enough to adjust her course forward. She's put in a proposal for a third book with Llewellyn. And she continues to collaborate musically with her husband, in addition to providing artwork for the www.nathanieljohnstone.com website and designing logos, shirts, and CD covers for the band. She has no plans to branch into new ventures any time soon. "I think I'm good right now. There are so many things I already do, that I'm feeling the need to hunker down a bit more and cover some specific areas more in-depth." I look forward to reading her summary of 2017... and all the magical highlights.

For more information about Laura Tempest Zakroff, please visit her websites.
Art - www.owlkeyme.com
Sigils - www.magodjinn.com
Witchery - www.moderntraditionalwitch.com
Author - www.lauratempestzakroff.com ■

which is quite different from the chaos magic-inspired route. I also enjoy doing custom spell paintings and sigils for people. I get so many stories back about how that work has manifested in their lives, which is the best kind of reward!" A spell painting is a spell within a painting, while a sigil is a carved, drawn, or painted symbol that is believed to hold magickal properties.

Her first book "The Witch's Cauldron" is scheduled to be released this coming May. "It's part of the 'Witch's Tools' series from Llewellyn... the largest seller of New Age/Metaphysical books in the US." This

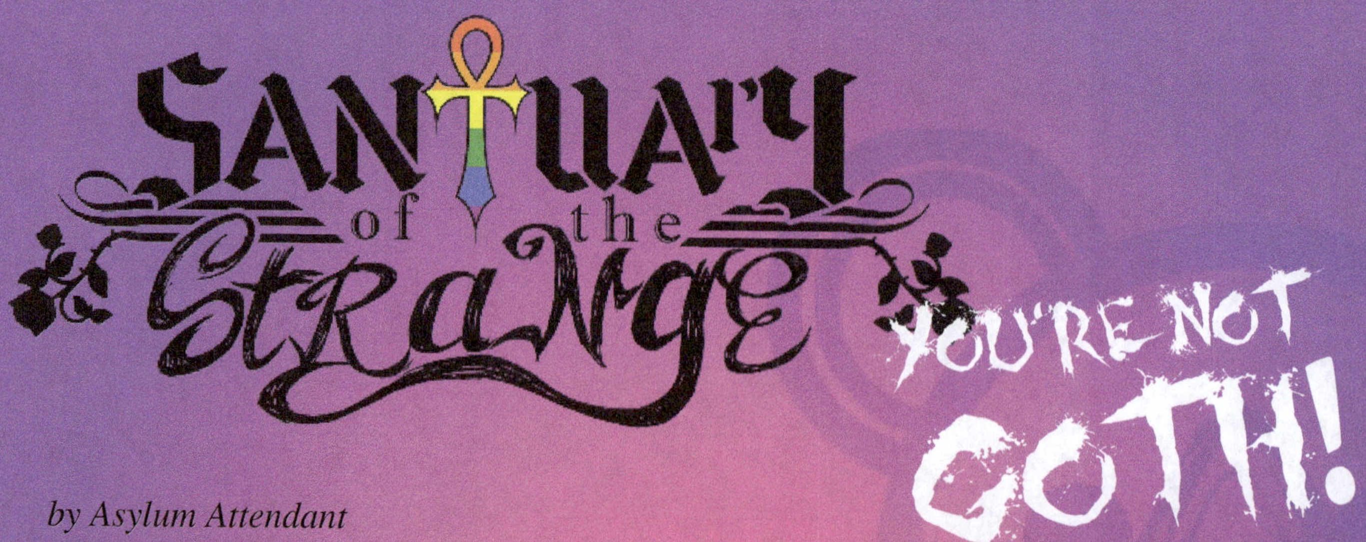

by Asylum Attendant

Essentially everyone I encounter outside of the Gothic subculture are certain that I am not Goth. They say I'm too positive and happy to write dark poetry. They say I dress too normal and professional at work to love PVC, platform boots and fishnet. They say I can't listen to both Lady Gaga and also enjoy Depeche Mode. These rigid opinions can really wear on a person and make them question who they think they are. Am I Goth?

The kicker is that all of the people I've met who call themselves Goth have never made me pull out my official Goth card to prove what a darkling I am. They recognize that Goth encompasses so many different fashion styles, music genres and mindsets that it would be silly to bar someone entry into the subculture for smiling. The normal people in my life try to reel in my individuality while my alternative friends take me as I am. That is an important distinction to make. Most of the population wants everyone they encounter to look and act just like them, even if they preach for diversity. Alternative people generally welcome the unusual and are open to learning about various cultures. They think my cutesy, glittery spin on Goth is intriguing, not silly.

I work full time in an office and the required attire is business casual clothing. Most days, I'm lucky to get there on time since I'm nocturnal. I'm certainly not going to spend a ton of time on my hair, makeup and clothing. I also want to be as comfortable as possible for the next eight hours. My fellow employees see me wearing a sweater and khakis and think I'm just like them. Wrong. But, since they rarely see me in edgy clothing and don't know a lot about my private life, I can't really get mad about the confusion. Once I disclose that I am in fact Goth, jaws drop and people shake their heads in disbelief. I thought my pink and black hair was a hint that I was alternative, but I guess not.

Something that's always bothered me about being alternative is people thinking that I'm trying so hard to be different. No, I didn't gravitate towards the Goth lifestyle to appear mysterious or get attention. Who would choose to be judged and humiliated by others for wearing makeup and feminine clothing? I want my outside appearance to match how I feel on the inside. This also means that I'm not going to conform to what a stereotypical Goth should look like. I'm not going to wear dark colors every day, though I do most days. That doesn't mean I've traded in bats for unicorns. I'm constantly evolving just like everyone else.

The good news is that for every co-worker who assumes I worship Satan after learning that I'm Goth, there is another that patiently allows me to explain what Goth actually is. Some people are never going to think I'm Goth enough and that only encourages me to throw more pastel skulls their way. BubbleGoth sounds a hell of a lot better to me than Instagram chic.

Just saying. ■

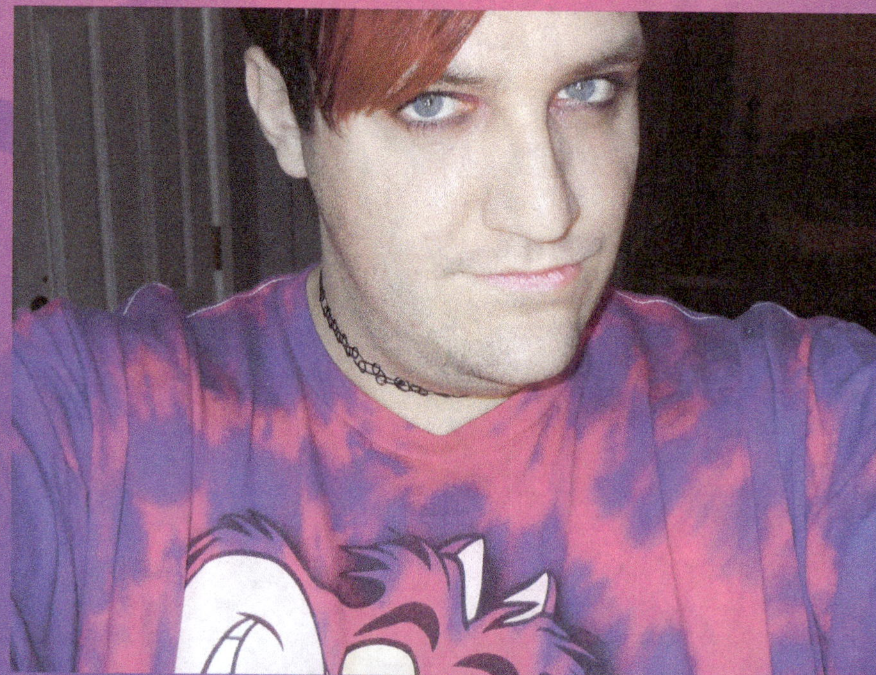

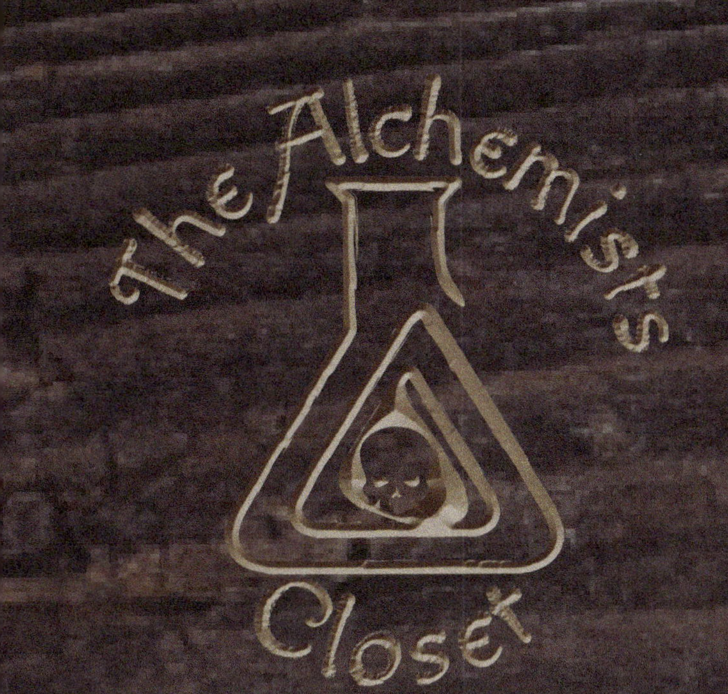

by Michael Jack and Xxx Zombieboy xxX

Bee Stings/ Bug Bites

Being a Pharmacist in a retail setting, over the course of the Spring and Summer months, the most common customer questions I get relates to bee stings and bug bites. It is very common, and even more so depending where you live. I personally live in a valley within the Appalachian Mountains, so bugs are numerous. In this installment of the Alchemists' Closet, my cohort Zombieboy and I will discuss what to look for and how to treat this frequent malady, or in most cases, minor annoyance. The treatments are simple and the products are easy to obtain. The real trick is knowing what to look for, and deciding if the bite/sting needs medical treatment.

First, let's tackle bee stings. I think we have all gotten stung at least once in our lifetime. They suck, hurt, and can be quite painful depending on the insect that impaled you with its stinger. Obviously, if you are allergic to bee venom, this situation can become very scary. For now, let's say you aren't allergic. Rule number one is to get the stinger out, because it contains venom and toxins.

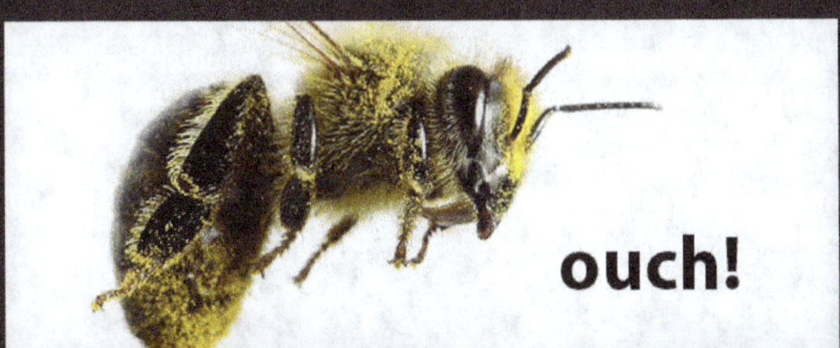

The longer the stinger is in, the more you will get. A tweezers and possibly a magnifying glass is all you need. Make sure to wash the site afterwards with soap and water. The treatment is simple...use a cold compress to take down the swelling if there is any. Over the counter steroid creams will relieve any pain or itching from the site. I always recommend a 1% Hydrocortisone cream, and you can pick it up almost anywhere. Even most gas stations sell it. Don't go for the brand name. Save a couple dollars and get the generic. It works the same. Your other option is an over the counter product called After Bite. This ammonia-based product will relieve the pain/itch immediately, and it comes in a convenient dab-on tube that easily fits into your pocket or purse. It also acts as an astringent, so it helps in multiple ways.

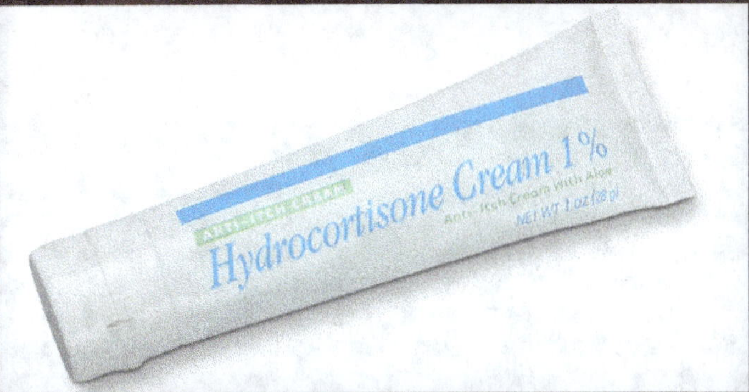

Now, let's say you are allergic to bee stings. I recommend getting tested by a physician to gauge the severity of your allergy. Some can be life threatening, and will require you to keep an Epi-Pen with you at all times. If you have only a minor allergy, an over the counter anti-histamine will be enough to offset the symptoms. I recommend Benadryl (diphenhydramine), or any generic of this product. Benadryl has withstood the test of time, and no product before or since has proven as effective in minimalizing or eliminating allergic reactions. Keep this on hand at all times, because it has many uses. If you are unsure if you are allergic to bee stings, and get stung, here are the signs to look at for: hives, trouble breathing, swelling of your lips, tongue, or throat, nausea, dizziness or fainting, or rapid heartbeat. If you experience one or more of these reactions after being stung, take the Benadryl and seek immediate medical help.

Bug bites are very similar to bee stings in the pharmaceutical approach to treat them. The trick is making sure whatever it is that did bite you doesn't carry any harmful diseases, because many do. It is also helpful to know what insect-carried diseases are common in your area. For me, it's the almighty deer tick, and he can transmit Lyme disease. The problem I discover is many people notice the red bump well after the fact, and have no idea what bit them. In general, Hydrocortisone cream alone, or with oral Benadryl, will get rid the itch/pain/lump. Nothing further is needed. After Bite will help here as well, and luckily you now have a tube in your back pocket. Again, you can use cold compresses if there is swelling.

If the simple treatments aren't working, or the site looks much worse than a simple bite, or is worsening, seek professional advice. You don't have to visit your doctor. You can come to see me, your local Pharmacist. Remember, I deal with bite related questions all of the time. If I think the reaction is severe enough, I may tell you to go to the emergency room or see your doctor. 9 times out of 10, however, I'll be able to help you in store. The things you want to look for are excessive

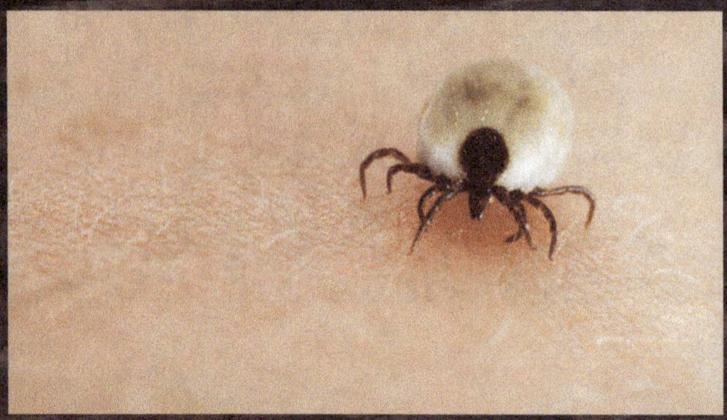

swelling, pain (and I don't mean just a dull annoying pain), redness, hot to touch, and/or pus or pustules. If the area starts developing a rash that resembles a bulls-eye, go see your doctor. Whether it is Lyme Disease, one of the many spider transmitted infections, or Rocky Mountain spotted fever, most insect born infections can be cured with a simple round of antibiotics. Knowing when to use more than a compress and a steroid cream is the key, and if you are unsure, seek out someone who does.

Now, before I turn this over to Zombieboy, and he tells you to pee on your insect bite, remember...that is now unneeded since you are carrying After Bite. You are welcome. Zombie...

*Sounds of fluid running

Zombie? ...ZOMBIE!

HUH?! *Zips Up

Oh! Ello' there! So you got ants in your pants or something else fabulously nasty bit you? Well, let's see to it. Growing up in the south, I have had to deal with flying, biting, stinging and generally other pesky things all the time. I've probably been bitten on by every critter known to the region and then some. Fortunately, most are no threat, they are just annoying. I would like to begin this verbose discussion by reminding everyone out there to PLEASE be kind to the bees! If you are concerned about allergy and see a hive, please get someone from the area to come and move it. Do not harm the bees. They are shrinking in numbers and vital to us all!

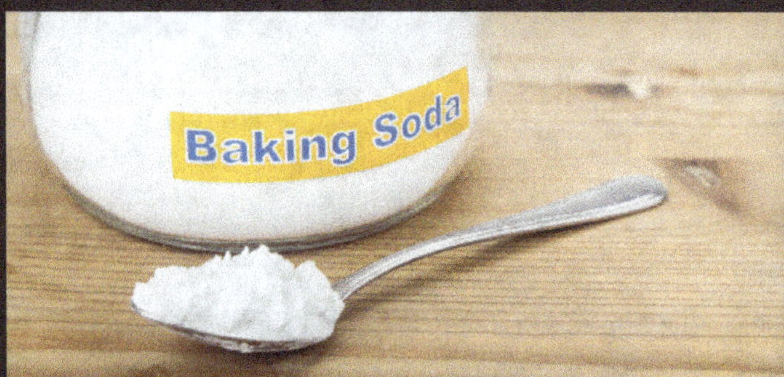

*Climbs down off of beer box

Again, let's pretend you got stung by a bee, wasp or hornet. And for now at least, you are not allergic. Honestly, if you were, my first response

would be the same as Mike's. Epi Pen and Benadryl, and possibly the emergency room. Let's move on. The two most common stings are bees and wasps. Fortunately, there are some great and easy remedies out there. Mike was not far off when he caught me peeing on my arm (I am flexible) to relieve the sting. And it is proven that urine can sometimes be a thing. There is something better though. For a bee sting, try using a solution of bicarbonate soda. For a wasp use a mix of diluted vinegar and lemon juice. Both will help take away the burning. If the stinger is still in you, it doesn't matter which flying offender got you, you should remove it as soon as possible. Contrary to popular myth, this is easy to do. Flick it away or scrape it away with something like a credit card. Do not pinch it however or use tweezers. Just flick it off of you. Ironically enough, their honey is an anti-inflammatory and a pain reliever. So, if you get stung, the bee made you something for it. So bee nice to the bee.

A quick word on scorpions. East of the Mississippi, there are no known venomous ones. As someone who has been stung twice by these critters, I assure you there is no need to panic. Just watch for signs of allergy as with all bites and stings. West of the Mississippi however, there can be more of an issue. Without writing a whole article on these beasts, let's just say out west, go to a doctor immediately.

Bites and stings in a more general outlook have some very simple home remedies. First, use an ice pack. The tried and true mother cure all works well to relieve the sting and the itch. This is across the board! If there is swelling, I have often heard it said that elevating the area of the bite will relieve the swelling.

There are some highly effective things you can apply right to a bite area as well. Tea Tree Oil works wonders and it is an antibacterial. Lavender and coconut oils also help to relieve swelling and itching. You can also use everyday toothpaste in a pinch because the menthol has a cooling effect on the area.

In the Caribbean, my mother had an old treatment for stings. She would mix water and milk and soak a compress with the mixture. It actually worked quite well! Another thing she used were tea bags. We always had plenty of those around, and after a little research, I discovered that tea can actually extract at least some of the venom from the bite area.

Basil can be a reliever as well, for crushing the leaves of this plant releases a camphor if placed directly on the site.

Finally, I want to make a mention of stinging caterpillars such as the saddleback. These guys can hurt like touching a live electrical wire. If you get nailed, try using tape to remove the spines.

In all cases, try not to scratch! And if you got nothing else available, well...

*Unzips. ∎

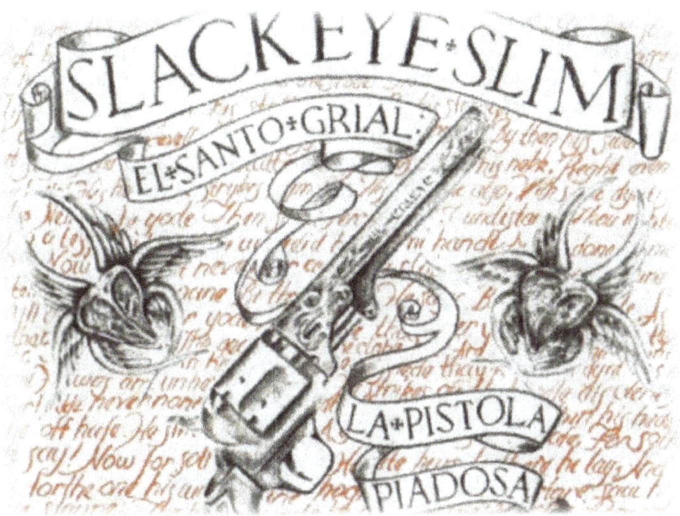

by *Sergio Manghina*

The so-called Gothic-Country is still a subterranean river to be discovered. "El Santo Grial: La Pistola Piadosa" (Spanish, "The Holy Grail: The Pitiful Gun") is one of the more precious nuggets hidden under its sands.

Joe Frankland, aka Slackeye Slim, comes from Ohio, but is currently based in Colorado. His voice is baritonal, with a touch of asperity, very remarkable and perfect for the genre. Compared to the excellent previous "Giving My Bones To The Western Lands," this disc is a further step towards an even more harsh and rough kind of death-roots-sound.

The narrative unfolds through fourteen short but intense chapters, which constitute a real concept album about a certain Drake Savage, his gun and a divine mission of vengeance to be pursued.

There are some monologues ("The Chosen One" part 1 and 2), a Johnny Cash style ballad ("Judgement Day"), the Mexican flavors of "Introducing Drake Savage" and the mambo-punk of the title-track. But, the album also contains a formidable series of vaguely spaghetti-western tunes ("Prayer," "Vengeance Gonna Be My Name," "El Mundo, Mi Enimigo," "Make It Right," "A Song Called Love"). And let's not forget about that carnival-luna park-waltz called, "Come One, Come All."

Above all, "El Santo Grial" is a great example of genuine Death Country, eclectic and soaked by punk-roots that screw to the bones. Because Slackeye Slim is sincere, essential and able to destroy in a second decades of asphyxiated Nashville sound and mawkish country-rock.

The old frontier is really a dangerous place. It is often dusty, bad, dirty but deeply proud of its own mythology, where a pitiful gun could be the extreme remedy, even blessed by God. ■

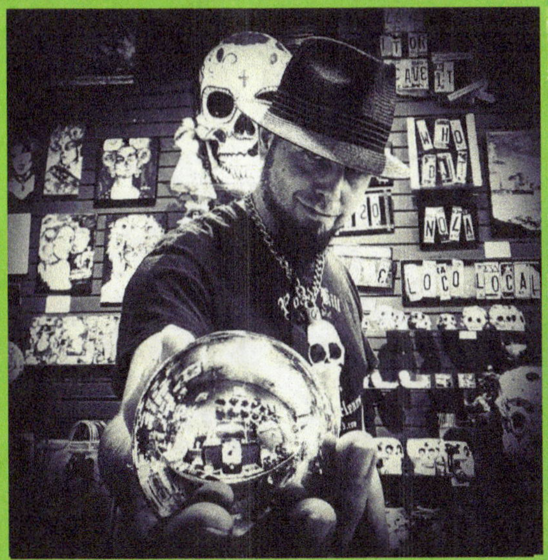

The *Dirty Show* CLEANS UP!

The Dirty Show, held annually in Detroit, came and went over a couple weekends in February with all its raunchy and naughty splendor. With sellout crowds for 2 of the 4 nights, the show brought all types to view the erotic art and live shows. This year's show, similar to the past 4 years, was held at the illustrious Russell Industrial Center, which was just recently temporarily closed due to failed safety inspections. Now in its 18th year, The Dirty Show had modest beginnings, from small spaces in a hotel to the massive size this year that featured over 300 pieces of erotic art. Besides the art, one could get whipped by a dominatrix or have their picture taken while riding an enormous rocking penis. The onstage entertainment included male and female burlesque dancers from all parts of the USA, and many from Detroit. These burlesque dancers all had very special routines that often called for audience participation. Throughout the grounds were go-go dancers in cages, and an area for rope artistry.

I was there to document all the gorgeous people and sights for 2 of the nights. Here's just a small taste of what I saw. ∎

by Mike Pfeiffer aka Digital Racket

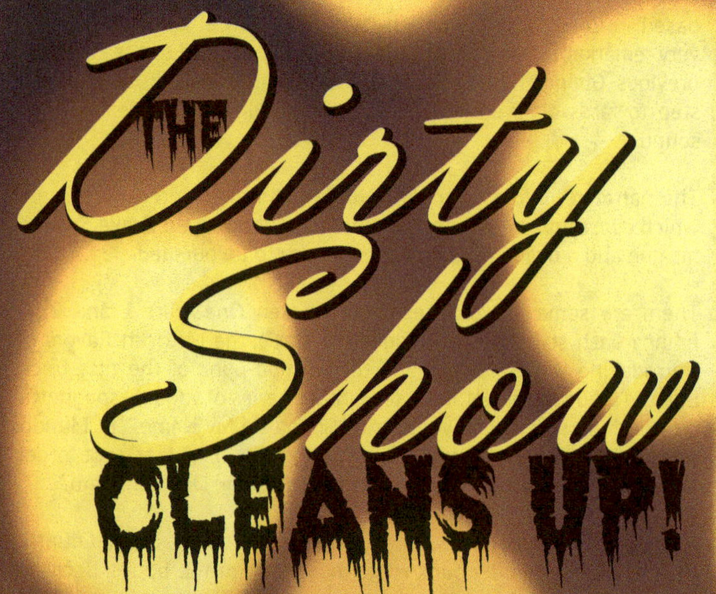

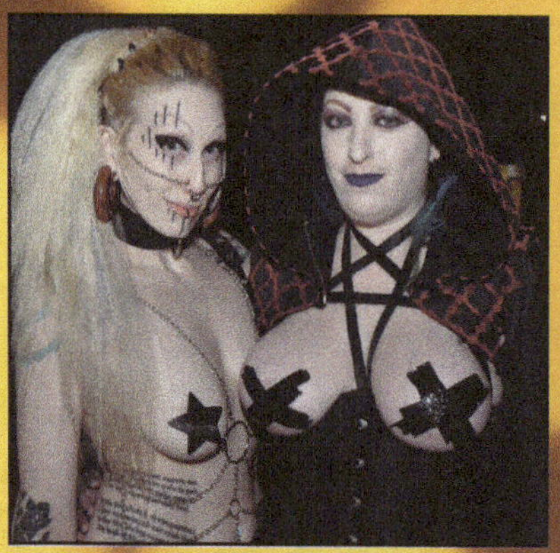

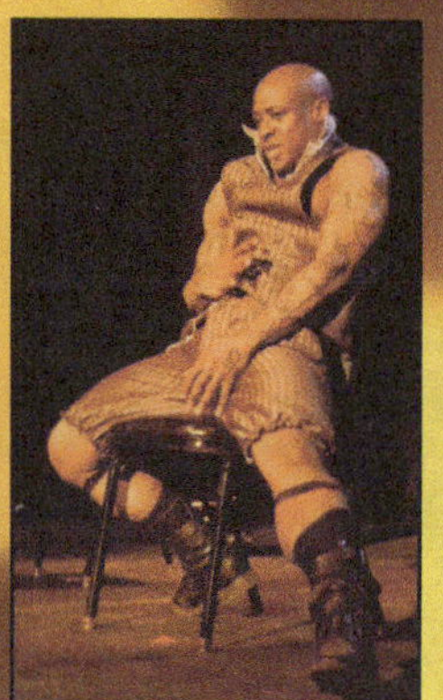

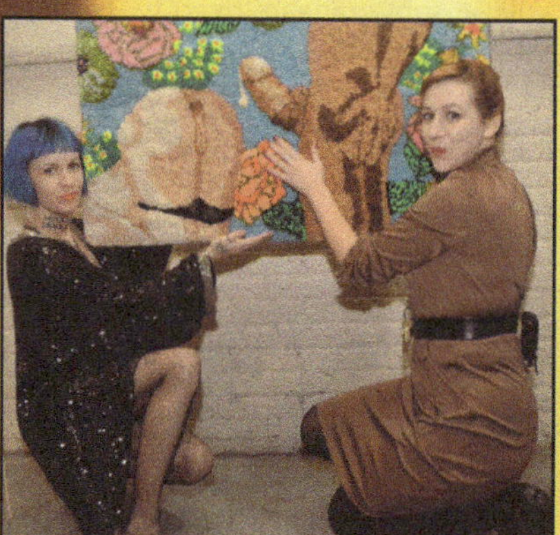

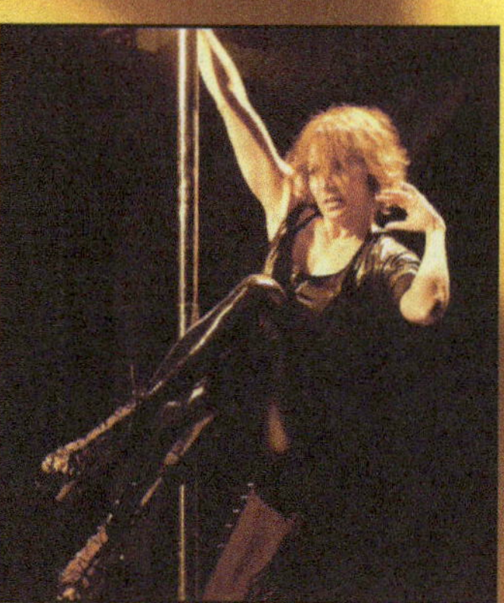

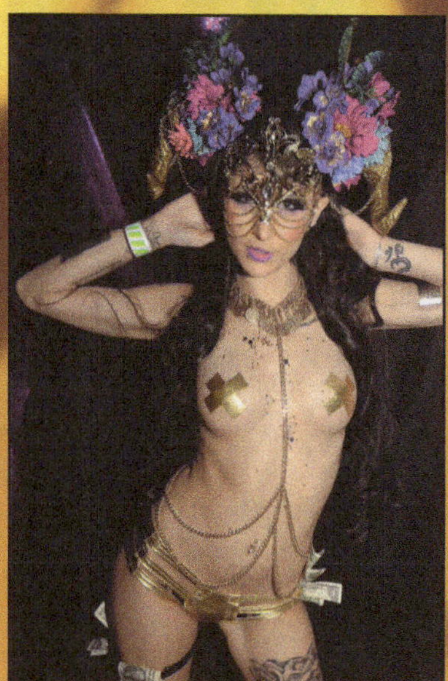

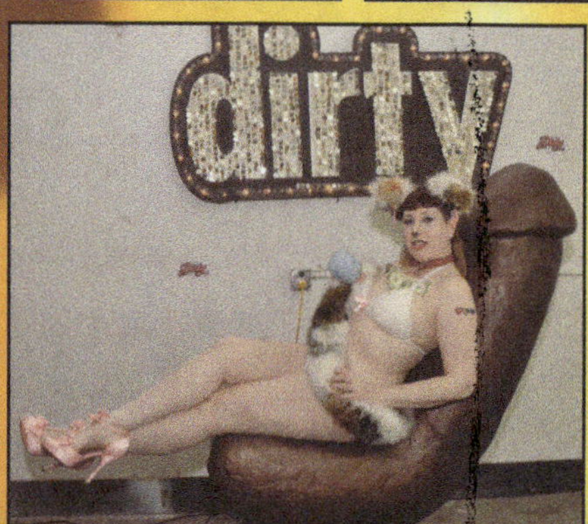

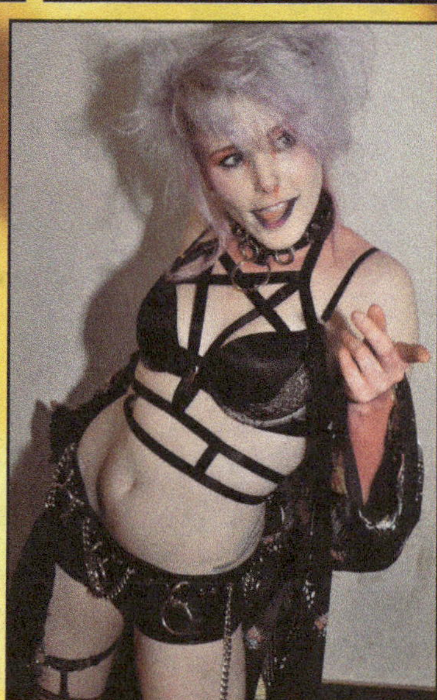

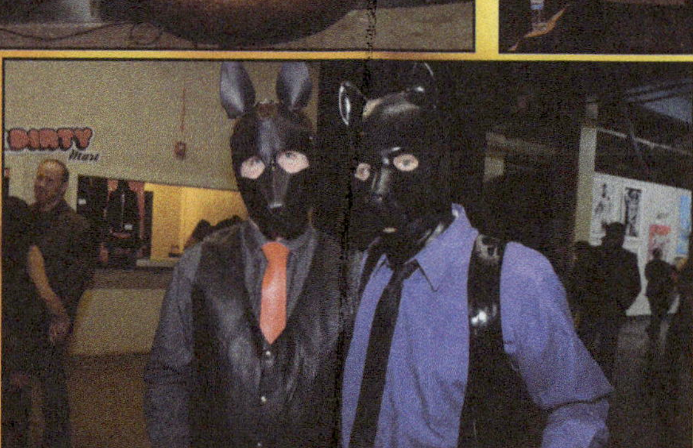

B L O O D Y
MARVELOUS

BLOODY HELL SPOCK!

by Xxx Zombieboy xxX

"When trying to come up with a Science Fiction themed Bloody Mary Recipe for this issue, I had a little trouble. My first attempt was to do a Star Wars themed one with Luke's "blue milk" in mind. Be damned if I was able to find a way to make this drink blue. I may come back to that challenge. My next idea was a solid black one, but I decided to save that for the future. Therefore, I present to you the BLOODY HELL SPOCK! Green like Spock's Blood, and hotter than mixing matter and anti-matter cold, may it make your blood boil!

1 pound tomatillos husked, trimmed, and quartered
1/2 pint (about 7 ounces) green tomatoes
1 cucumber roughly chopped
2 tablespoons freshly-squeezed lime juice
2 jalapenos diced (Because Pon Farr)
1 Thai Chile halved
1 teaspoon kosher salt
1 teaspoon Cajun seasoning
2 ounces Svedka Vodka (See advertising campaign)
½ ounce of Tequila
1 teaspoon prepared horseradish
3/4 teaspoon green hot sauce
1 teaspoon Worcestershire
1 Pinch of celery seeds

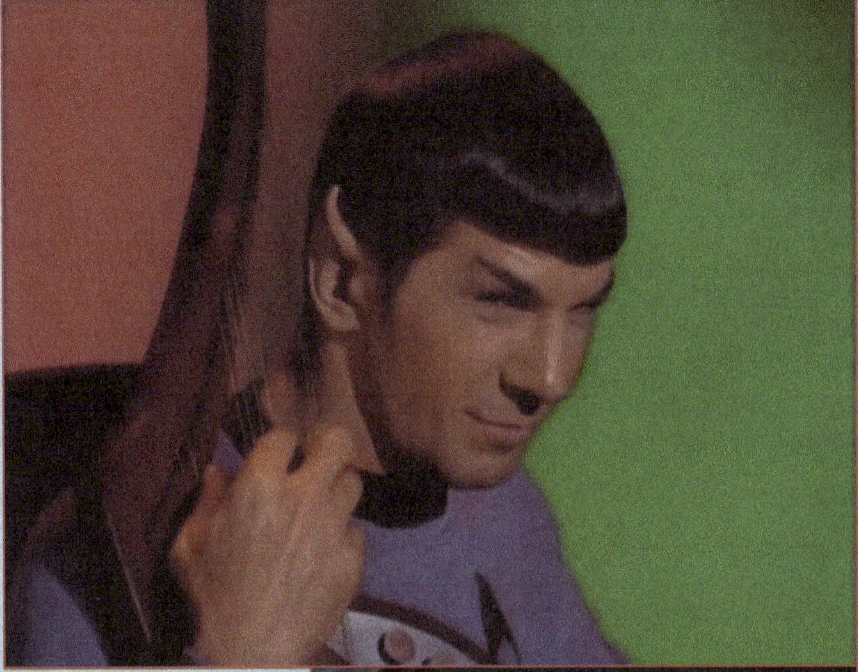

To create the base for the Bloody Hell Spock, take the tomatillos, tomatoes, the cucumber, tablespoons of the lime juice, chile, the diced jalapenos, the teaspoon of Cajun seasoning and the teaspoon of kosher salt in a blender and process until smooth, at least 33 seconds.

Salt the rim of the glass with more Cajun seasoning. The contrast between the red and green looks cool. Tastes good too. Combine 4 to 5 ounces of the Base with the vodka and tequila, the horseradish, hot sauce, Worcestershire, celery seeds, and juice from the lime wedge in a shaker. Add ice to fill halfway then stir until the shaker is cold, about 10 stirs. Pour the drink and ice into a serving glass, garnish to your liking. I use spicy pickle wedges and spicy green beans for this one. ■

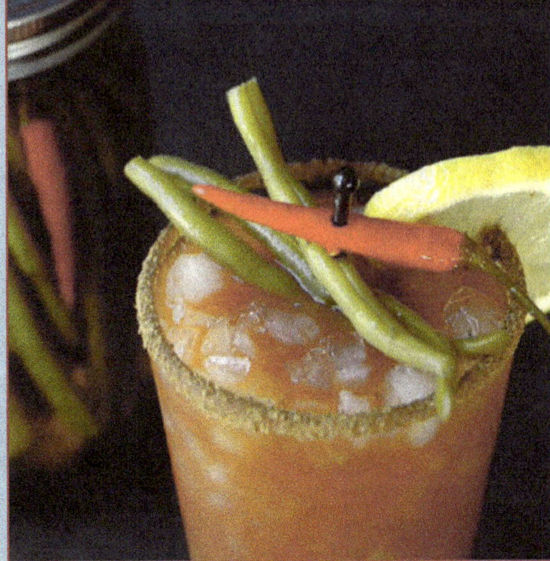

A DECADE OF
Dark Beauty
RazorCandi

by Michael Jack

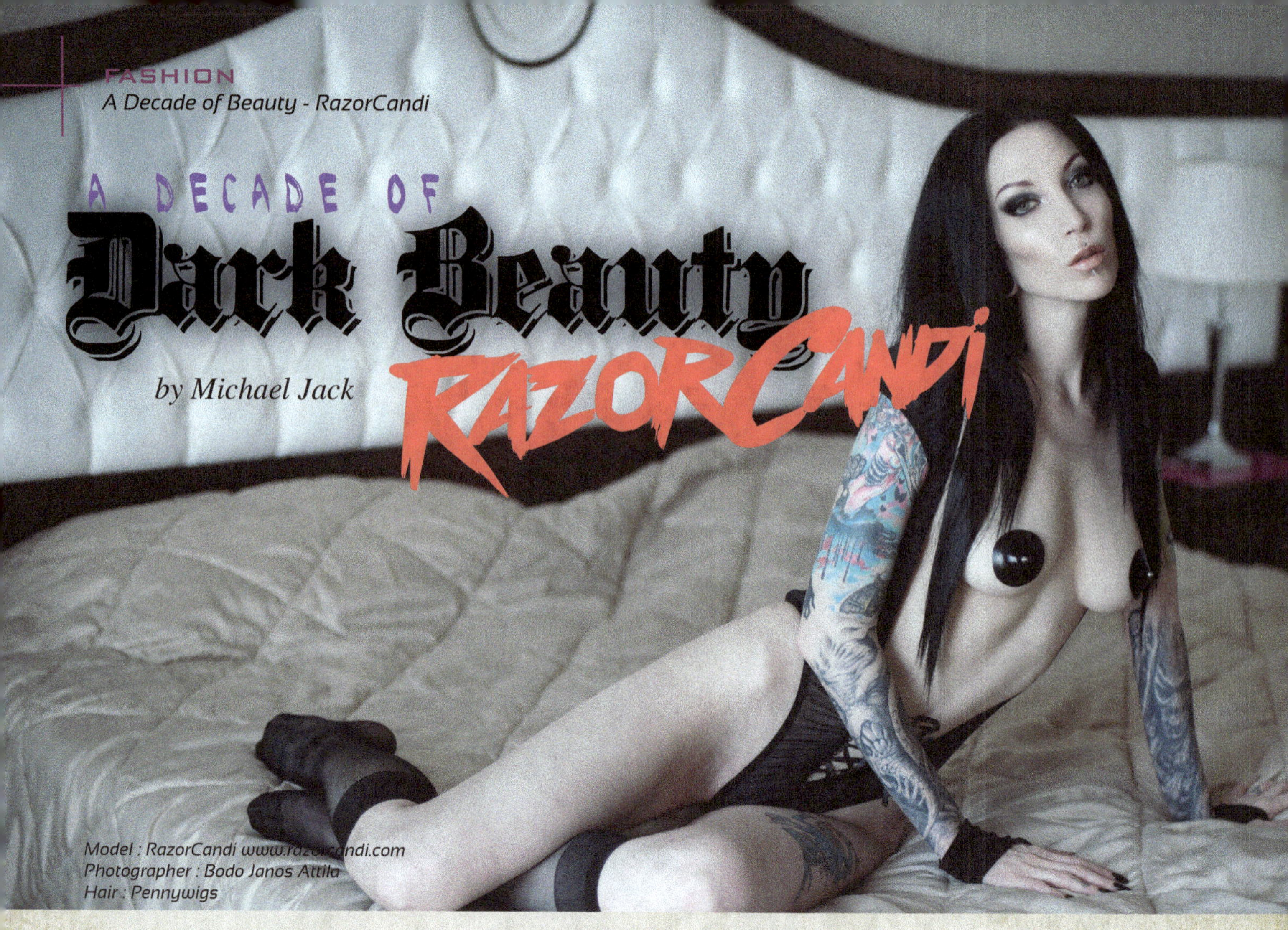

Model : RazorCandi www.razorcandi.com
Photographer : Bodo Janos Attila
Hair : Pennywigs

Being and Editor and a writer, I spend a ton of time on the computer simply doing research. There are two facts I have come to accept. One, no matter what subject I am researching, I will come across an article written by Carpe Nocturne's own Amy Townsend from her old blog Stripy Tights and Dark Delights. Two, no matter subject I am researching, I will quickly come across pictures of the woman I must consider to be the most recognizable face in dark alternative modeling, RazorCandi. I say must, because her online presence is completely staggering. If you don't believe me, pick any subject related to Goth, and hit Google image search. See how quickly a picture of RazoCandi pops up.

Kym (RazorCandi) has now spent a decade creating some of the most fantastic imagery for the darker cultures. Many of her photo shoots are iconic. She has worked with so many incredible photographers, and her concepts are always completely outside of the box. RazorCandi's skill with make up and hair artistry sometimes defy logic, giving her the ability to completely alter her appearance from one shoot to the next. So when she announced she would be releasing a hard cover coffee table art book of her most memorable photos, I was ecstatic, yet entirely bewildered at how she could even choose which photos to include and which to leave out. I needed to contact Kym and find out, and gather more information about this exciting project.

When I caught up with incredibly gifted RazorCandi, she was fresh

I just find something very tantalizing about darkness combined with sexuality.

off an international move from Transylvania to Austin, Texas. Kym was busy adjusting to her new surroundings, getting new equipment, and putting together and promoting her new art book. I don't think she ever slows down. Amidst this must be chaos, RazorCandi took time out to answer some questions for me, and I couldn't be more thankful. I have been a long time admirer of her work, and am familiar with almost everything she has ever done. Now, I get to present my interview to you...the iconic RazorCandi.

The very first question I had to ask was about the coffee table art book, and where the concept came from. To my surprise, this was something Kym had her sights on for quite some time. She explains, "The coffee table book was something I had dreamed about doing for a while now. A few years back I had actually put out a trilogy of small photo books with my most memorable photos while living over seas. It was really the best option I had at the time, but my aspiration was to eventually put out a beautiful hard cover coffee table book with over 100 pages. I finally had the opportunity thanks to Blue Blood and jumped on it!"

As for choosing the photos, she had help deciding...the Blue Blood team. In RazorCandi's words, the reason she used their help in the selection process was because, "I always find it easiest to let others be the judge since they see my work with fresh eyes." Asked about her most memorable shoot, Kym replied, "Right now my favorite

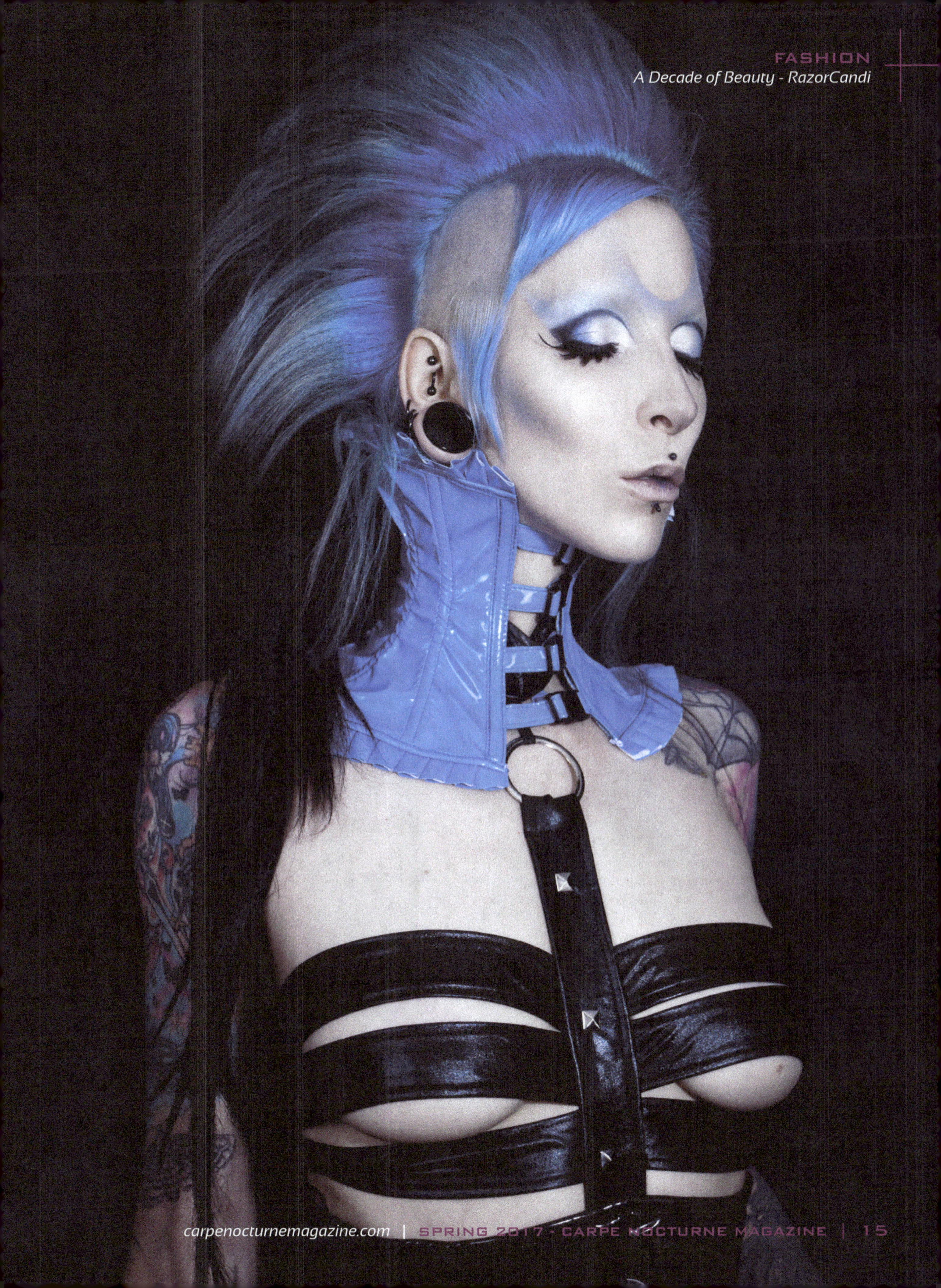

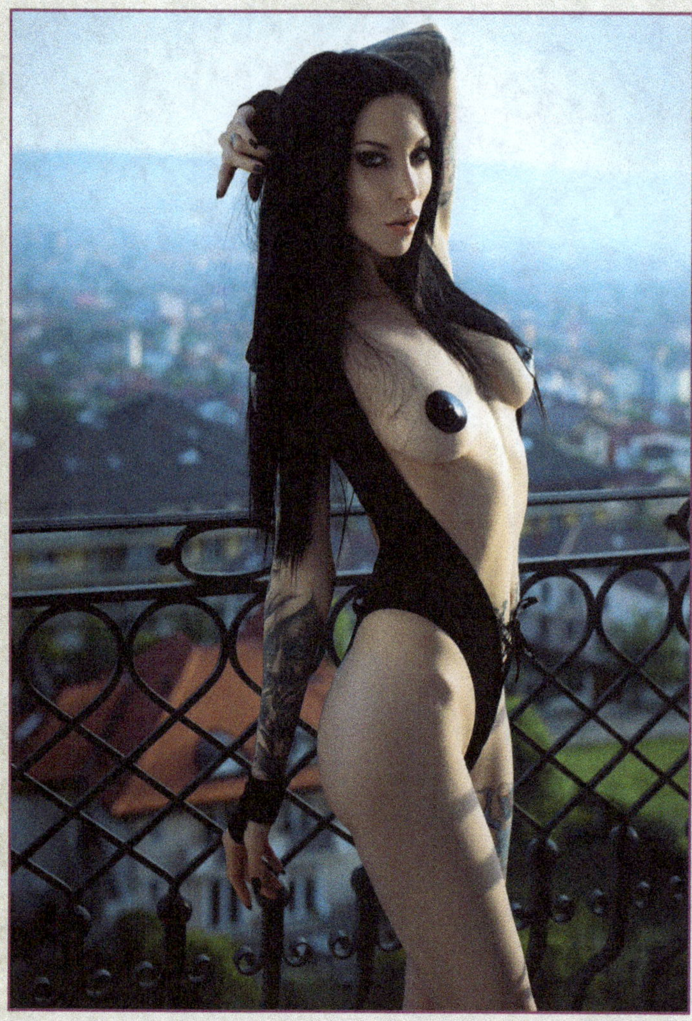

For me, as a fan, and as an Editor of a dark culture magazine, I am most astonished by RazorCandi's ability to change her appearance. Sure, there is always her high cheekbones, which Kym and I both agree are her most distinguishable feature, but sometimes that doesn't even give away it is her under the persona she chose for a particular shoot. Kym is like a chameleon. I had to find out where all of these concepts came from, and if she ever ran out of ideas. RazorCandi replied, "I

I feel that modeling is very much about being able to fit into any look with ease and confidence.

certainly try my best to keep my looks varied. I feel that modeling is very much about being able to fit into any look with ease and confidence. I'm not really sure if I'll ever run out of looks because I'm continually inspired. Even when I find myself in a slump with creator's block, something or someone will always come along at some point to inspire or awaken something new in me."

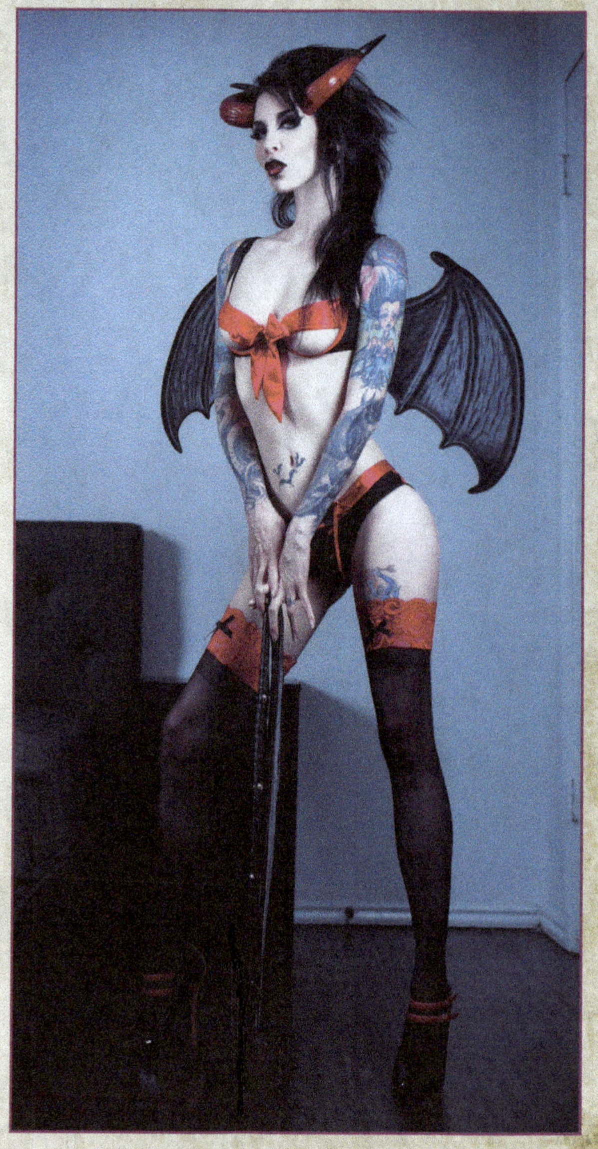

and most memorable shoot is probably Liberate Tutemae Ex Inferis. I really love dark themes. I just find something very tantalizing about darkness combined with sexuality." I think many of Carpe Nocturne's readers will agree with that statement.

The book itself is 172 pages, and full color. The majority of the work was shot by Kym's own personal photographer, but others are included. One of those additional photographers is Kym's twin sister, Eden Pepper. If you follow RazorCandi, you'll have seen more than a few photographs of these near identical siblings posing side by side.

To fund this project, Kym turned to Kickstarter. Many artists in the darker cultures have turned to this avenue, and I am always proud to see the response. RazorCandi exceeded her goal. When asked what this kind of support from her fans means to her, Kym responded, "I'm still amazed that my campaign did so well. To be honest, when I launched it, I really had my doubts and wasn't even sure I'd hit a thousand. Knowing that so many people want this project to happen means so much I'm not even sure how to put it into words. For the longest time I was feeling that people just didn't want me on the internet. Between having my Facebook page reported and banned to simply just struggling otherwise to make ends meat with modeling, this has really changed my perspective on my fan base. I really feel very loved right now :)"

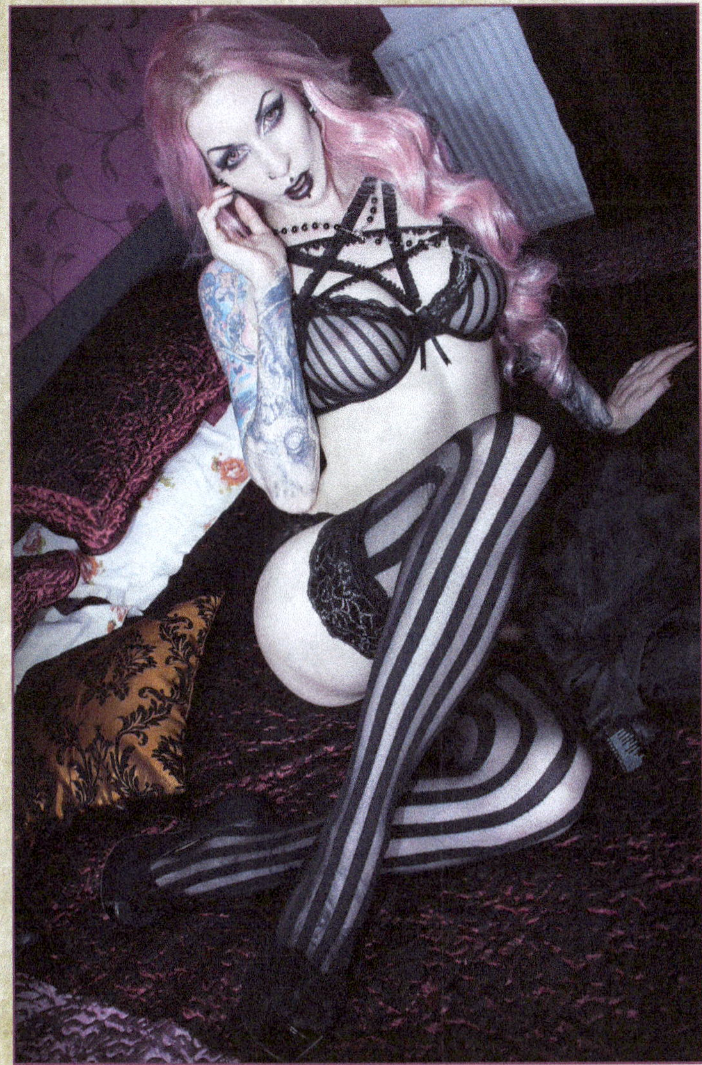

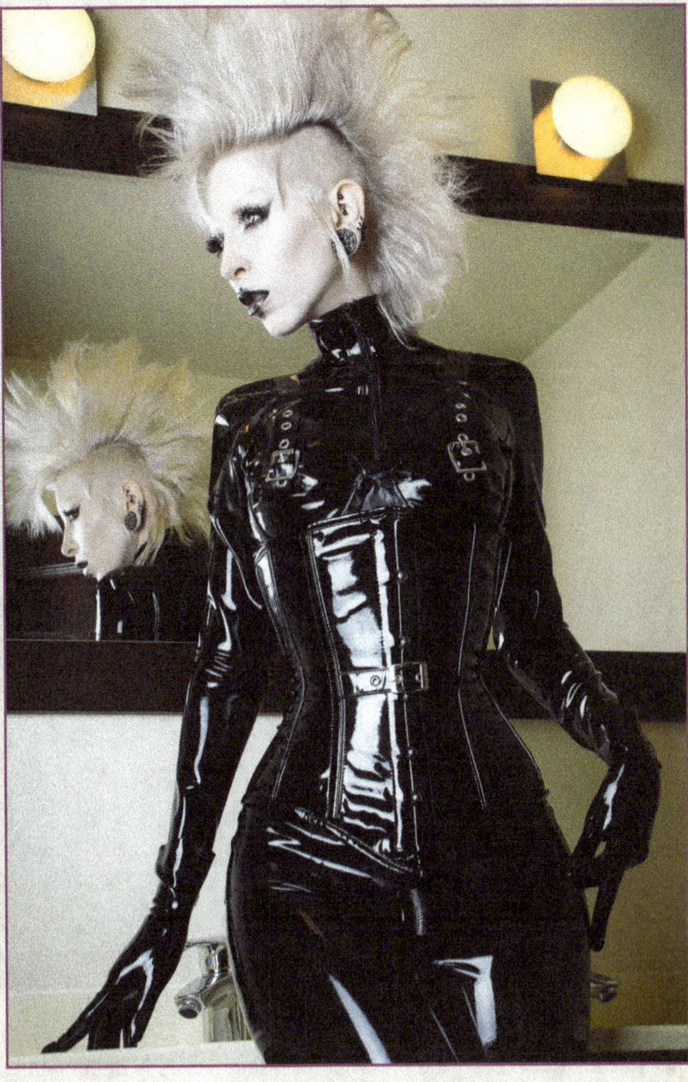

Kym's alabaster skin makes her a natural fit for the darker themes she shoots. Yet, and many people are not aware, along with that skin tone comes natural red hair. Like many models of her hair color in the alternative and Gothic genres, she rarely uses it. Instead, it's usually died. This is a topic I have been curious about for a long time, and have even considered writing an entire article on it. Why don't redheads in the darker cultures use their natural red hair? My guess was it's the challenges associated with the makeup artistry for the darker themes they shoot, and Kym vindicated my theory. "You're absolutely right in your assumption about natural red hair not fitting into darker themes, at least for me that's how I feel. I've done some looks and dark themes with my natural red hair color, but overall I don't feel that it has the impact that black or other funky shades may have."

Although RazorCandi spent the majority of her career shooting dynamic non-nude Gothic, Punk, and Deathrock themes, she eventually turned to nude modeling to pay her bills. As many alternative artists will tell you, it's financially hard to make a career in this industry. Along with Kym's decision, came new roads of opportunity and a broader market for her work. When describing the transition and how it affected her fan base, Kym explains, "It wasn't a hard transition for me mainly because I was in my late 20's when I decided to start, so I was well matured and ready for the step. I've never had a problem with nudity and I'm confident about my body and sexuality, but I suppose if I could make money not having to take my clothing off I'd probably prefer it. I don't like to downplay nudity and sexual themes when its comes to art because I feel it is artistic in its own way, but I also feel that it can sometimes take away from what I'm trying to convey through my appearance. While nude art does help pay the bills, I'm happy that I can also make a statement while doing it. As for my fan base, I think the transition was probably harder on them than it was on me haha. While I may have lost followers due to my transition, I think I gained a lot too."

> *I feel that our appearance is an outward expression and the biggest symbol of freedom.*

This answer brought me to my next question, which is something I

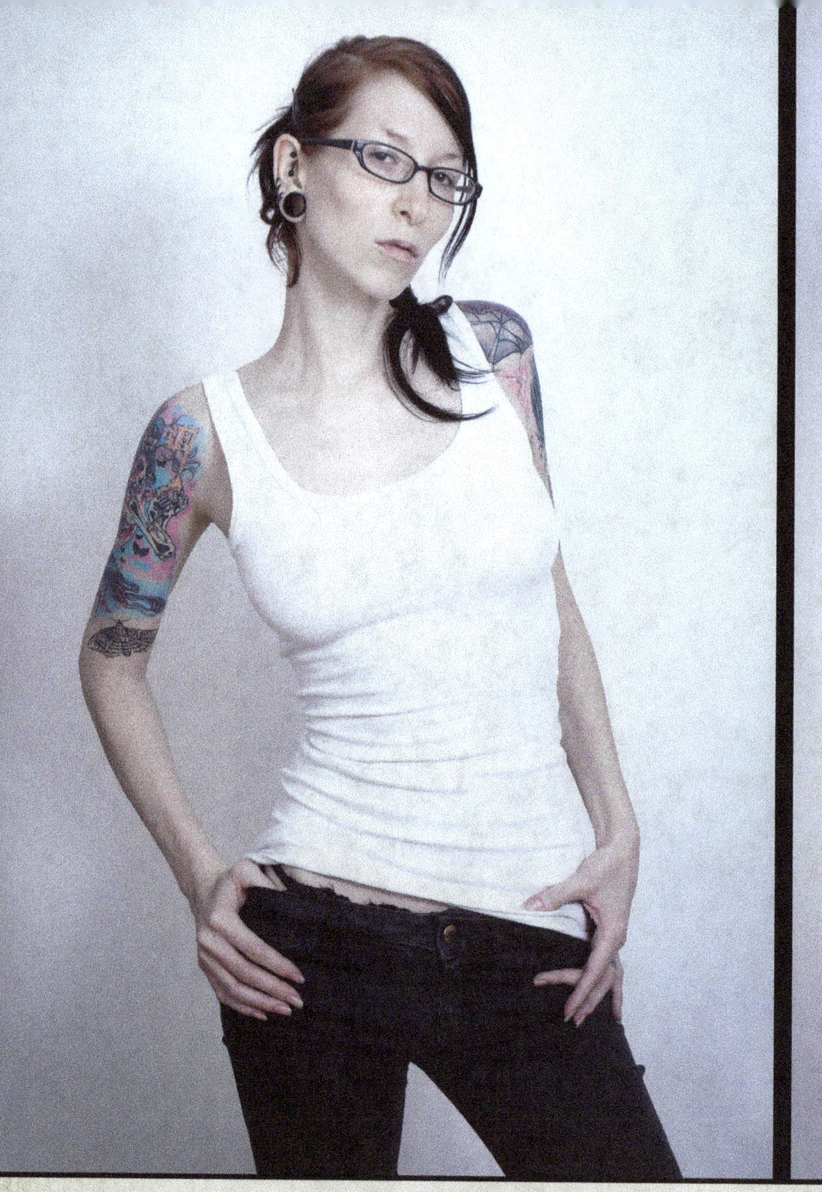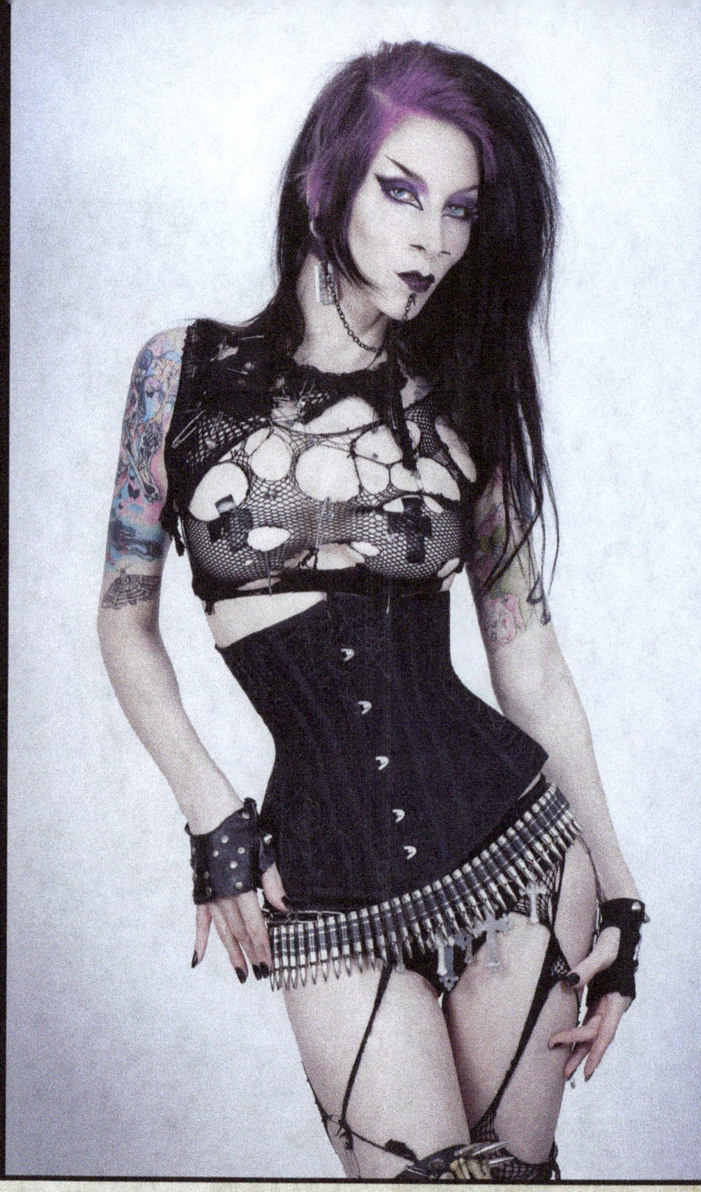

have been concerned about for a while now…Goths being viewed by many as a sexual fetish. I know what RazorCandi does is undeniably art, but I needed to know her thoughts on the subject. Her reply explained a different side of the equation, and one I didn't necessarily consider…

"Even though some may find the label "fetish" offensive, I'm fine with it because I know I do a niche look. So the way I see it, if someone who prefers Goth over other forms of erotica, that makes my work more unique. On the other hand, I've met many people who hugely emphasize on my details which is surprising because usually I think people look right past them or don't notice. I feel that an artist's body of work speaks for itself, and even if I am sought out by Goth fetishists, my work still has something about it that will set me aside. I think I feel most disappointed when people don't realize I'm a one woman show as in I don't work with a team of designers, hair stylists, make up artists or location scouts aside from the few collaborations I've done in the past."

Maybe that is the most remarkable thing about RazorCandi overall. It is just not the looks, the styles, the sometimes bizarre themes, the can-be-downright twisted ambiance of the set, the polarizing Gothic fashion she displays, the wildly varied hair colors and styles, the impeccable make up artistry she expertly applies, the attention to detail she has, and the incredible diversity of the concepts

she creates…it is the fact she does it all herself. Any one of these aforementioned tasks are difficult enough. RazorCandi has mastered them all. With her seemingly unending talent, RazorCandi has provided her fans (and future fans) with already a decade worth of mesmerizing dark art, and soon to be bound in a hardcover art book. I asked her about her legacy, and Kym responded, "I'd be happy if my legacy would not be forgotten and remain memorable in the Goth scene. My biggest pride is the knowledge that I've helped people, whether it was just making someone feel more confident about themselves, or finding acceptance within the alternative scene through discovering my work. I feel that our appearance is an outward expression and the biggest symbol of freedom. If years from now my work continues to inspire people, then I can proudly say I feel very accomplished!"

RazorCandi has one final note for her fans:
"For those of you who want to keep updated about the project art book release, you can follow me on IG @ Razor_Candi or my new Facebook Page (www.facebook.com/RazorcandiOfficial). I'm also in the process of launching a new crowdfunding project on Patreon for help towards creating better dark art sets! Now that I am back in the USA I have access to a lot of great designers and other sources for shoots but I need the funds to be able to bring my haunting projects to life! You can read more about it on https://www.patreon.com/RazorCandi "■

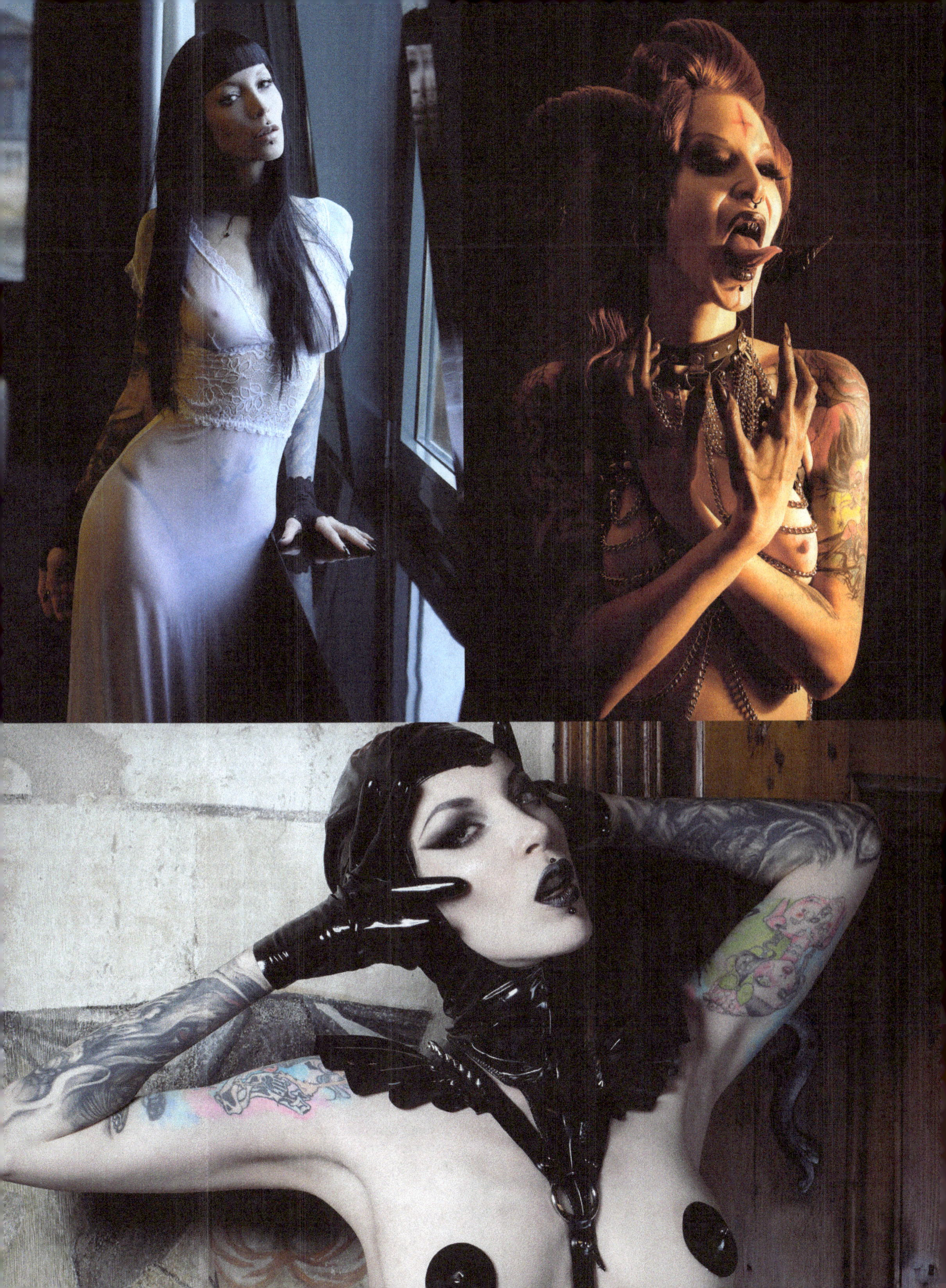

MINIMALISM
AND *Makeup*

By Amy Townsend

Once back in the mists of time when I used to blog a lot, I used to receive dozens of messages from younger Goths and scene newbies along the lines of "I'm not comfortable wearing heavy make-up, does this mean I can't be a 'real Goth'?" Well, let's not get into the 'real Goth' thing because who has the time (or the patience), but suffice to say that not every Goth (or black-clad, darkly inclined person) wears make-up from day to day, although of course there are many who do. And come to that, more than a handful of notable faces well-known for their skilful, dramatic make-up, whether worn on the daily or for special occasions. Siouxsie Sioux's heavy eyeliner. Rob Smith's smeared scarlet mouth. Adora BatBrat's false lashes, fangs and eyeliner swirls for days. Just to name a few.

Whilst festivals, photo shoots or clubbing might warrant a heavier application of maquillage, I think it's probably a fairly safe bet to say that many make-up wearers have a fall-back, basic 'everyday' look, because as much as we may want to look a certain way, we also have kids to drag up or work to get to at a reasonable time. The everyday look is one that we can swipe on through bleary eyes at crazy o'clock in the morning and then fall out the door. Some of us may not be able to wear our preferred style of make-up every day because of dress codes or practicality (if you're a lifeguard, for example, it seems a waste of time to glue on false eyelashes before work), and some, Goth and non-Goth alike, simply don't want to wear make-up, for various reasons.

Heavy make-up is perhaps thought of as a staple of the Goth scene, but in recent years a trend for minimalist make-up application has begun to emerge. Dramatic, vampy make-up, whether in the time-honoured

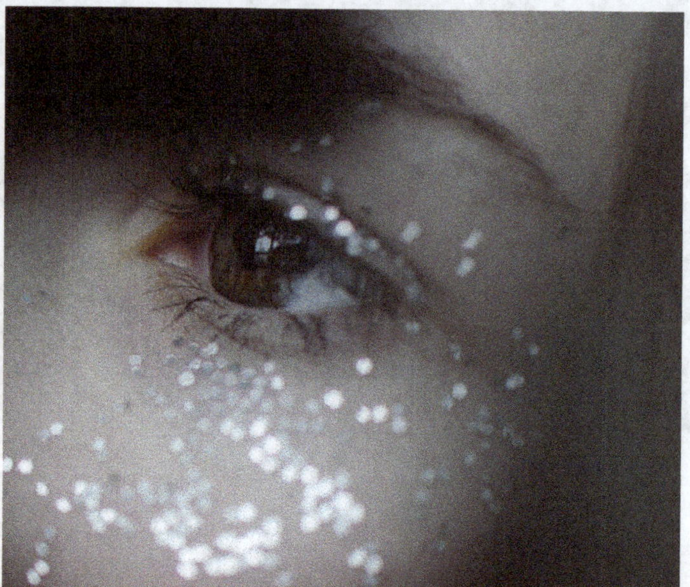

Goth style of black, black and more black, or kids on the internet today with their HD brows and Kim K contouring, has the potentially rather daunting effect of making you unrecognisable without it after long-term wear, even to yourself. I spent my teenage years building up my 'tolerance' to stronger, more elaborate looks (though sadly my skill in applying them did not increase proportionally, as I felt it ought to), and eventually after a good decade of daily eyeliner came to find my face intolerable without it. This is not an enjoyable feeling.

On the one hand, make-up can be empowering - whether as a transformative mask, to turn you into the person you want to be today, or simply to unleash and enhance the inner you and make you feel good in the mornings. The cheering power of a good lipstick is not to be underestimated. But on the other hand, when you feel shackled to the bathroom mirror and can't appreciate your own face without eyeliner, sometimes make-up feels more like a tyranny than a treat. I gave up wearing all make-up for six months, and yes, okay, I felt like an eyebrowless potato for a very long time, but the freedom to just roll out of bed in the morning and get on with my day felt

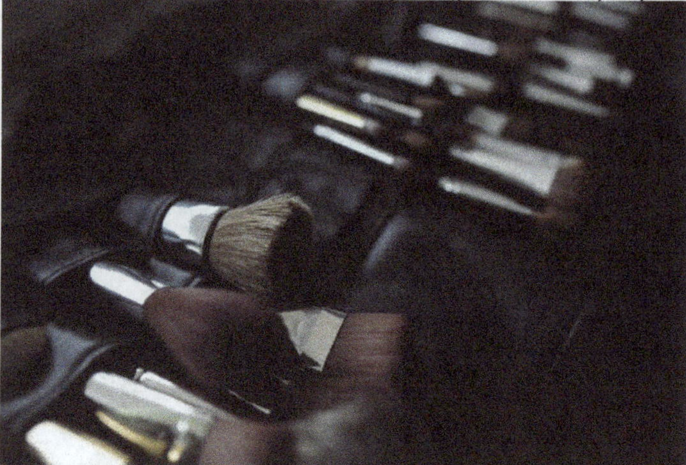

absolutely wonderful, and I have not since been able to commit to a heavy-duty routine. Lip balm, brow pencil, blush (because I like it) and a swipe of mascara and I'm good to go. Sometimes I feel like playing about a bit more, but mostly I don't.

Of course, painting on a new face over your own face has never been everyone's thing. The natural (or natural-er) look has its own place in the Goth scene, be it doll-like, ethereal, faerie-esque or Victorian-maidenish - more so perhaps since the early 2000s when more people began to draw inspiration from Japanese Lolita looks and vintage, retro and burlesque stylings. However, with the ever-growing influences of body positivity, 'radical self-love' and third-wave feminism strongly present on social media, the burgeoning predilection for a minimal make-up application or even a bare face could also be said to hearken back to the early era of Goth, when it was still closely enmeshed with the punk scene. Punk make-up looks, as we know, had little to do with enhancing one's appearance in line with conventional ideas of beauty, and more to do with rebelling against societal standards, particularly for women. Perhaps – smug supermodel #nomakeup #iwokeuplikethis Instagram posts aside – in a time of selfies and Snapchat filters, a naked, unadorned face is in some cases used as a statement of strength, a rejection of such standards and a claiming of personal freedom from a tiresome primping routine. ∎

Prancing around with
PAWSTAR

by Sonnett57

The underground community is certainly known for some of the most beautiful, outrageous and eccentric fashions. Although elaborate and aesthetically pleasing, the corset, fish nets, pirate shirts and pointed boots can become a little monotonous day after day. There are those that are comfortable with this look, but also those that need a little more flavor. Each month I am required to dig into this realm of textiles to wear something different and within a theme. I have searched and searched for years to find that special furry outfit that would not make me look like some sort of strange muppet, but something that was cute, classy and sexy all in one. I finally stumbled upon the amazing line at the Dark Arts Festival here in Salt Lake City. The merchandise was being sold to be by an intriguing DarkFox Fursona that was very informative about his wares. My search was over. Pawstar had been revealed to me and I was soon covered in fur. Pawstar serves many genres with pieces that move between them with ease. Your furry, fetish, and cosplay needs will be met with no limit to your creativity.

Before we get into things, let me clarify what a Fursona is, as some of you may not know. Enlightenment is crucial in today's age and accepting one's identity is key to finding harmony with others and yourself. A "fursona" is the depiction of the animal persona of an individual. It can be based off of real animals, mythology, or other fantasy creatures. People often base fursonas off of qualities that these animals have or exhibit, and it allows members of the furry fandom a great amount of self-expression.

When asked about his fursona, DarkFox says, "My fursona is mostly a monochrome red fox (vulpes vulpes) with yellow eyes." He feels that it is pretty vanilla compared to some of them out there. As for the personality DarkFox says, "I identify with the playful an inquisitive personality of a fox. I also scavenge food from my friend's meals and I love eggs!" He goes on to say, "The color scheme of my fursona just fits a lot of my wardrobe."

Now that is out of the way, let's focus on the company. The name Pawstar says it all about these creative business partners. The title is an imaginative splicing of two figures. DarkFox says, "Pawstar is the literal combination of a stylized animal paw (between a cat and a fox) as well as stars." The logo of the paw was a combination of the skills that Vixis-Nai and Darkfox compiled, and the stars represented

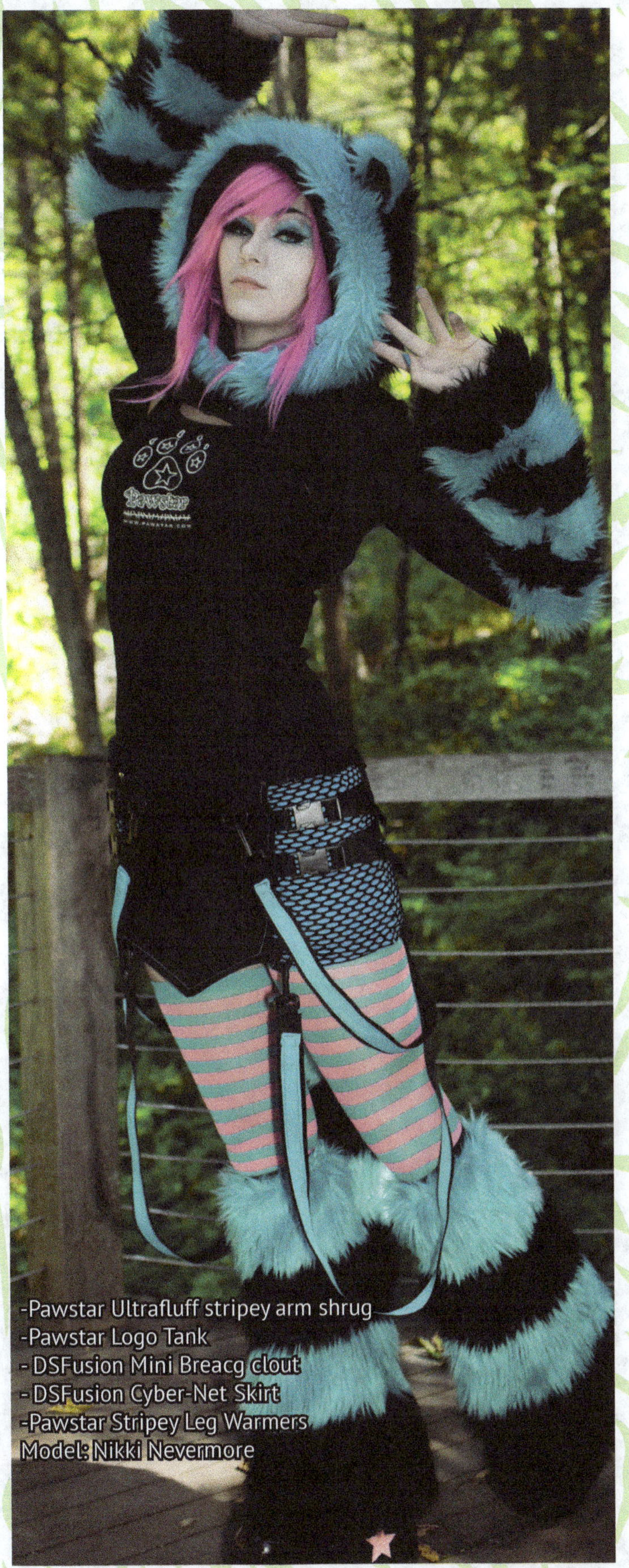

-Pawstar Ultrafluff stripey arm shrug
-Pawstar Logo Tank
-DSFusion Mini Breacg clout
-DSFusion Cyber-Net Skirt
-Pawstar Stripey Leg Warmers
Model: Nikki Nevermore

- DSFusion Uber Spike Goggles
- DSFusion Reflective Cyber Mask
- DSFusion custom Plate-X Collar
- DSFusion Symbol Arm Warmers
- DSFusion Transfigurator Skirt
- DSFusion Reflective Symbol Leg Warmers
Model: Nikki Nevermore

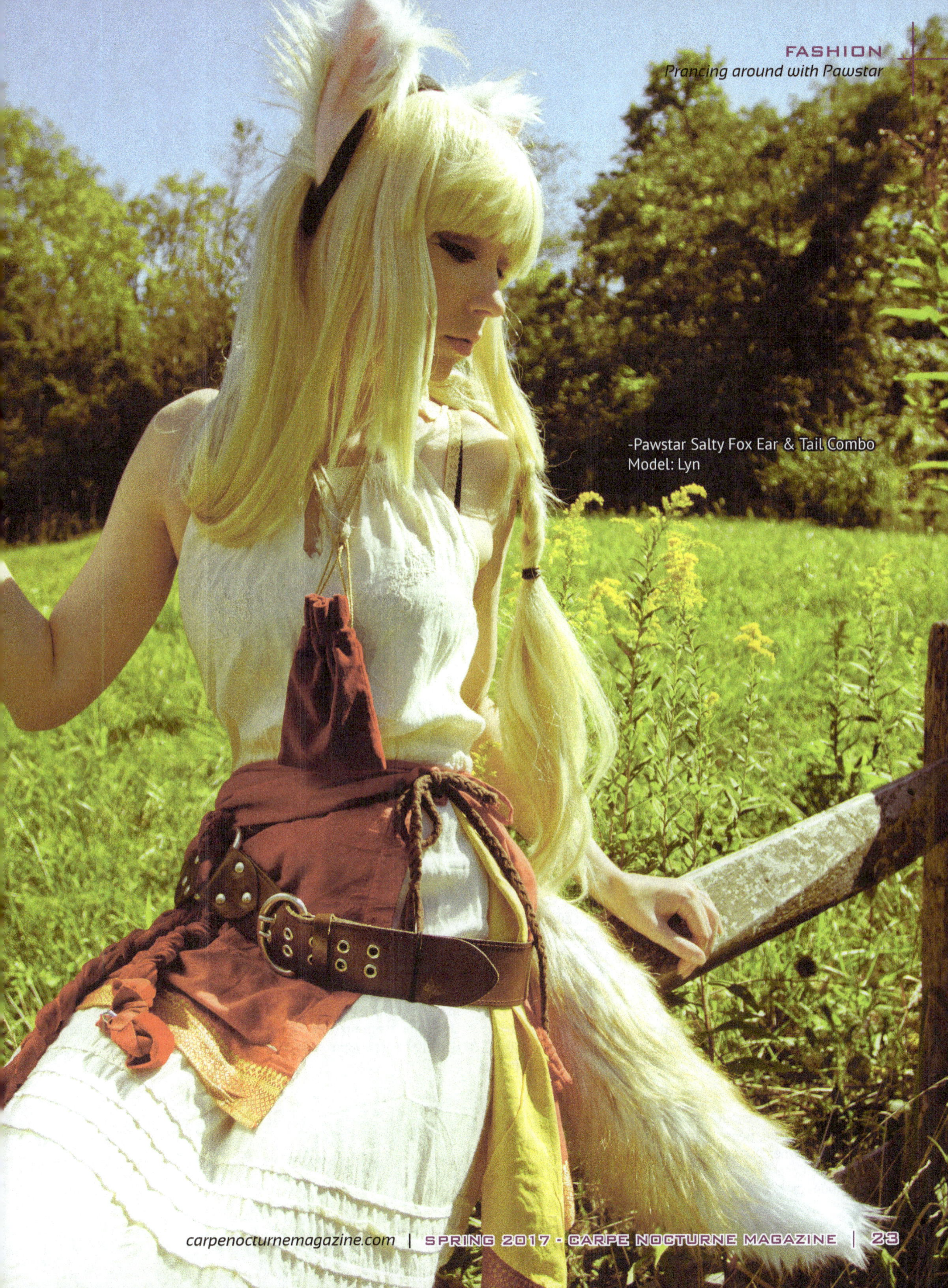
FASHION
Prancing around with Pawstar
-Pawstar Salty Fox Ear & Tail Combo
Model: Lyn

the awesomeness that could be if these things were brought together. Pawstar is growing fast, and currently has a sister brand, Darkstar Fusion (DS Fusion for short). DS Fusion is geared towards the cyber, gothic, industrial, and future-wear apparel group.

With an almost 15 year tenure shows that this company knows what they are doing when it comes to innovating ideas, quality, professionalism and customer service. As to how the company was started, it appears as if it came out of a personal fashion need that led to success. Co-owner Vixis-Nai has always been a DIY machine, and decided one day that she wanted a hat with kitty ears. She made it and thought it was very cute and decided to try and sell it on eBay. Darkfox added leather collars to the mix and slowly the company grew. Quality assurance is also a factor in success as their new prototypes are put through rigorous testing to ensure they meet their standards. DarkFox says, "We pride ourselves in the fact that all of our products are handcrafted in the USA and carry a lifetime manufacturer's warranty against defects."

With their headquarters based in Zion, Illinois Pawstar has become a top manufacturer of quality costume apparel and accessories. Their company has been in business since 2003 and currently has 15 personnel working for them, creating amazing looks on a daily basis. DarkFox says, "Fancy fashion forward. We look for a lot of aesthetic in the current fashions and we try to push the envelope and see what

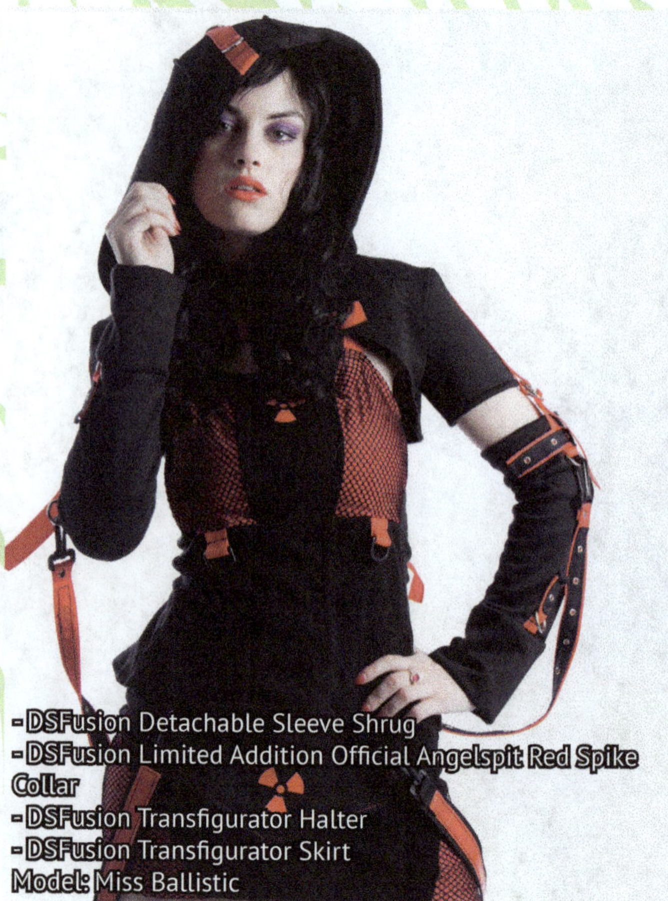

–DSFusion Detachable Sleeve Shrug
–DSFusion Limited Addition Official Angelspit Red Spike Collar
–DSFusion Transfigurator Halter
–DSFusion Transfigurator Skirt
Model: Miss Ballistic

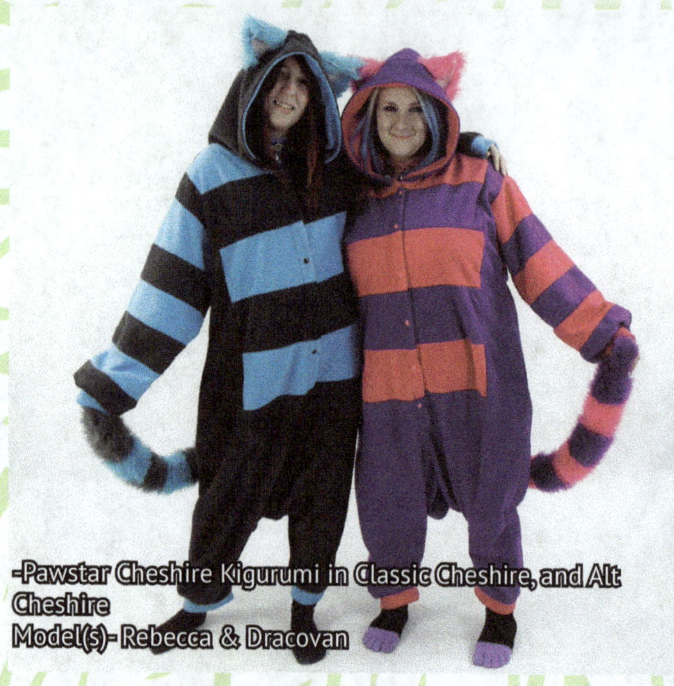

–Pawstar Cheshire Kigurumi in Classic Cheshire, and Alt Cheshire
Model(s)- Rebecca & Dracovan

we can do that currently isn't being done." Pawstar fashion draws inspiration from bright colors, dancewear, and animal styles while DS Fusion looks into the world of dark fashion, cyber styles, and future forward club-wear.

They make their products out of a variety of materials but primarily focus on synthetic fur, fleece, and leather. When asked to describe the fashion, co-owner DarkFox says, "Pawstar's fashions cater towards the Anime and Cosplay interest groups, but has crossovers into other interest groups as well."

Pawstar also cares for the communities they serve. When asked if they donated to charity, DarkFox says, "All the time! We prefer animal-related causes because we feel they tend to get overlooked, but we also have donated to causes like the Fukushima disaster relief, LGBTQ awareness, and children's cancer." Quality goods with quality minds creating them. I don't know about you, but it always makes me feel better when I do my retail therapy with companies that take care about what is important.

You can find Pawstar items at a myriad of places. The easiest of those would be on websites like pawstar.com, amazon, etsy (stitches by pawstar), crunchyroll, ebay (pawstarstitches), dsfusion.com which leads to DS Fusion's etsy store. I know it seems like a lot, but do not fret. You may find all Pawstar links are on pawstar.com's home page. Pawstar and DS Fusion brand products are also sold at about 30 conventions and trade shows across the U.S. yearly. They have also marketed special events and tours as well, with their latest being a DS Fusion team-up with the band Angelspit for the "Cult of Fake" tour. Be sure to grab yours soon. ■

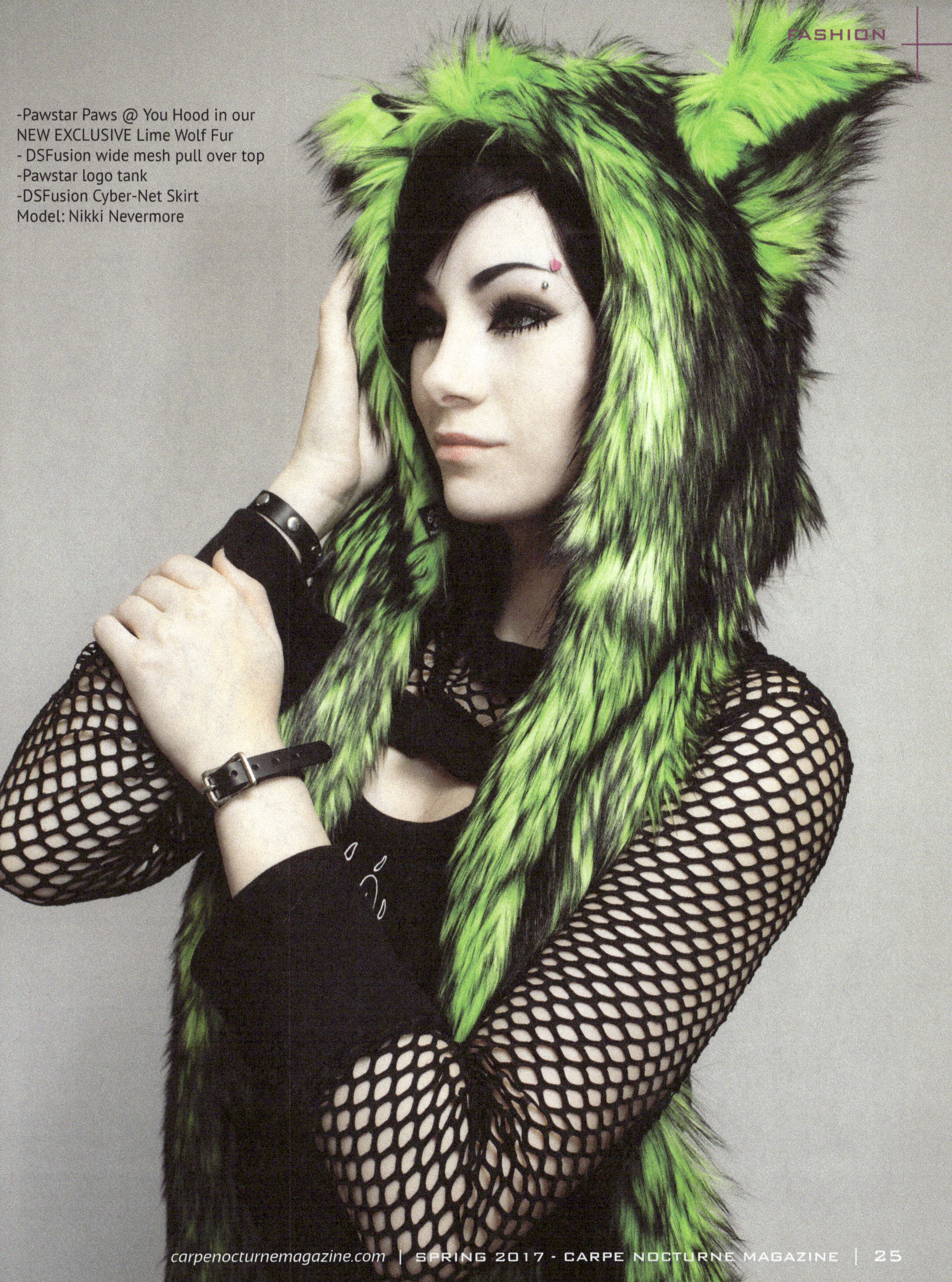
FASHION

-Pawstar Paws @ You Hood in our
NEW EXCLUSIVE Lime Wolf Fur
- DSFusion wide mesh pull over top
-Pawstar logo tank
-DSFusion Cyber-Net Skirt
Model: Nikki Nevermore

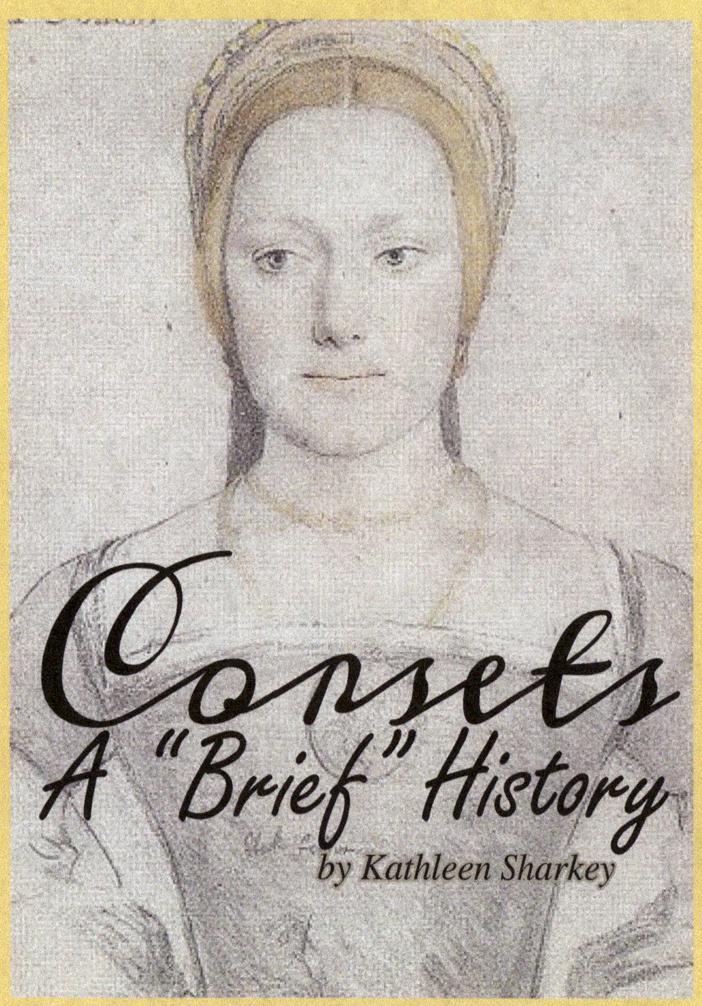

I decided to write this article because I have heard so many contrasting opinions about corsets. Some people think that they are the most brilliant invention and wish that they would be brought back into fashion mainstream. While others see corsets as a demon best left in the past, a torture device used by women who didn't know any better. Having worn the corset's cousin the bodice I have my own thoughts on the matter. So I thought I would look into the history of the corset and give you a little background to make your own informed decision.

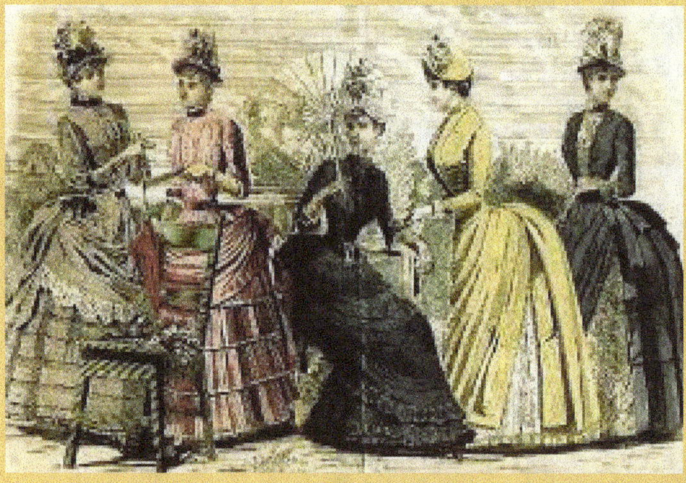

Seeing that talking about underwear from any time period is definitely taboo it can be hard to find a whole lot out about their everyday use. I have gathered much of my information from the internet, so a grain of salt must be accepted. One thing that many of the pages I have visited agree upon is that the corset was not used to draw in the waist as much as it was to flatten curves and lift the bust

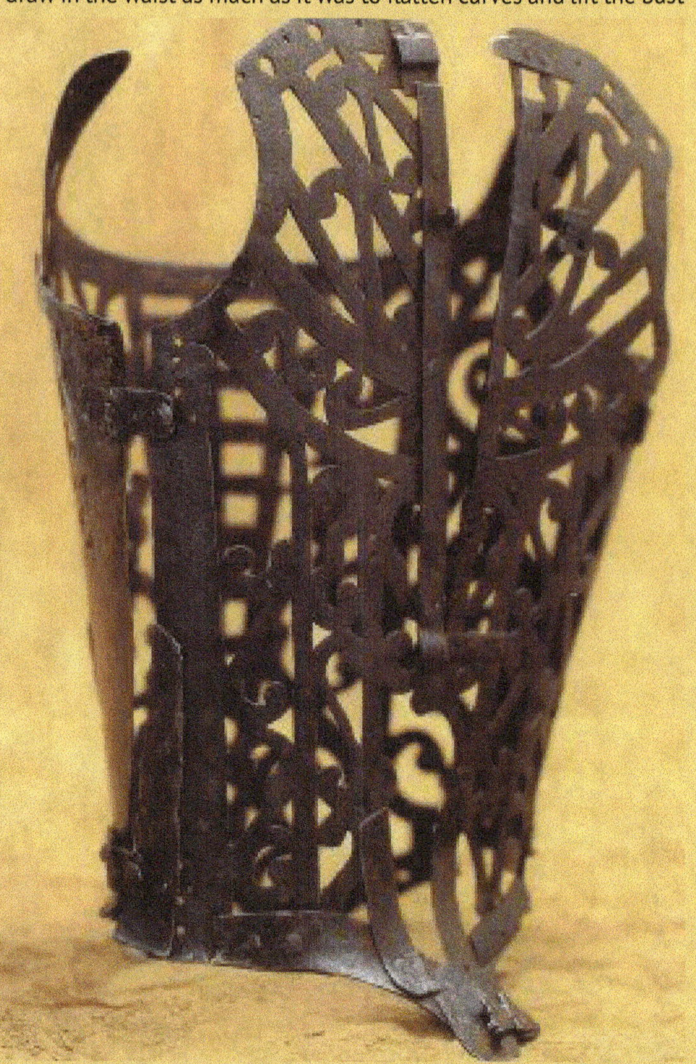

line. This created a conical or cylindrical shape to a woman's body and allowed the body to fit the fashion as opposed to the fashion fitting the body type.

Corsets, in various definitions, can be found throughout history but seem to have reached an apex during the 16th century. Instead of corset it was known generally as a "payre of bodies" and this is when the corset seems to have become separated from other pieces of the undergarment construction (http://www.elizabethancostume.net/corsets/history.html, Drea Leed). As stiffening seems to have become more and more important in the construction of the corset pockets were sewn into the garment and reeds, bone, wood and sometimes (though rarely) steel stays were slipped into the pockets. Looking at these corsets one can see that the corsets were wonderful for great posture as the arm holes where placed farther back stopping the wearer from any contemplation of slouching. Some of the more negative routed informational sites have pictures of corsets that look like torture devices from the 16th century made out of strong metal it seems to be well documented that these crazy contraptions were more than likely used for spine and or back problems and were not worn every day.

By the 17and 1800s the corset was the primary breast support undergarment. It still smoothed out curves but this was not its primary purpose. But as the Victorian era came along a change in fashion did too. The industrial revolution made fashionable clothing more obtainable to the masses, and so it made the corset more obtainable as well. I will pause here to say this, the Victorian era, like the Elizabethan era long before it were different times from the one in which we now live. I know this statement seems extraordinarily obvious but I say it because we cannot put our own modern day biases upon the lives and underwear of those over a decade ago. Diet, nutrition and general body sizes where generally a world different from that which we now know so I had to keep this in mind when I perused the fashion and corsets of the Victorian era.

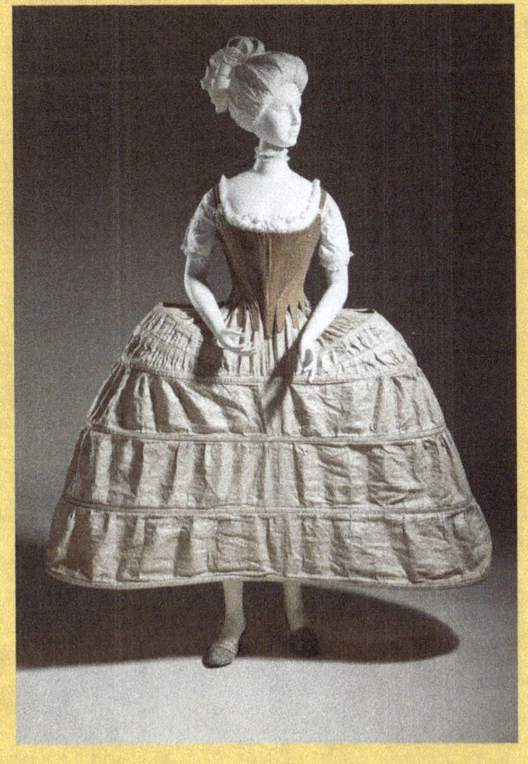

The fashion of the time in 1850s was definitely the hour glass figure. Bust lines were larger and hips were wider but waists had to be proportionally smaller. The corset aided in this creation and made it easier for larger women to attain the fashionable proportions like their thinner counterparts. Women began wearing corsets early in their teens, for posture perfection and to "train the waist". These corsets came below the waist to, seemingly, add size to the hips. Corsets were being worn by pregnant women to aid in support of the weight in front of them. This was probably due to a lack of back muscles due to the initial wearing of corsets which stiffened the spine without the aid of those muscles. It was during this time that the medical practice began to vilify the corset.

Some of the issue doctors had with corsets were probably accurate. Shortness of breath caused by displacement of the lungs by corsetry probably did cause an increase in fainting spells. Displacement of organs would have definitely occurred and could have caused a variety of issues. Bones strapped into tight corsets at an early age were bound to be deformed by the pressure, and as I have already stated certain muscles that would not be used due to the supportive intention of the corset would deteriorate. But perhaps a good deal of the villainy of the corset was due to its nature as an undergarment and the sexualization of undergarments.

The 14 inch waists of the Victorian era, like the size zeros of our era were the exception not the norm. Fashion was the decision of the wearer and some of the later fashions were ever stranger. Eventually the corset seems to have resigned its reign to the bra, this is probably due to the need for metal during the 1st World War. Women became increasingly more active and the constrictive nature of the corset did not allow for freedom of movement required. So I say go out and wear that corset, but understand it probably won't look the same on your frame at it did on Great Aunt Matilda in the late 1890's because Aunt Matilda was wearing corsets for most of her life. Don't judge women for being ignorant for wearing corsets while wearing your six inch stiletto man killer heels. Wear your fashion and be the beautiful you that you are. Big women are beautiful in corsetry, thin women have beautiful curves too. Short women and tall women have their own amazing symmetry, it is what we do with it and how we decide to wield our beauty that empowers us. Take notes from our ancestors and deny your own complacency. Fashion is our decision, our beauty, our power and what we define as beauty is not how others define it. The one thing that this article has taught me is to not judge a fashion by its detractors, rather educate yourself and find power in other people's definition. Go forth and be the beautiful you that you already are. ■

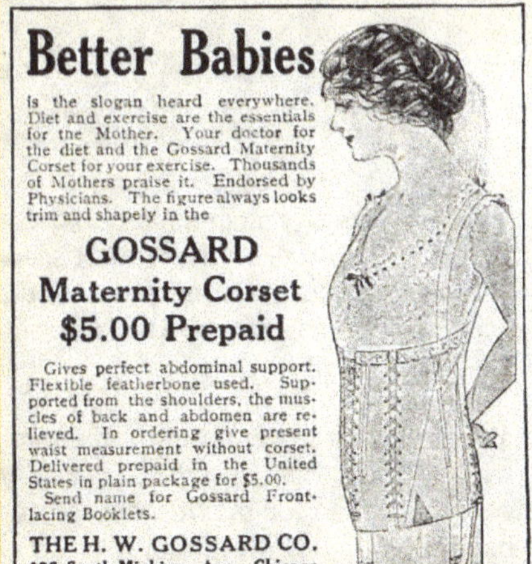

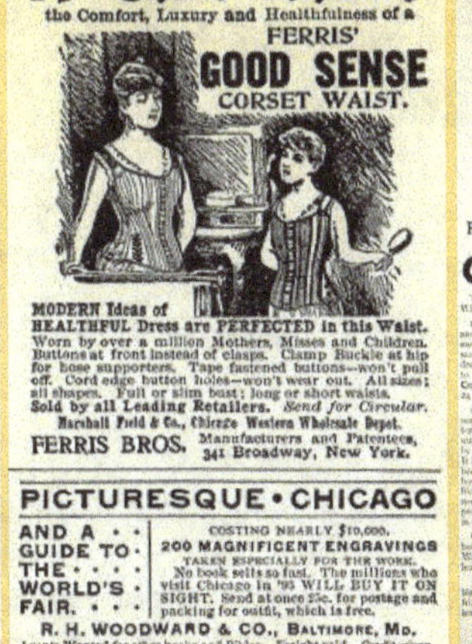

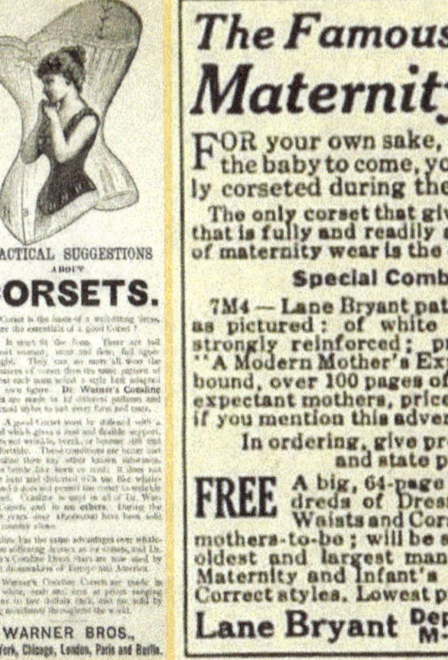

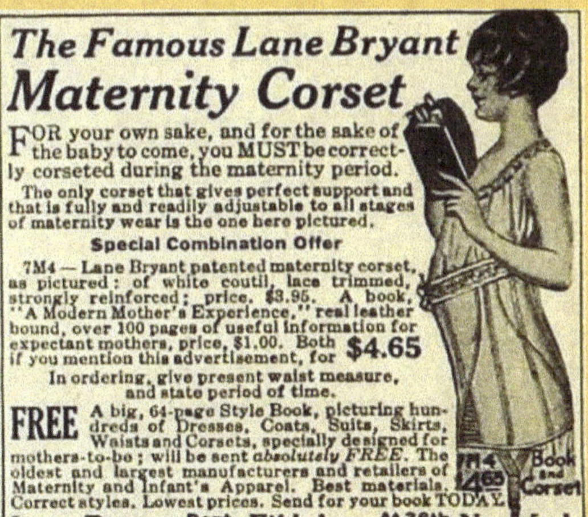

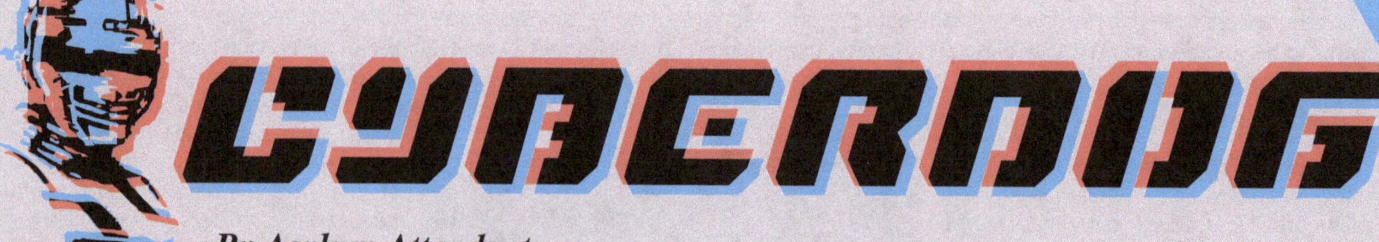

CYBERDOG

By Asylum Attendant

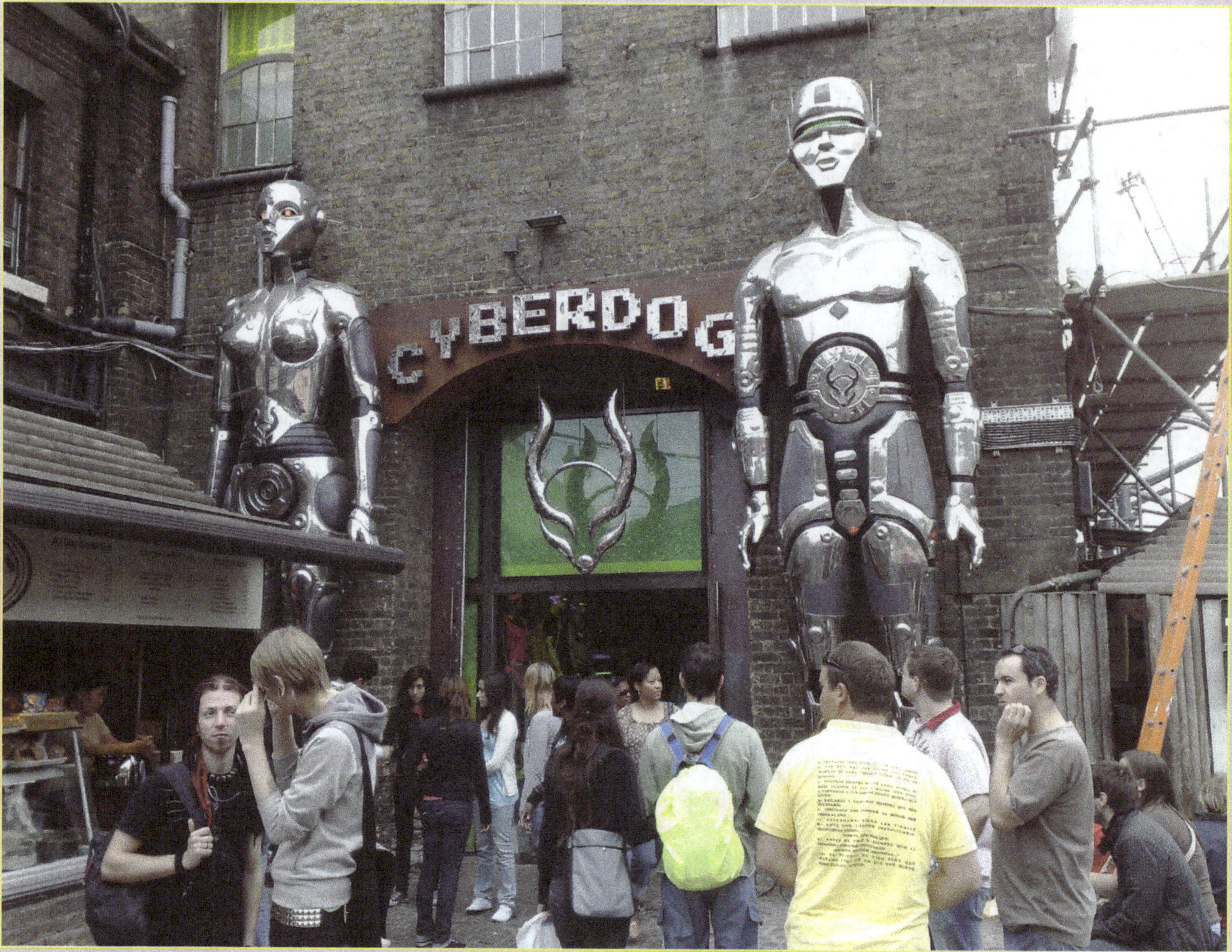

Putting together the most stellar outfit for that warehouse rave you have been dying to go to might not be the easiest of tasks. Sure, you could dip into the nearest sex shop for furry leg warmers and neon fishnet tops, but what if you want to elevate your look? I don't think showing off your entire kandi bracelet collection on your arms would help the situation either. There might be a fashion mecca for space aliens such as yourself if you live in the UK or have an internet connection. Ever heard of Cyberdog?

Cyberdog is a brand that specializes in futuristic club wear that would make any CyberGoth gasp. The brand was created in London in the 1990's by partners Terri Davy and Spiros Vlahos, with their main inspiration Chi Chi the Space Chihuahua serving as the company logo. They sell everything from light up shoes to holographic backpacks. If it glows in the dark or would be trendworthy on the nearest space station, then you can probably find it at Cyberdog. You can shop the brand online, but this is one techno utopia you have to visit in person if you ever stop by Camden Town.

Visitors are greeted by two giant robots at the entrance to the three level store, which is simply badass. Once inside, the electronic tunes are pumping, the black lights are raging and you might come across a pole dancer or two. You are barraged with a whirlwind of fluorescent colors in all directions and employees in wild outfits. Cyberdog is so

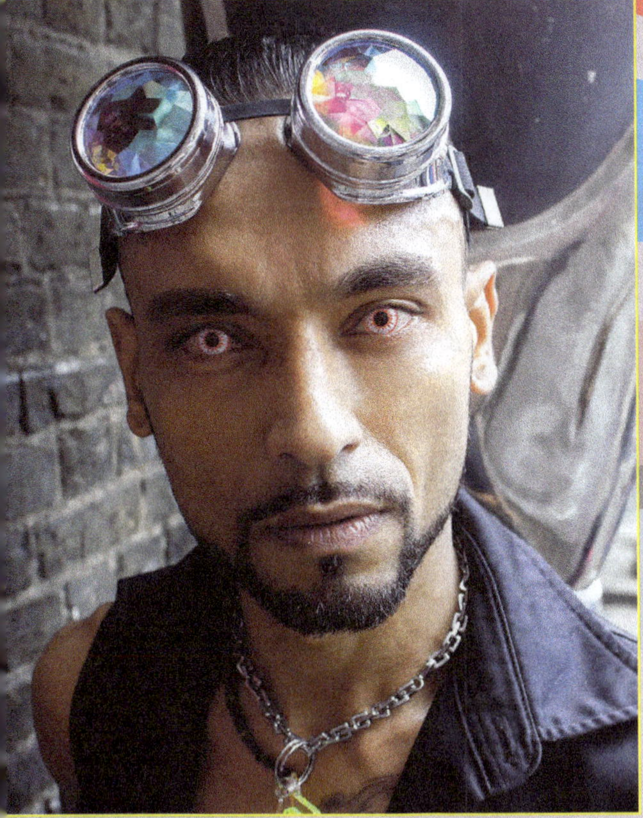

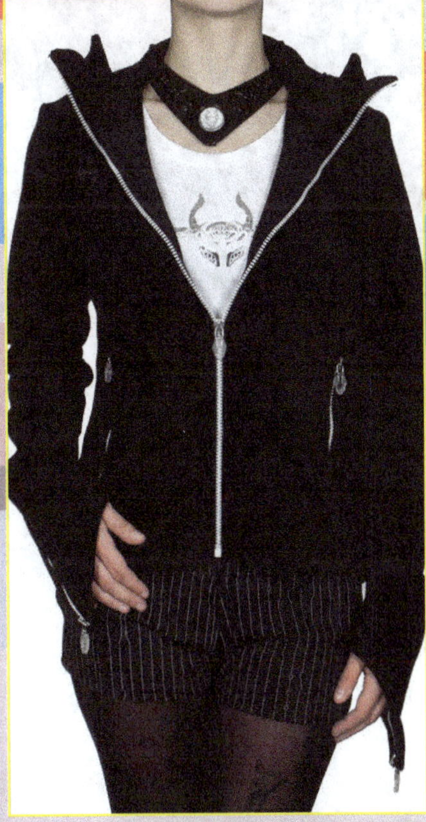

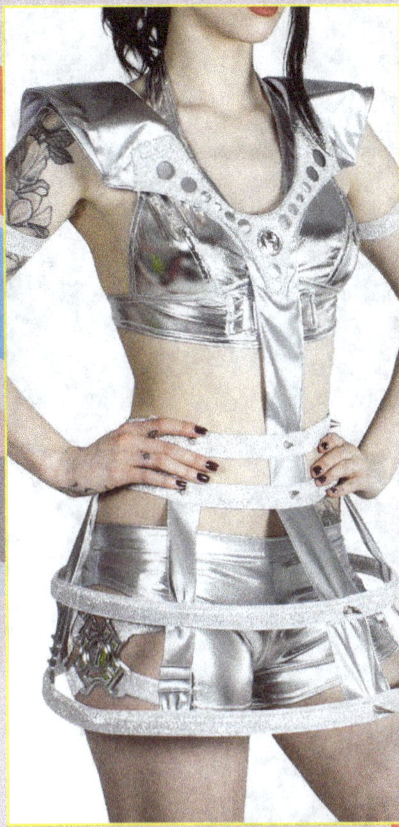

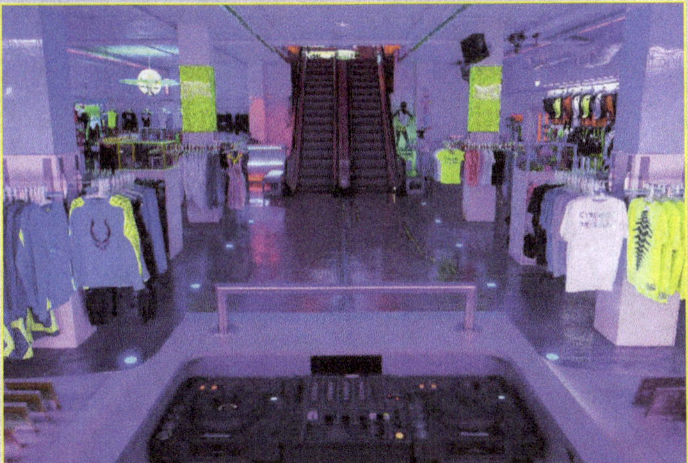

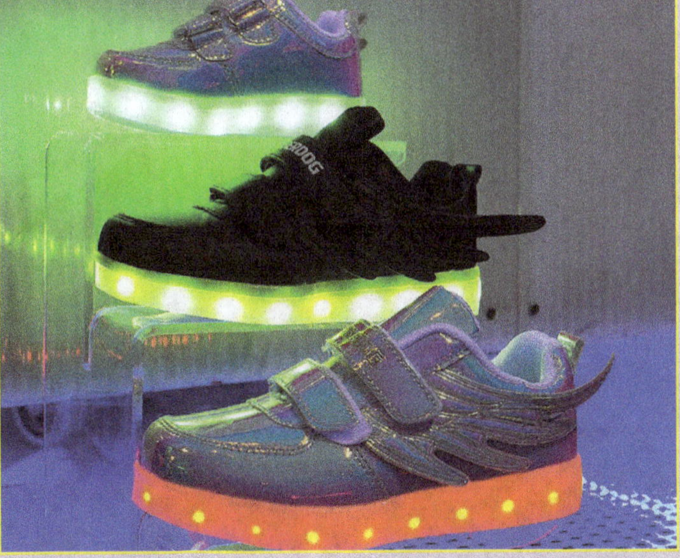

much more than just a clothing store. It is a one-of-a-kind hangout spot for tourists and alternative types alike.

Cyberdog crafts the most intriguing mixture of textures, patterns and materials in their clothing pieces. Where else can you purchase light up t-shirts with removable battery packs that are sensitive to sound? This is some next level shit people. Yeti costumes and skirts shaped like UFOs are just the tip of the iceberg that Cyberdog has to offer to its eclectic customers. They have plenty of black latex and vampy items to accommodate any nocturnal animals roaming through this electric playground. There are even adorable moon dresses for the kiddos!

Cyberdog even launched the adult brand Futurelovers in 2012 for all of your fetish and sex toy needs. This is a brand unafraid to push the envelope. I think my favorite items are the kaleidoscopic goggles, the bat jacket and anything made of silver lame fabric. I realize now that I have seen celebrities wear Cyberdog stuff before, so it must be a very popular and well-respected brand. They have tapped into a market that keeps growing as electronic music festivals become more and more widespread. Fashion is a huge part of rave culture and adds to the euphoric adventure.

Brighton and Manchester also boast Cyberdog stores, so hit them up the next time you visit the UK or shop online at http://www.cyberdog. net. When the aliens invade Earth, I truly believe this will be their first pit stop. ■

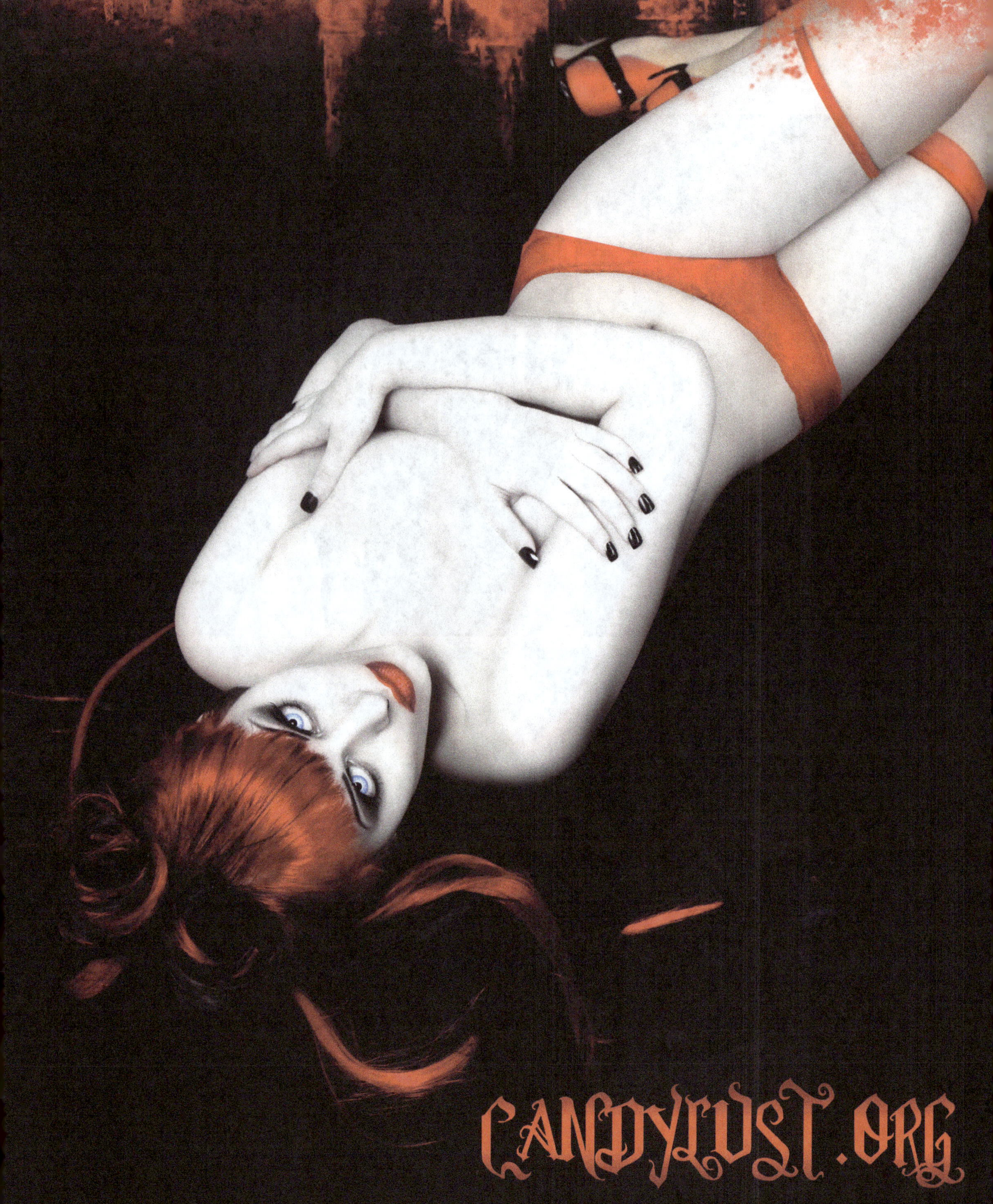

CANDYLUST.ORG

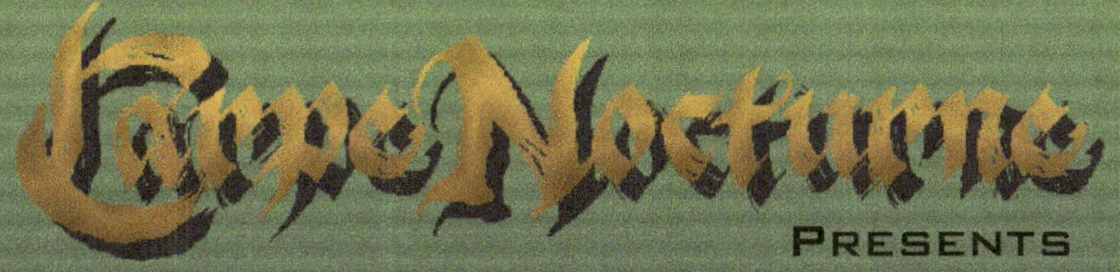

VISCERAL Attractions

If you are a model, a photographer, a cosplayer or a designer and would like to have your work featured in Visceral Attractions, contact the editor at fashion@carpenocturne.net.

THEMES

SPRING - SCI-FI
SUMMER - STEAMPUNK
FALL - GOTH
WINTER - FANTASY

/VIS(ə)RəL/ -

coming from strong emotions;
not pertaining to logic or reason.

Visceral Attractions is Carpe Nocturne's official Fashion insert, spotlighting the most unique and decadent counter-culture fashion designs out there.
Every quarterly issue features full page spreads of fashion, fetish and cosplay photographs to the theme of Goth, Fantasy, Sci-Fi, and Steampunk.

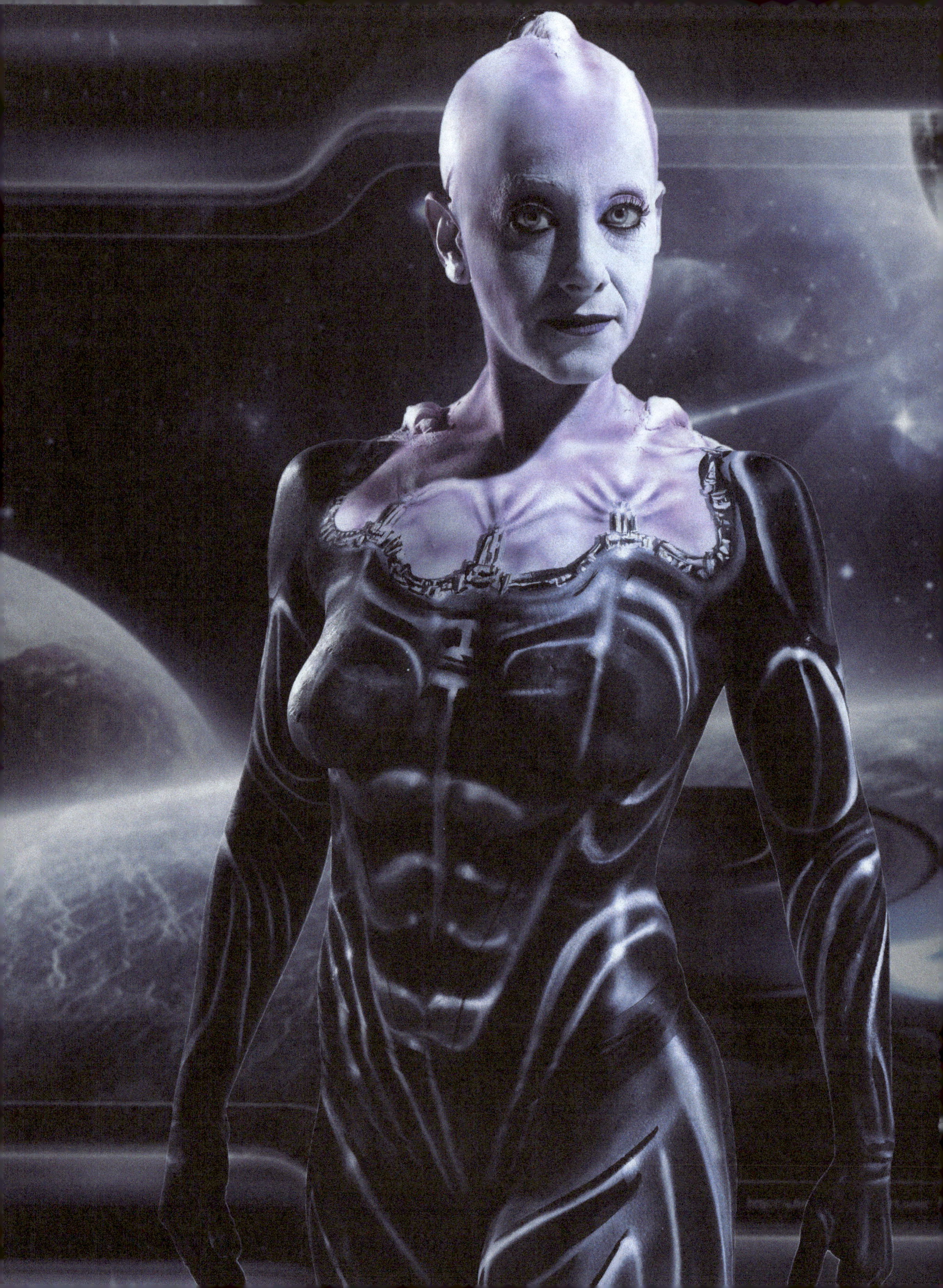

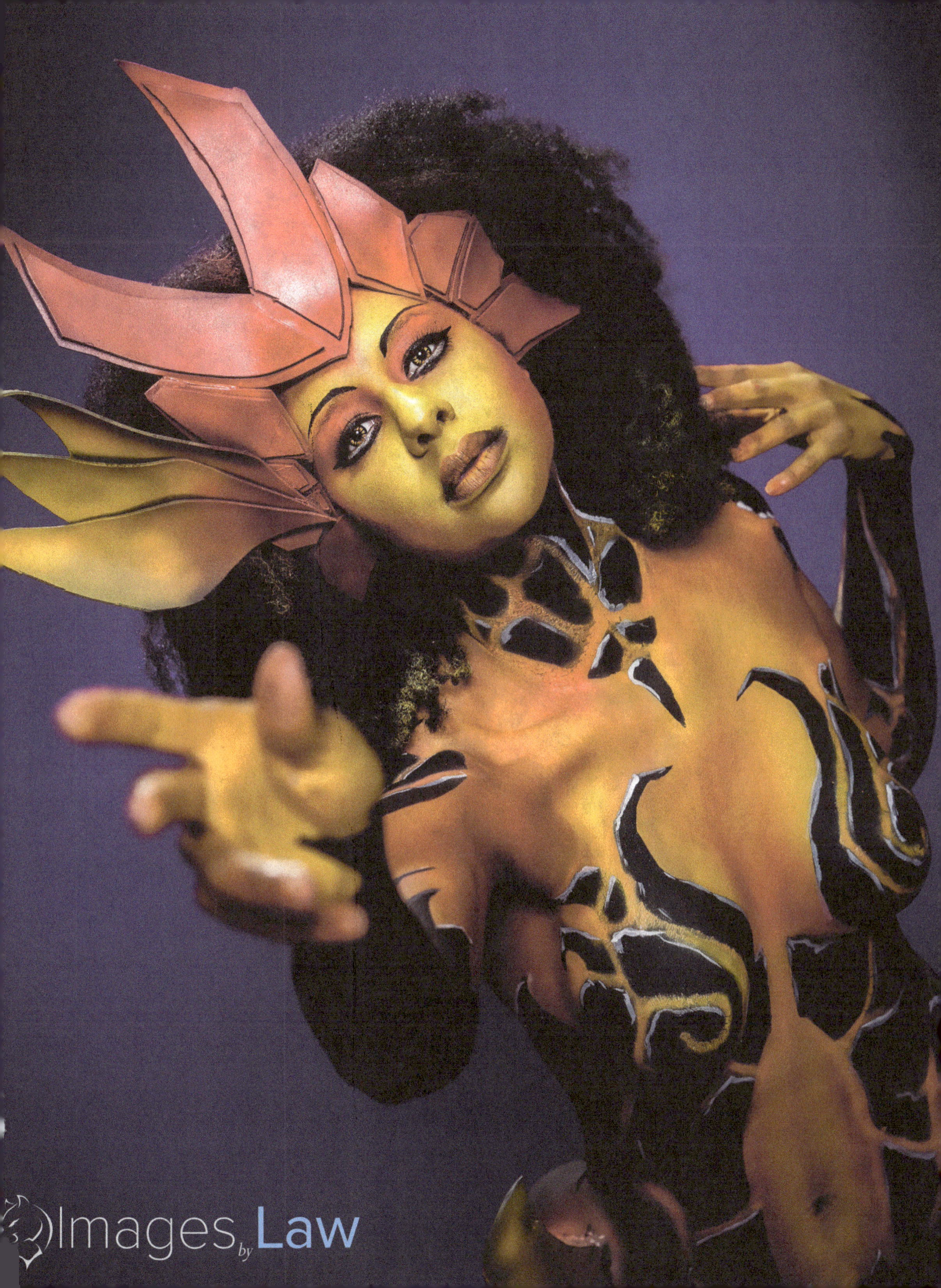
Images by Law

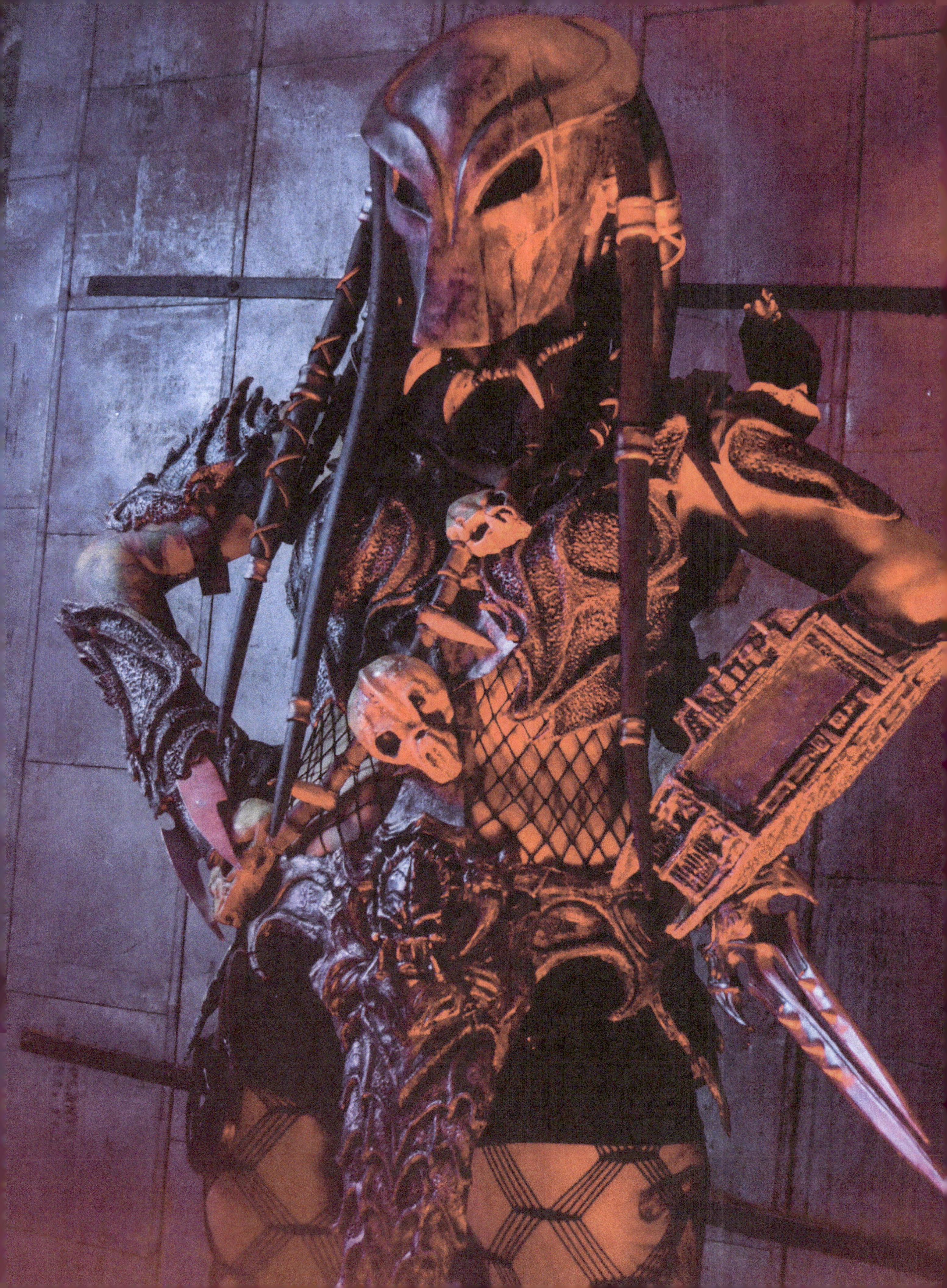

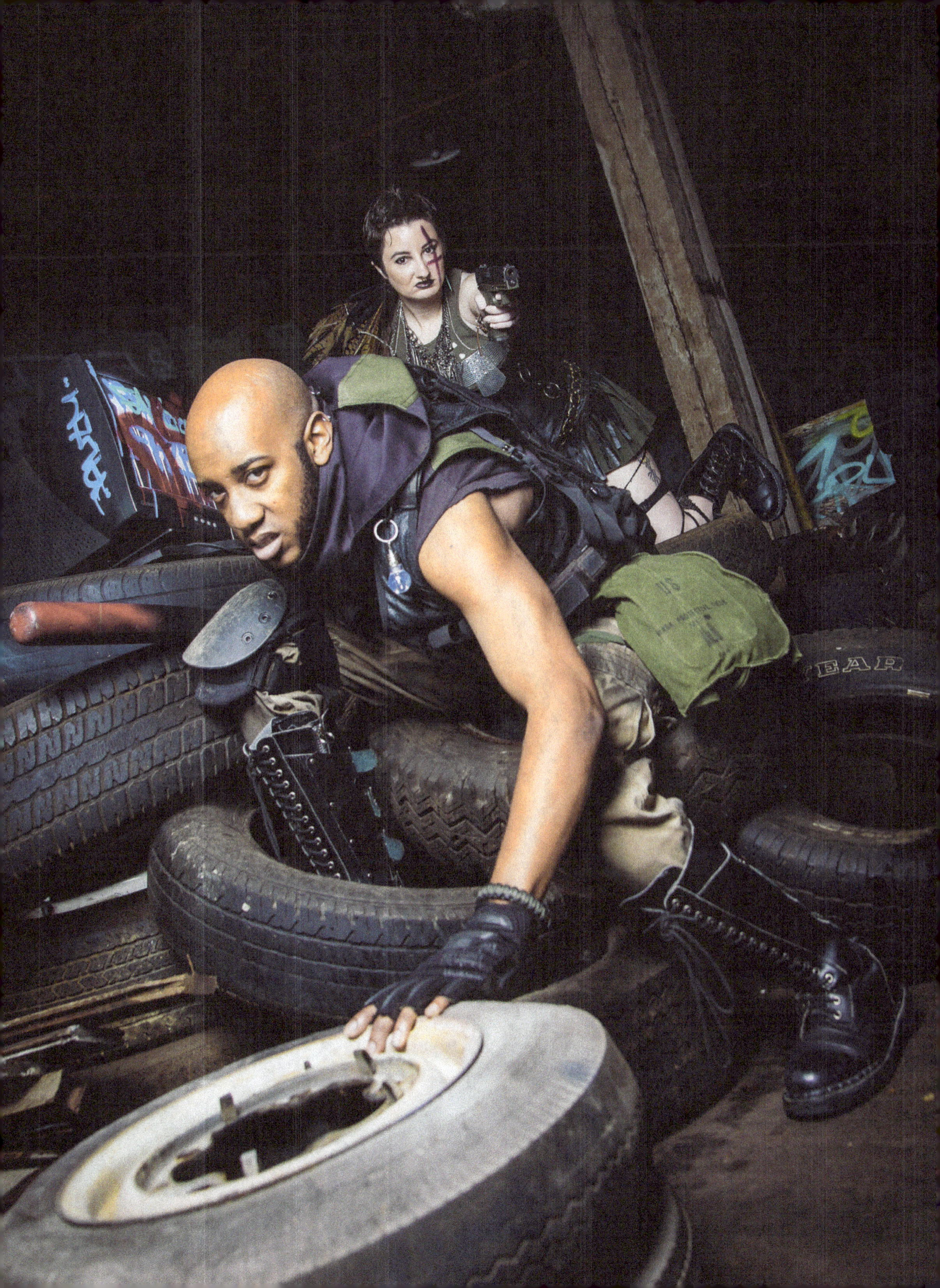

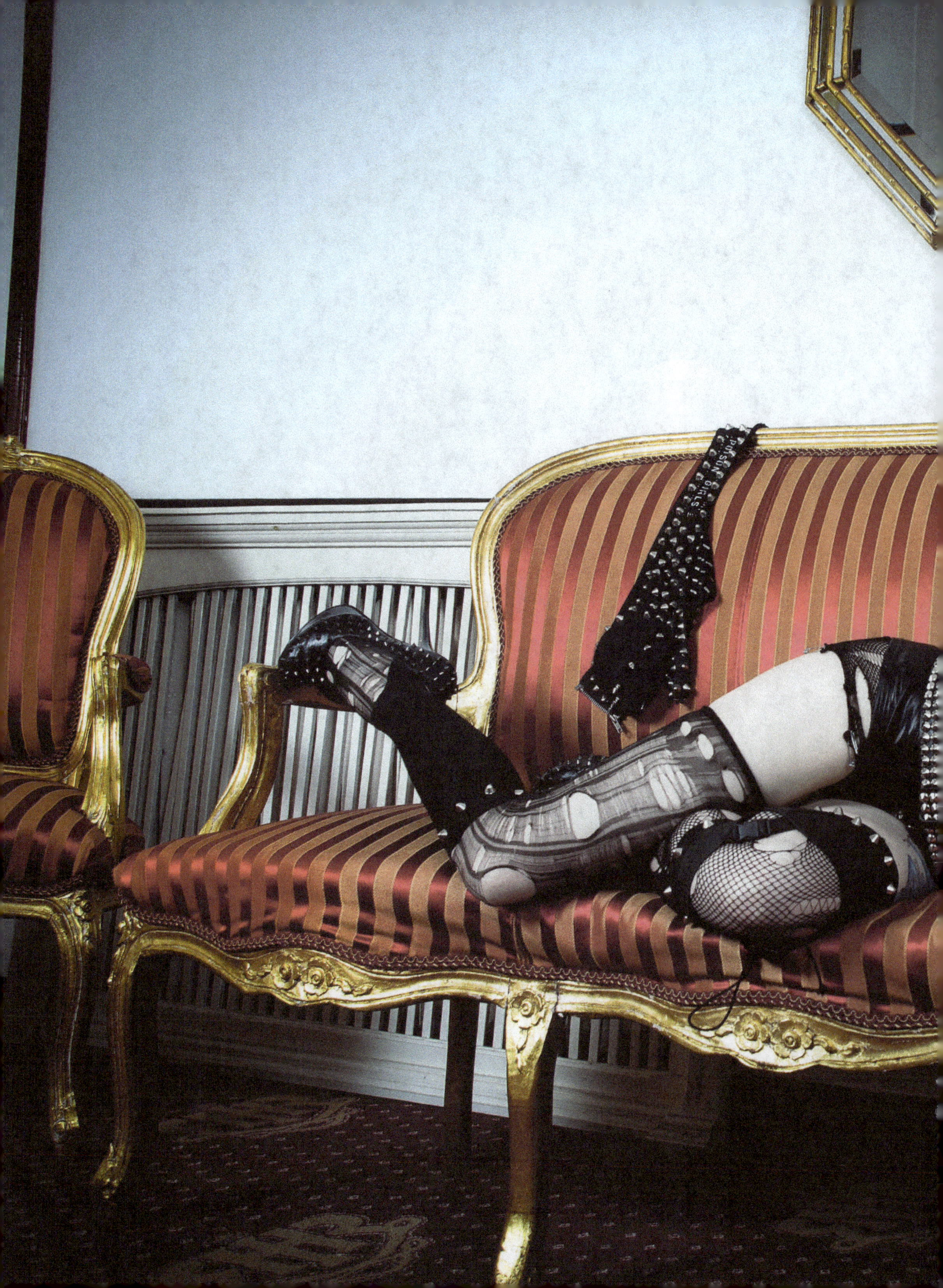
POISON GIRLS

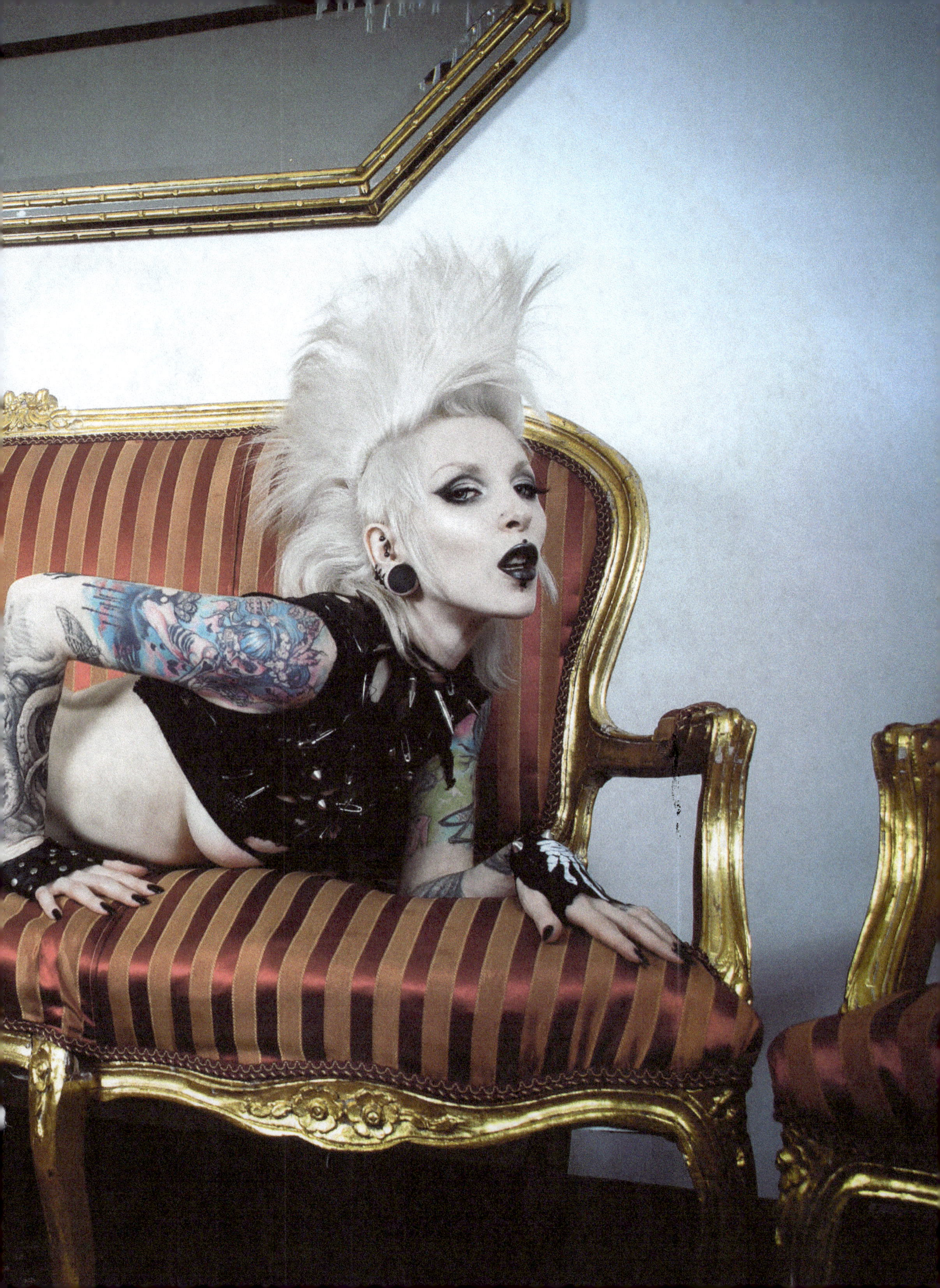

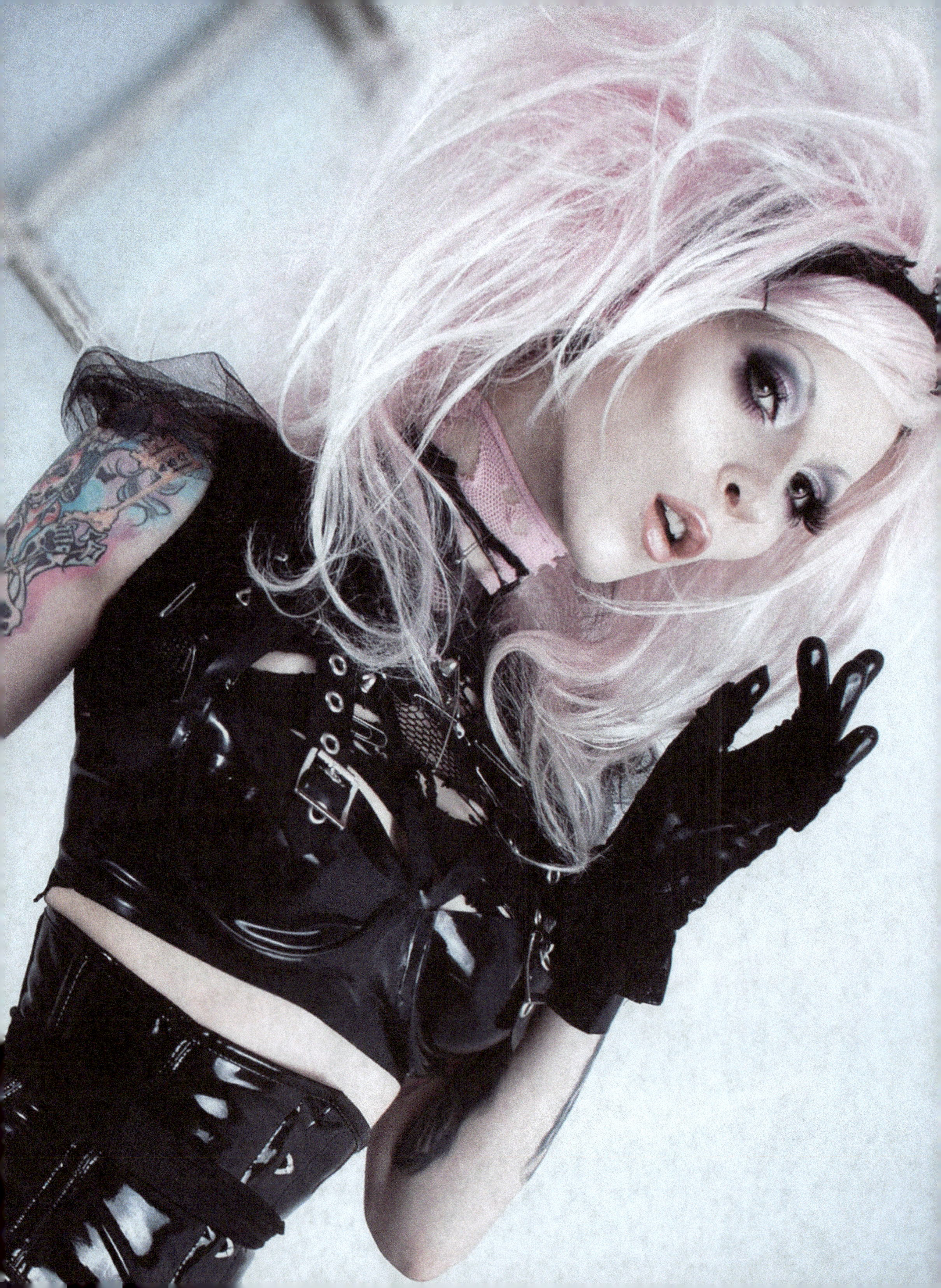

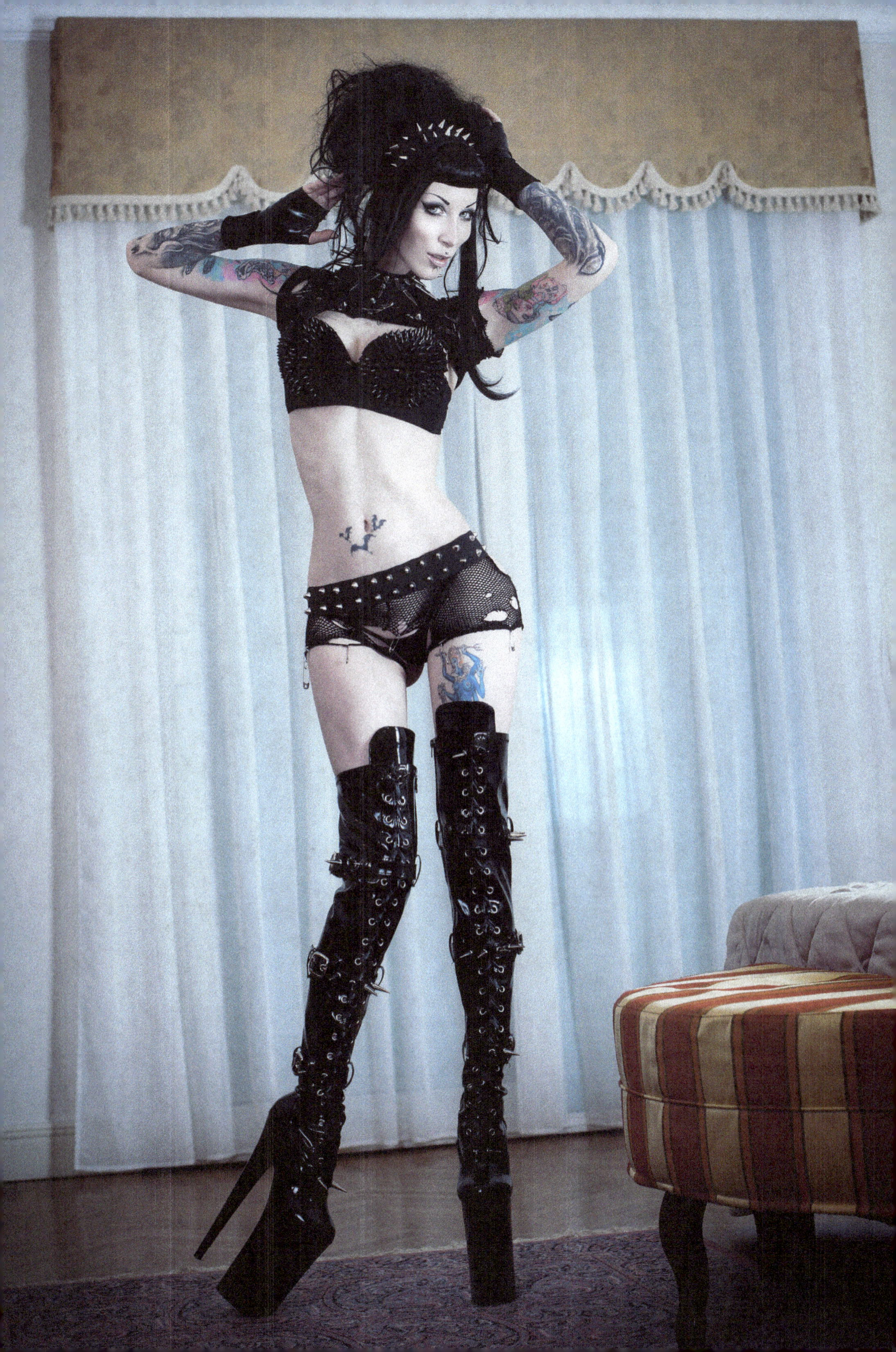

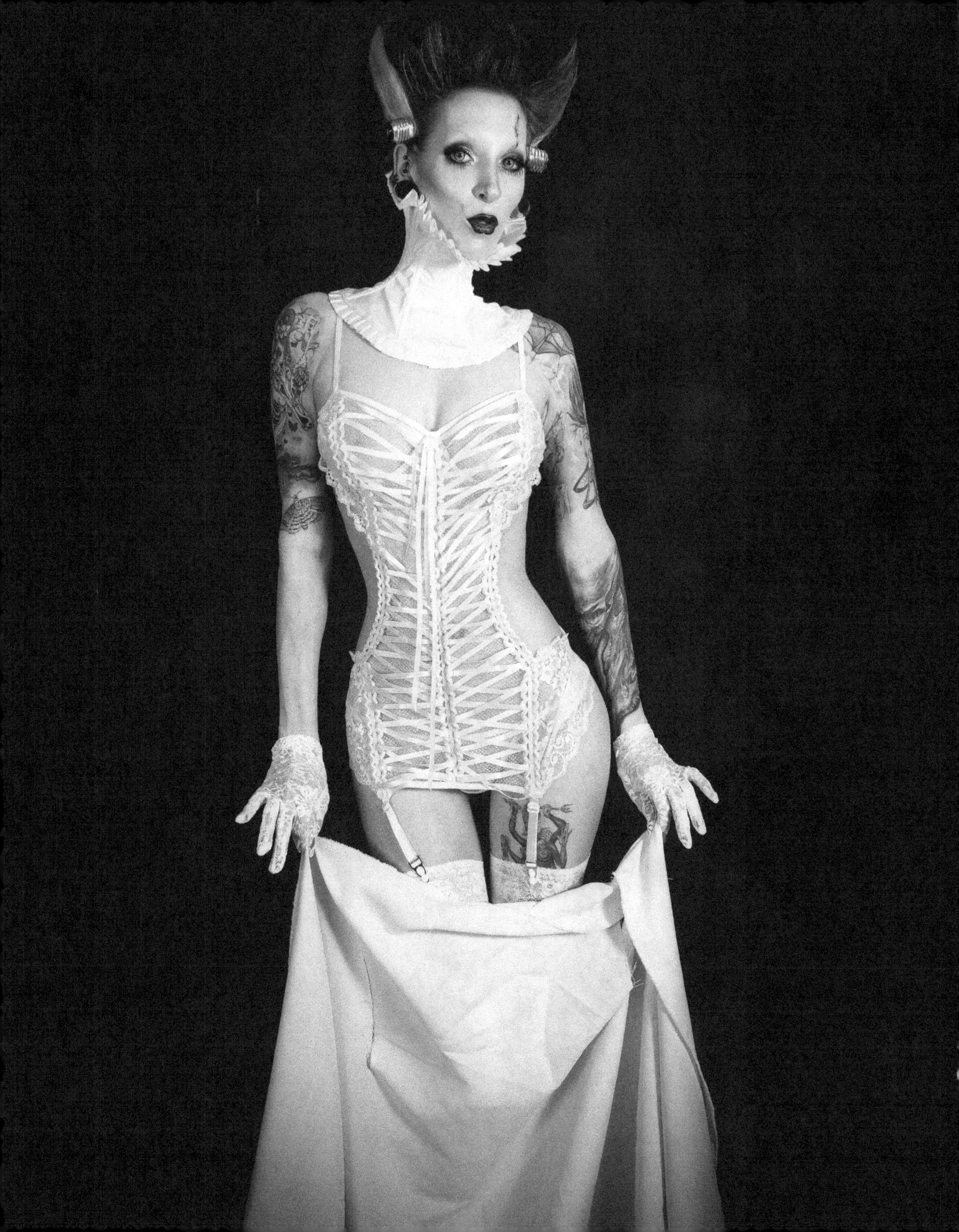

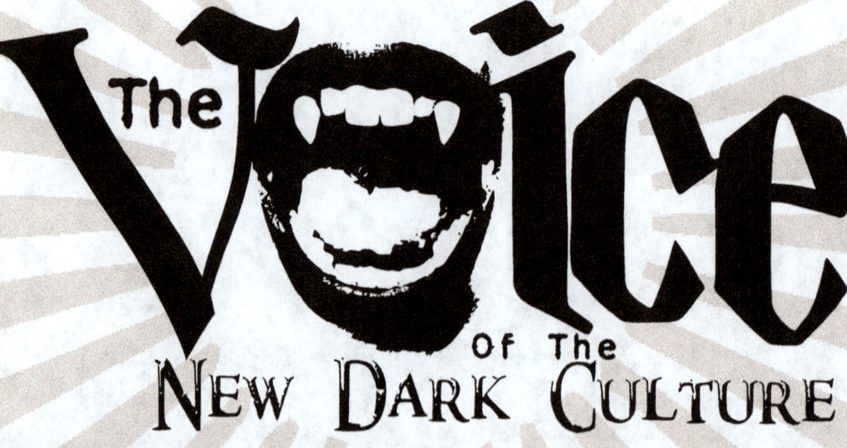

*We are not children anymore.
Save the games for the playground.*

by Chirality

Here we go, more dating editorials. I have been dealing with this way too long to not want to do it anymore. I am sure the reader will chuckle at some of the antics I have encountered, and if I repeat myself, I will apologize. One thing I will say to everyone: BE TRUE TO YOUR WORD. Stop the games. We are not children anymore. Save the games for the playground. Seriously, grow up... man or woman up.

until he called me a good "friend." Two years later he is hitting me up. I asked him point blank if his last relationship just didn't work out and he was back to me. I am worth more, we all are.

My friend met someone about two years ago, but he didn't want anything. They run into each other recently, and what do you know

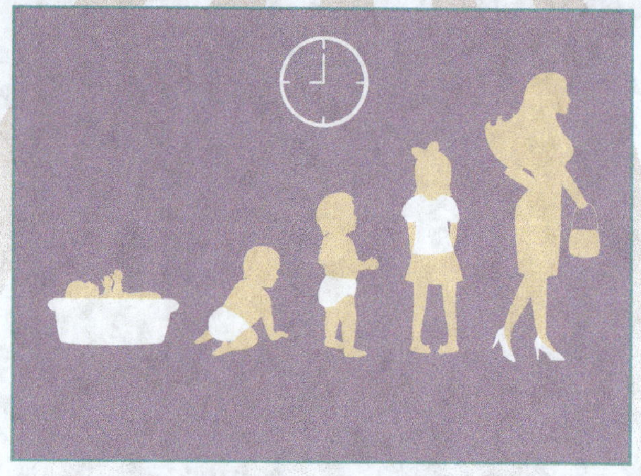

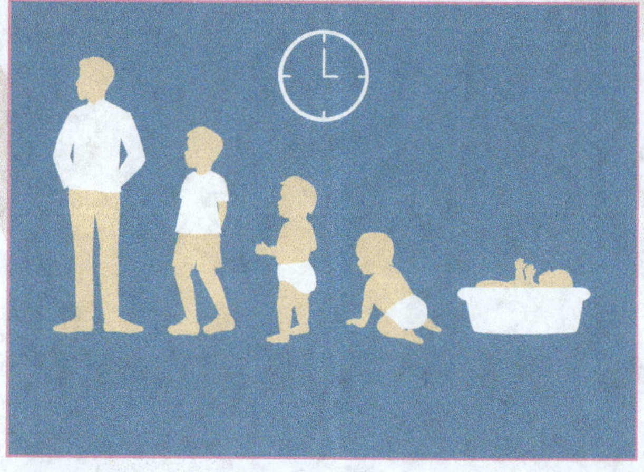

If you do not want a serious relationship, then say that and do that. Do not string someone along for your own personal enjoyment. Your words are gold; if you want to tell someone you love them, do not take it back like it's a scarf. These words and actions affect how the person handles the next relationship.

If you have personal issues going on, then deal with those BEFORE you enter into a relationship. Sometimes, however, you will find someone who will be able to handle the highs and the lows. Life is a roller-coaster. You need to find the person who will handle the ride with you, if not, then leave them be. Life situations change and looks fade. People really need to stop looking for perfection, otherwise you will be very lonely.

One thing I am so sick of is being a boomerang girl. What I mean by that is, I will meet someone and will date for a bit. Then, for some reason, it ends. The person will date around, and not meet their perfect person, so they look to me and come back to me. Good 'ol me. When I call the person out, I always get an excuse. I will no longer be a boomerang girl. There was one guy I dated and I really liked him

he messages her. Still, he is not looking for anything and then gets upset when she has things to do. So, she is not a priority, but you need to be when you are clearly not looking for anything? How does this make sense?

Dating is not easy, even though we all think it is. With sites like Bumble, Tinder, Plenty of Fish and the list goes on, it is so easy to give up on someone and just move on. I find this philosophy terrible because people are worth more, and people lose the chance to meet someone awesome. We are not our looks or our money. Life changes, you will not look like this forever. Give people a chance. I cannot tell you how many guys I have had to block because they send me messages with NO response and harass me. One guy messaged me four times, then asked why I was not answering him. Stalker much? Why am I obligated to message you? Why if I am not interested do I need to give you attention? Stop telling me to smile in my pictures. Stop telling me to date you. Stop sending messages where you cannot spell or just say "mmmm," and for the love of God, a dick pic has NEVER worked! ■

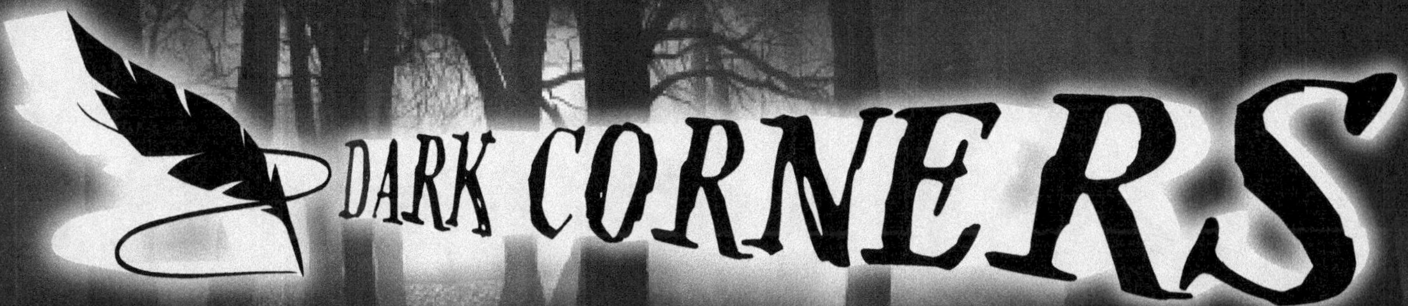

~From the darkest corners of our imaginations, soar the most beautiful creations....

The March of Asher

Earth caked beneath each fingernail,
Desire to break through the vale.
My next rake is with more earnest,
Yet I continue to fail.

The landscape bathed in shadows,
Blurring all signs of detail.
The stench of life stains my clothes,
It's wretched... it's deceitful... it's stale.

Determined against fate to bulldoze,
Every lie that paves the way before my toes.
Against your wishes I'll be at peace yet,
Crafting a world of my own.

Grinning as I unearth a cassette,
It's contents a sword of freedom sown.
Built using instruments of sorrow and
sweat,
The tape began to hover with a moan.

I walk to the world from inches of soot,
With the sound of failing cardiac output.

I am the enemy you so long desired,
So, see you soon with the weapon I've
acquired.
Bleek is my vision now that I am inspired,
Soundwaves will crush your dreams until
you've expired.

My form grows erratic with the rise of the
choir,
Rejoice as we leave footprints in the fire.

by Ninja

Everlasting Winter

The colder I become,
My soul feels more and more numb.
Warmth I cannot recall,
Confronted by this icy wall.

Damaged is my skin,
From fingers long and thin.
The scars will stay on my body;
Weakness I embody.

Misfortune possesses those close to me;
Health decays rapidly.
Death creeps in when it is darkest,
Barraging the feeble the harshest.

Entrapment breeds hopelessness,
The frigid air filled with loneliness.
Motivation has no light to grow,
Melting like grimy snow.

An avalanche of boredom,
I cannot overcome.

by Asylum Attendant

The Fallen of the Walls

Sometimes the wall is shaking...
I can feel it in my veins.
Vibrate to my heart.
Dancing the symphony of perdition.
All is frozen in this moment.
Hard days bear to each earthquake
as if it were the last.
The last that it will shoot down my door.
The last that it would make me lose
strength
and will silence my breath, to fall into the
abyss.

by Einsam Vuk

Think your poetry is good enough
to be published in Carpe Nocturne?
Send submissions to
mj@carpenocturne.net
subject line "Poetry."
All submissions must be under
250 words, and will be judged by
Managing Editor, Michael Jack and
Assistant Managing Editor, Zahara.
The best entries will be featured
in our next issue along side of our
very talented staff. ∎

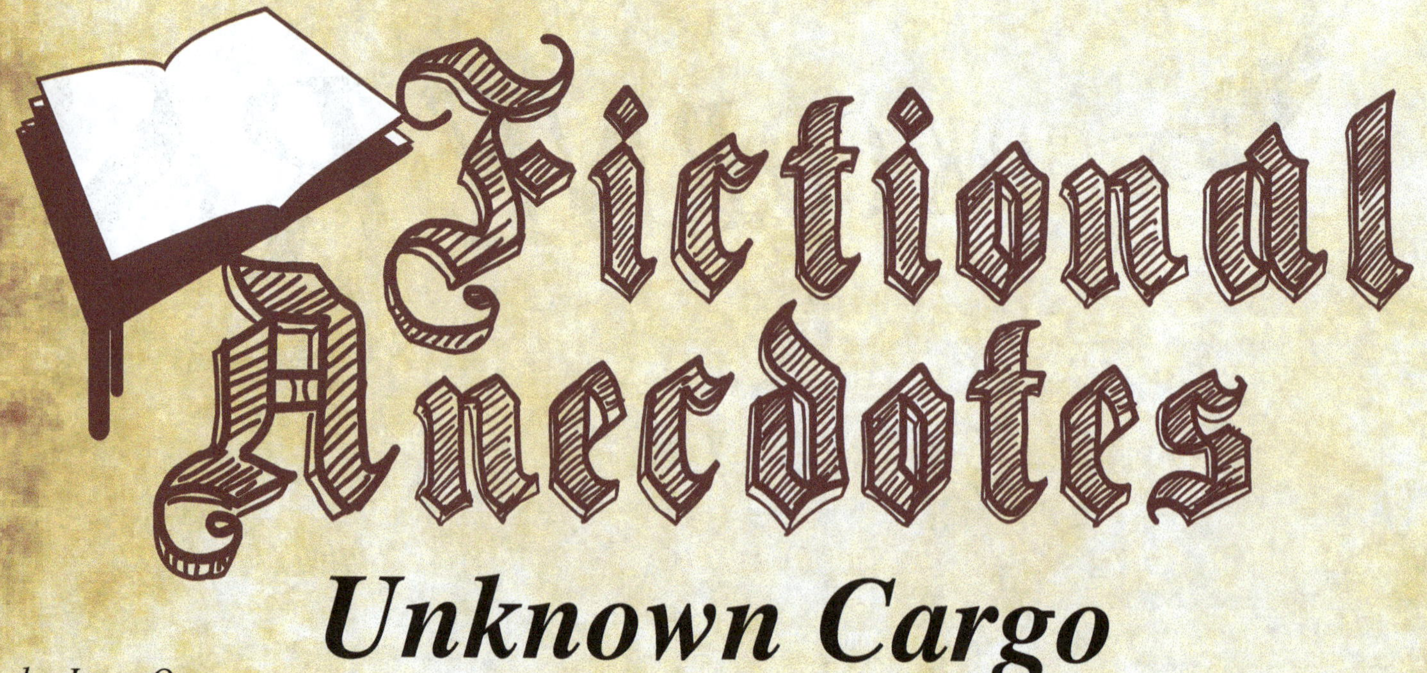

Unknown Cargo

by Jesse Orr

My name is Ridley.

I work on board the SS Tremain, one of the largest interstellar warehousing barges in the National Fleet. Originally, I was a part of a team of programmers who perfected the Automated Master Integrator system, or AMI. When we were done, there was no part of our fleet that was not controlled by AMI, and the team was dispersed to monitor her performance in different places throughout the galaxy. I was assigned to the Tremain because of the volume of materials the warehouse stores, and the fact that AMI oversees all of it. We orbit AMI's base planet, where a control station on earth transmits AMI's will all over the fleet.

three is all it takes to run the huge Tremain. The three crew spots are a Systems Analyst (me), Warehousing Manager, and Ship Manager. I monitor AMI's performance; the Warehousing Manager keeps track of what is being received, and where AMI is storing it, while the Ship Manager stays up on the bridge and oversees the well-being of the barge itself. AMI handles the life support systems and navigation of the Tremain, but the Fleet Admiral insists upon a fail-safe being installed on every vessel which will place control back in the hands of the crew.

Tonight, an automated cargo pod is scheduled to arrive and be stored in the hazardous materials corner of the barge. Its destination is a

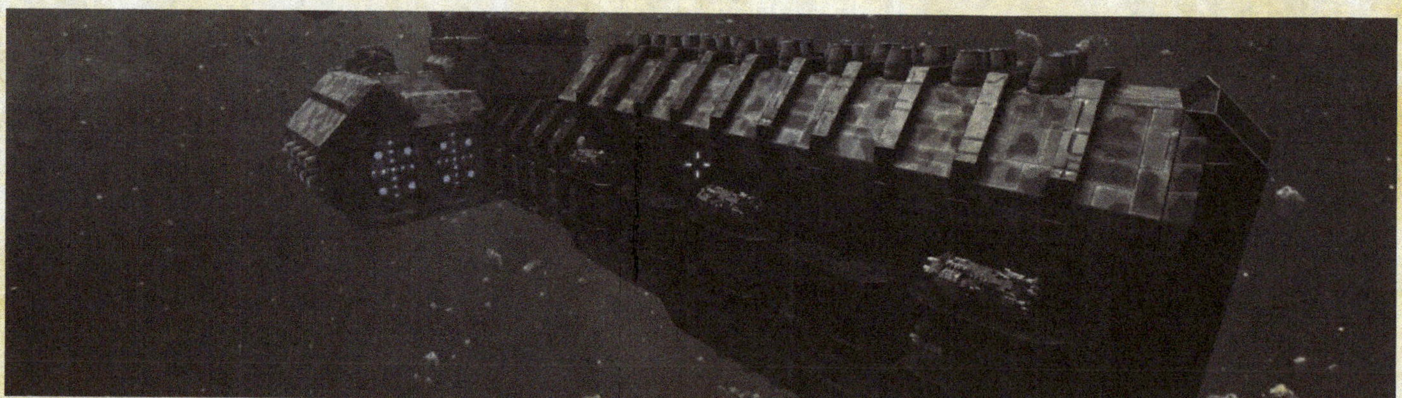

After almost a year of AMI running things, there is nothing we can't handle, nothing we haven't seen or can't anticipate. Most of the human portion of the job is repairing any robotic malfunctions, a skill AMI still lacks. Even those, though, are easily predicted, and maintenance takes place on a preventative basis rather than as-needed. Costs have been slashed to the bone and a skeleton crew of

research center on a distant planetary system, and a representative will be arriving within hours to take custody of the pod and its contents. The Ship's Manager forwarded the order to the Benedict, the Warehousing Manger, who sent me a copy to verify that AMI had processed the order properly. She had, just as always.

Exactly at the prescribed time, the automated pod's signal is picked up by AMI's radar and the tractor beam locks onto it. I can see the bright red markings associated with a high maintenance cargo, and a white skull stenciled on the side. I glance at Benedict, standing beside me gazing through the porthole as the pod grows closer and closer to the cargo bay door.

"What's in it?" I ask.

He flips open his folder and ruffles some sheets of paper. "Subject D21AA23, EXPERIMENTAL SPECIMEN. Do not open pod, is all it says on the manifest," he says, and rolls his eyes. "Would it kill them to provide us with a scrap of detail?"

"Probably," I say, without much interest as the pod snuggles up against the Tremain. According to the manual, we stand by and observe AMI bringing the pod into the cargo bay. There must always be at least one person to take over in case of an emergency.

We watch as the cargo bay is pressurized and the main rolling door opens to reveal a pod whose hatch has been warped until it barely fits in its place. The skin of the pod looks as though something inside has been at it with a large hammer.

"What the…" Benedict exclaims, and starts forward.

At that instant, the door blows open with an explosive force, leaving a dark hole behind. Inside the pod is darkness. A living darkness which moves and breathes, and now begins to spill forth from the pod like oily smoke. With a will of its own, it moves across the concrete floor of the cargo bay like a snake. Before Benedict can do more than take a reflexive step back, it has enveloped him completely. Across the room, the pod's door ricochets off the wall and clatters to a halt.

As quickly as the smoke has swallowed Benedict, so it lets him go. I don't hear myself scream when I catch sight of his body hitting the floor but I must; seeing something so dead, so sunken, lifeless and twisted that had moments before been a person, and not screaming is not an option. The smoke slides across the floor toward me, and just as I am realizing I am seconds from becoming just another shriveled

pile of remains, the emergency cargo bay airlock slams down in front of the advancing smoke, barring its way. The Ship Manager must have triggered them, the only other living person on the Tremain. He must have been watching the operation on his monitors. I sprint for the stairs leading out of this cargo bay and glance behind me. The emergency door is built to withstand the vacuum of space, but even from here I can see the smoke slowly seeping through invisible cracks in the door's seal.

By the time I get to the bridge, warning lights are flickering. Alarms are sounding. George, the Ship Manager, rushes past me to flip a number of switches on a panel marked in red. "I don't know what in the hell was in that pod but it's gotten into the ship's AI unit," he says, and real fear in his voice. "The fail-safe is malfunctioning, I can't override it."

"Let me see if AMI can stop it," I say, and pull my control screen out of my shoulder bag with shaking hands. "She has a virus scan program that should seek and destroy any irregularities." I open AMI's control interface and activate the virus scan. It has never been used except in tests, but has never failed a one. I watch as the virus scan sweeps the ship and zeros in on two abnormalities.

"Wait a minute," I say, and now my shaking fingers are cold and clammy to match the growing sense of dread in my stomach. "This can't be right. Let me scan it again."

This time, the screen does not obey my touch. Instead, it grows hot beneath my fingers, so quickly I am forced to drop it instinctively. Plasma screens in the bridge now display the results of the virus scan, magnified. There are two infections in the Bridge area. As I watch in horror, the options to Ignore, Quarantine, or Delete are cycled through several times before stopping on Delete.

With an explosive rush of air, the SS Tremain's every opening to the raw vacuum of space is thrown wide, exposing the pressure inside to the hungry emptiness surrounding it. The darkness rushing over my vision reminds me of the smoke for the briefest instant, before it swallows me whole. ∎

As I watched in horror, the options to Ignore, Quarantine, or Delete are cycled through several times before stopping on Delete.

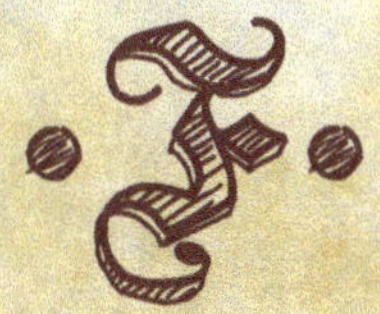

SPOTLIGHT

FEATURE

There are a lot of truly talented people out there, especially in our culture. Some use this talent simply for passing the time and personal growth, while others develop their talent to create services, works and objects for others to enjoy. Some post their creations on their website and never try to sell their works, while others use their talents to supplement or create their income. Carpe Nocturne Magazine admires, respects, and supports YOUR TALENT!

Whether you are creating to sell or only for personal enjoyment,
LET THE WORLD SEE WHAT YOU'VE GOT!
There is NEVER A CHARGE to be Spotlighted or Featured!

The feature within Carpe Nocturne Magazine spotlights artists, designers, photographers, crafters and others with a creative side.

Does your work relate to the subject matter of this publication. Whether you do what you do for self-enjoyment or to sell your craft, we support you.

Contact: art@CarpeNocturne.net
Subject Line: Spotlight Feature

ARTISTS • COSPLAYERS • CRAFTERS • DESIGNERS • MODELS • MUSICIAN • PHOTOGRAPHER

SPRING SEASONAL!

I actually find Spring confusing when it comes to seasonal beers. The reason is, there are just so many different varieties available. The rest of the seasons are clear cut…Winter is stouts and porters, Summer is lighter session beers with strong citrus notes, and Fall is Oktoberfests, pumpkins, and harvest ales. But what about Spring? I personally think brewers are trying to figure that out as well. Classically, you had many floral beers, sweeter fruit infused beers, and saisons. That is changing. If you look around at what your local breweries are offering for their Spring seasonal, you may find a pilsner, a Belgian, a Scotch Ale, or even a stout. I haven't decided yet if this is a good or bad thing, but I do know there are choices for every palette. I am going to pay honor to this diversified seasonal selection by jumping around to different styles, and more specifically, to beers that are a touch different than their associated styles. This is what I feel Spring in the beer world is beginning to represent, and again, it may not be a bad thing.

Seasonal: Founders Kentucky Breakfast Stout

From Founders Brewery in Grand Rapids, Michigan comes one of the most sought out and hardest to get beers in America, and for good reason. It is the Kentucky Breakfast Stout, and it is a limited-edition Spring release. This beer is always rated extremely high on every list I have ever seen, and it is the only beer I have ever seen Beer Advocate give a perfect score of 100 to. That says a lot. This stout is so well known in the beer world, that it is simply known as KBS. If you don't believe me, next time you visit your local beer distributor or craft six pack shop, just ask if they have the KBS. The person there will immediately know what you are talking about, and will probably laugh at you. The typical response is, "I got four cases in yesterday, and they were gone within a half hour."

The beer itself is made with an insane amount of coffee and chocolate, and then cave-aged in oak bourbon barrels for an entire year. Sound good? The results do vary from year to year, but I have never had anything less than an exceptional KBS, and I try it every year. The thing with

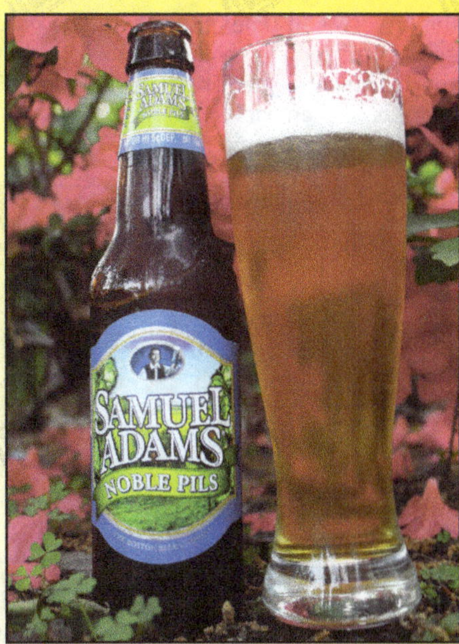
Sam Adams Noble Pils

Year Round: Samuel Adams Noble Pils

I think I have ignored the Boston breweries for long enough. This is about to change, and I am going to begin with the most well known craft brewery in America, Samuel Adams. They make many great products, but for this article, I decided to focus on the Noble Pils. Why? At one time, it was their Spring seasonal beer. Because of its popularity, this fantastic pilsner is offered year round, and many people couldn't be happier. If you a regular reader of this column, you should know I'm a big fan of the pilsner, so trust me when I say… this one is a touch different.

The Noble Pils is made in a true Bohemian Pilsner fashion, so you expect a certain honey-malt flavor to it. Yet, this Sam Adams offering goes well beyond. Because it was a Spring beer, the brewers added notes of citrus, floral, and pine to it. You would expect that from an IPA, but not a Pilsner. What you end up getting is a clear golden Pilsner with a lot of earthiness to it. I think the pine and malt dominate the flavor, but they are subtle. The citrus and floral essence balances the flavor. What you are left with is a very drinkable session beer that is a little more complex than your average low alcohol brew. Many people I have encountered don't necessarily love this beer at first taste, but many do. The ones who don't come to enjoy

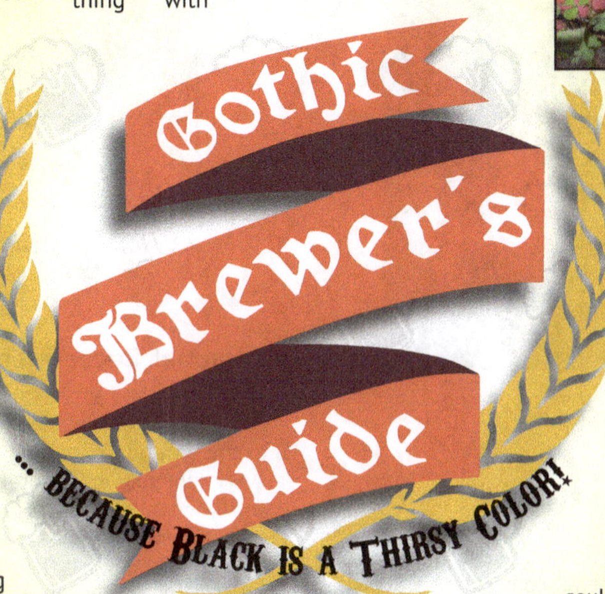

by Michael Jack

stouts, in my opinion, is it's easy to go overboard with one aspect of the flavoring. With the KBS, there is a remarkable balance between the coffee, chocolate, bourbon, and stout maltiness. There is even a hint of vanilla thrown in. The aroma perfectly expresses the ingredients, and the beer pours to a pitch black color with a tan head. The KBS is everything you want in a breakfast stout, and everything you didn't realize you wanted. This extremely hard to get stout is 12.4% abv, and will knock you on your ass. Drink only one, and try to spread out the rest over the course of the year. If you managed to score a four pack, chances are you won't be able to score another until next year.

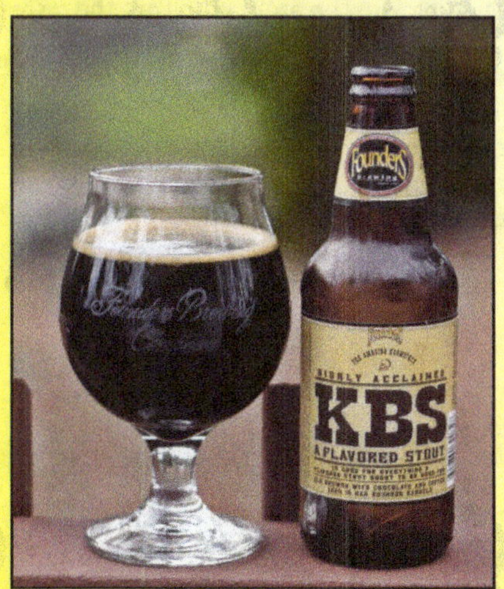

this beverage in time. You just have to let go of your expectations, and realize you are about to drink something a little different from your common pilsner. The Noble Pils is 4.9% abv, so throw back as many as you can handle.

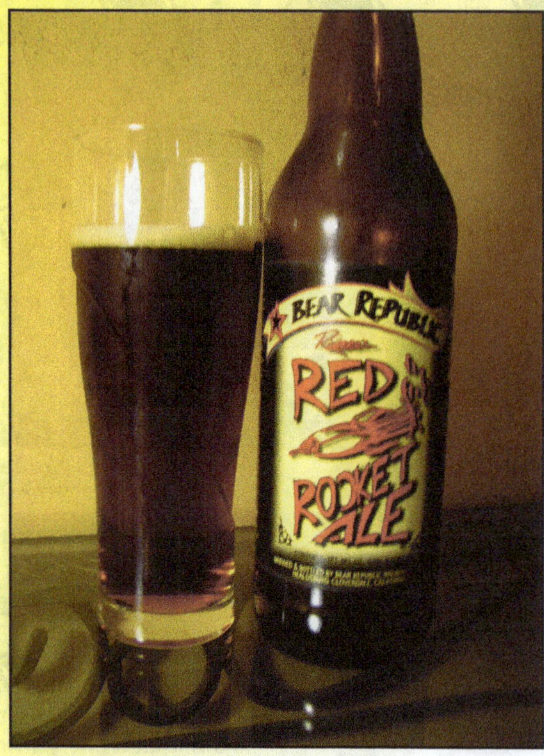

BR Rocket Red Ale

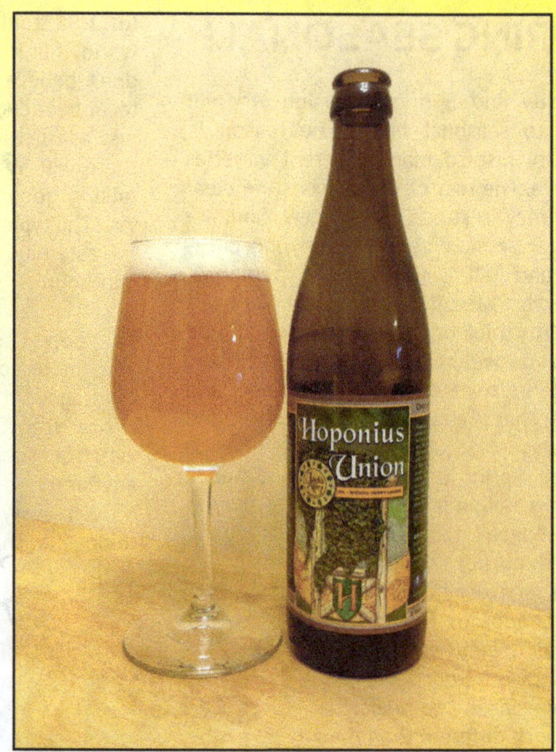

JA Hoponius Union

Theme: Bear Republic Red Rocket Ale

In my opinion, red ales may be the forgotten beer style in America. I see plenty of brewpubs offer them, I just never see anyone drinking them. I'm as guilty as everyone else when it comes to this. So, when I went to my regular tavern and saw the Red Rocket Ale on tap, I was curious. Mostly, I was curious because it was offered by Bear Republic, which is a phenomenal brewery out of Sonoma County, California. Their IPA, the Racer 5, is hands down one of the best on market. So, I asked the owner about the beer, and he responded, quite enthusiastically mind you, that it was the best red ale he has ever had. After that endorsement, I had to try.

The Red Rocket Ale poured to hazy reddish-caramel color, and reminded me a lot of the Scottish ales I had tried (although the Red Rocket is actually a blend of American and Scottish styles). If you haven't ever had the pleasure, the Scottish Ales are thick, and need to settle. Think of a clearer Guinness. The taste, well…I'm not exactly sure how to describe it, and from reading up on it, many people are in the exact same boat as me. The Red Rocket Ale is smooth with a slight bitterness. There is definitely malt, and either toffee or caramels hints to it…possibly both. Some people say citrus, but I didn't get that. What I do know is I enjoyed it, and the red ale was a refreshing change of pace from my usual. I don't think I would order the Red Rocket Ale every time I see it on tap, but I would definitely order it again. This beer is 6.8% abv, so it is good to drink in moderation..

Personal Recommendation: Jacks Abbey Hoponius Union

Every now and then there comes a beer that shakes the beer world to the ground. I'm talking an outside of the box beer that destroys every fundamental of brewing, and works. It doesn't happen often, and when it does, it gets beer lovers buzzing. Let me introduce you to this Framingham, Massachusetts brewery's incredible invention, the Hoponius Union. It is the world's first India Pale Lager. That's right, it's an IPL, and it is amazing.

Lagers aren't meant to be brewed with citrusy IPA hops…wrong. What amazes me is it took this long for someone to figure it out. The Hoponius Union is everything you would expect from a very good tasting IPA, but it's a lager. Mind blown. The aroma is citrus, the taste is hoppy and citrus, I mean…there is nothing not to love about it. The beer is bold, but perfectly balanced. You don't really notice the lager yeast too much, but it is there. The fact it is a lager means it won't dry your mouth out like an IPA can. If you are an IPA lover, it's an absolute must try. The Hopnius Union just might be the best of both worlds, and I have a feeling we are about to see an explosion of this style. This clear amber lager is 6.7% abv, but I doubt you can stop at just one. Try to stop at two. ∎

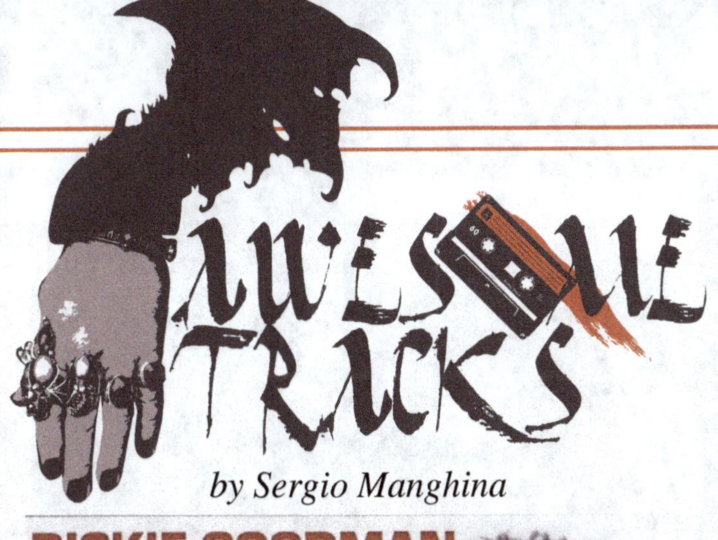

DICKIE GOODMAN
THE KING OF NOVELTY
WORKS 1956 - 1959

by Sergio Manghina

DICKIE GOODMAN
THE KING OF NOVELTY
Works 1956-59
Label: Cherry Red

It is well-known that, in the mid-fifties, the world was very different than it is today. Despite everything, America was an optimistic country about its future and all those wonderful things to come. The nascent Space Age drove millions of common people to interstellar journeys in their cozy living room. Some were scared for an imminent alien invasion as recently viewed at the drive-in. Rock'n'roll began its unstoppable revolution, drastically replacing a host of impeccable crooners with certain disreputable individuals and their thunderous electric guitars.

A guy called Dickie Goodman, from Brooklyn, had a stroke of genius. "I found the Martians in my home garden yesterday !" he (maybe) said. "I'll put them in touch with Elvis Presley !" He was a record producer, and in some way a visionary. With a partner in crime called Bill Buchanan - and a pair of scissors - he cut off some clips from the hits in heavy rotation, then pasted them into spoken commentaries and fake radio news about the aliens. The "Break ins" were born as a delirious game of answer (the songs) to questions posed by some actor voices. The effect of this stuff was funny, hilarious, at least at the time…

"Flying Saucers," part one and two were the first of a series of "experiments," then followed by countless imitation attempts by Mad Martians, Bobby Leonard, Spaceman and so on.

Dickie Goodman is still really little known today, and yet those techniques anticipate the art of sampling. This anthology is a re-discovery of his work, and a sort of "Rosetta Stone" useful to decipher those incredible years, even better than a sociological essay. ∎

Roadkill BY XXX ZOMBIEBOY XXX

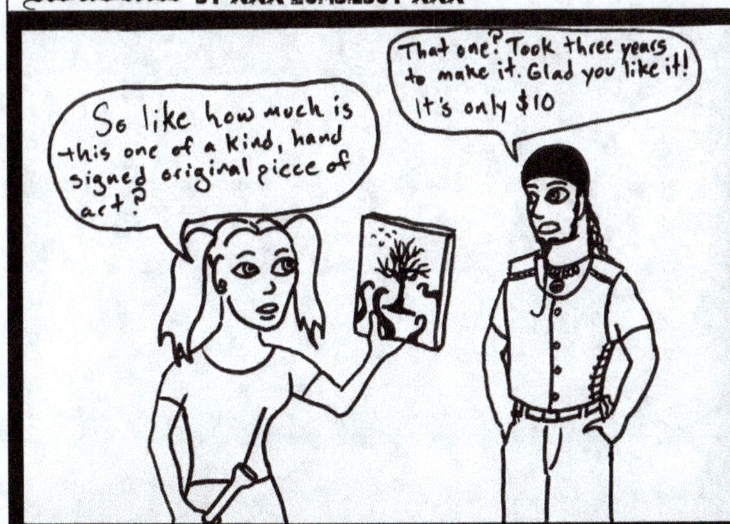

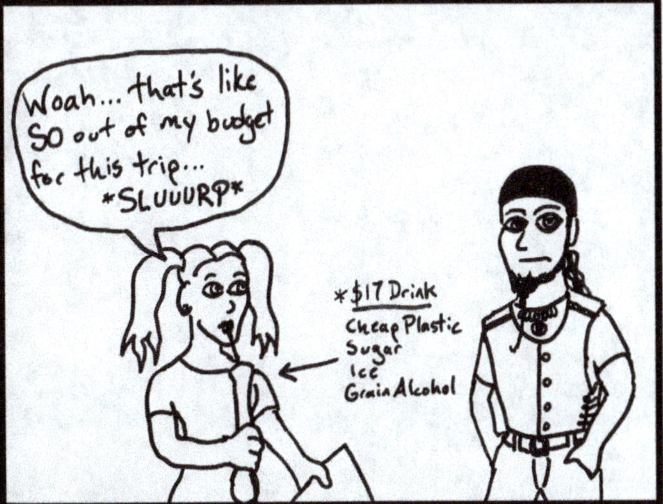

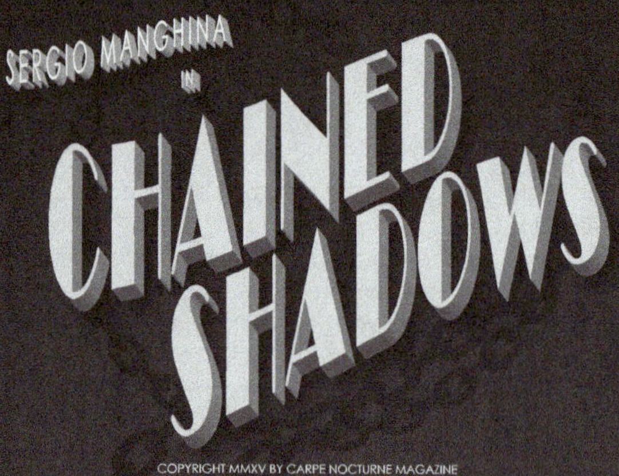

DAVID LYNCH, ANGELO BADALAMENTI, TWIN PEAKS, LOST HIGHWAYS, VIDEOCLIPS, FEMMES FATALES, CARS AND MUCH MORE...

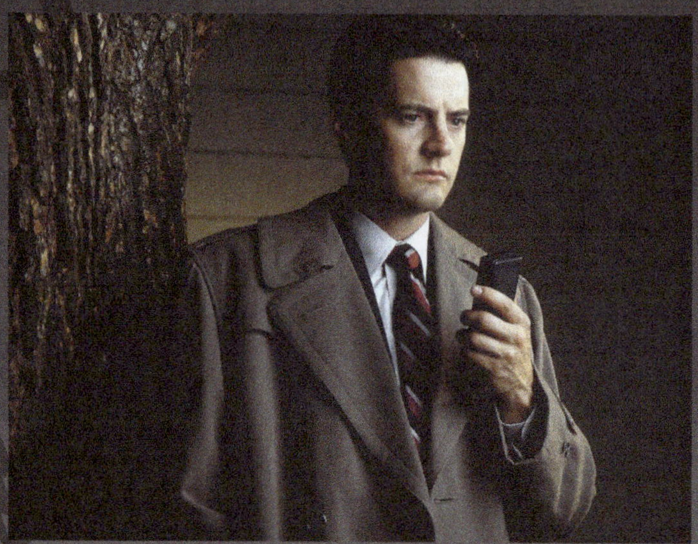

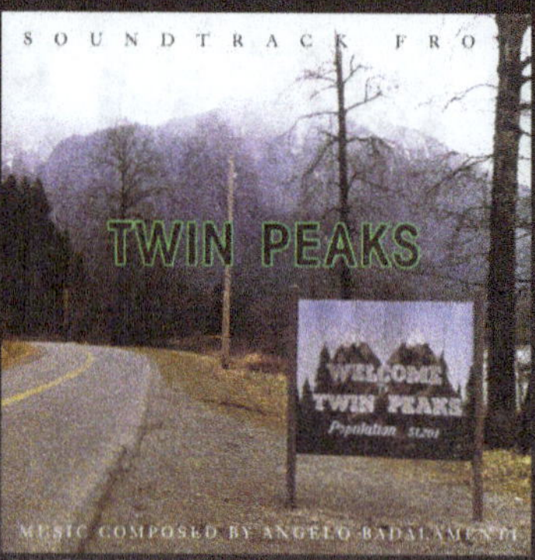

ANGELO BADALAMENTI
SOUNDTRACK FROM TWIN PEAKS
Label: WB 1990

Bizarre things, grotesque characters, forbidden spaces, strange rooms, dreams, nightmares, angels and demons... Lynch's world continually raises questions unanswered or - at least - without a clear answer. What is happening? What is real? What is not? The time is misaligned, the space is an open door, empty passage to many other doors. The world around can be familiar but slippery. Yet, all this is not so abstruse, or least of all meaningless, it is only a nowhere land that speaks using another kind of syntax. Just passing that door, like Alice through the looking glass.

The "Twin Peaks Theme" is evanescent, romantic, vaporous, nostalgic in that special way for something indefinable. There is a sort of slowness, that precise moment before things change forever. Those notes of twangy guitar mark the time dilation, dilute, circular, elusive. The "Theme" opens and closes the album, capturing in its web the noir jazz of "Freshly Squeezed," "Into The Night," "Dance of the Dream Man," and then the experimental escape of "Night Life in Twin Peaks." Anyway, "Audrey's Dance" is the true other highlight of the soundtrack. It is so nocturnal, obscure, atmospheric, filled with sinister premonitions, to appear as a stealthy and feline step in the dark, among velvet touches of vibraphone.

Angelo Badalamenti has marked the way for a lot of imitators and/or admirers, on the devious path of Ambient-Dark-Jazz. Lynch is himself musician and author of several works as a soloist. He shares with Badalamenti a remarkable influence on alternative and underground music, both aesthetic and substantial.

DIVERTED TRAJECTORIES

David Lynch and Angelo Badalamenti are like two different twins. Their works seem came out from the same mind, so are complementary. "Blue Velvet," "Wild At Heart," "Lost Highways," "Mulholland Drive," and naturally the intrigues of "Twin Peaks." Many of us are fans of this series since the beginning, and are eagerly awaiting the premiere of the new edition, after twenty-five years. "Twin Peaks" is a crime series, but also a sort of soap opera, characterized by an unsettling plot and deviated by continuous infiltrations - drop by drop - of Gothic, noir, thriller, horror, supernatural. An oblique world pulsates behind the curtains of that town, like closed eyelids, where nothing is as it seems and all has multiple faces. Moreover, not exactly reassuring.
The title sequence offers a catalogue of pacific cohabitation between civilization and wilderness, including: a robin, a waterfall, a factory, an empty road, the iconic town's welcome sign.

"Reality can be beaten with enough imagination," said Mark Twain. For Mr. Lynch, reality is a distorted mirror that often deforms minds, bodies and even places. Apparently, everything is normal and quiet in the city. Almost a slower version of the life that, however, hides a significant amount of secrets. The discovery of Laura Palmer's corpse, and consequently her double/triple life, removes the cover of the Pandora's box. The FBI special agent Dale Cooper is asked to resolve the puzzle of this murder case, soon becoming much more of an aloof, external viewer.

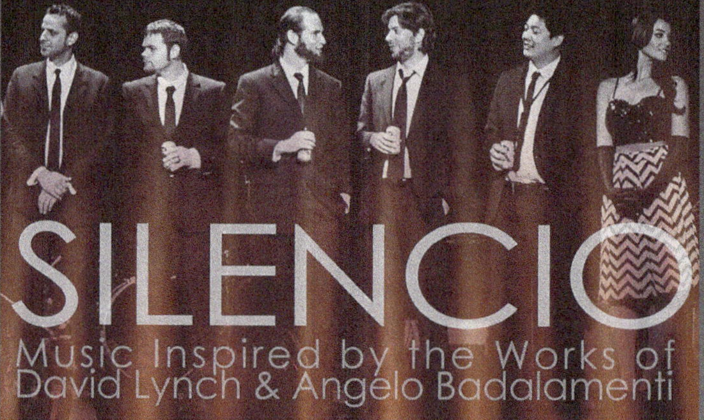

David Lynch is a true connoisseur of fine music, and hence, also pop-music, with a weakness for female singers. In his films, classic songs of the kind of "In Dreams" and "Crying" by Roy Orbison, "Blue Velvet" by Bobby Vinton are interpreted by women. Isabella Rossellini (however, not properly a singer) intones "Blue Velvet" in the homonym film, Rebekah Del Rio performs "Llorando/Crying," in Spanish. And then, Julee Cruise - the star of the "Twin Peaks" soundtrack - until Chrysta Bell, within the strange universe of "Inland Empire" in 2006. She's the last Lynch's muse.

STORIES AND VIDEOCLIPS FOR DISQUIETING SOULS.
Lera Lynn, Lykke Li, Lana Del Rey, Alison Goldfrapp, Inga Liljestrom, Dessa Poljak (Silencio), Chrysta Bell.

1-DRIVE by Lera Lynn. Her 1972 Chevelle 66 swallows the asphalt, illuminated by its own headlights, leaving back someone asleep in a motel room. There is a face with no name among unquiet shadows, neon lights scattered in pieces like falling stars and bars open all night.

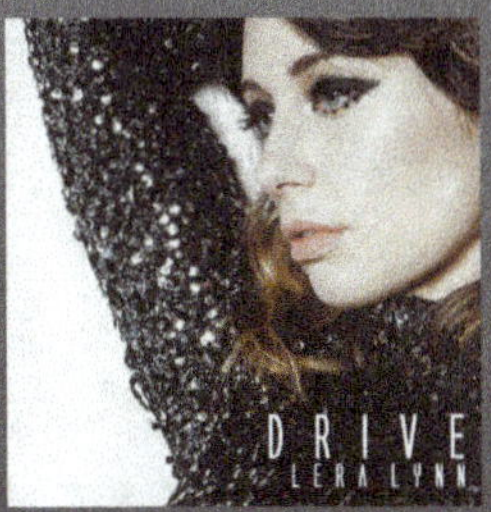

**LERA LYNN
RESISTOR
Label: Resistor 2016**

She's obsessed about time. She steals and then destroys all clocks or watches around. She's an instant of life camouflaged in the blackness, sometimes with a deep look, otherwise a distracted glance.

There is a solid line, and then a broken line, a twang guitar and reddish flash backs. Wild things run fast, and Lera runs into the unknown until the last burning frame, recalling an old road-cult-movie.

2-I'M WAITING HERE by Lykke Li & David Lynch. The road is a clean cut in the middle of desert, caught between the daylight and the imminent shadows. The twangy guitar drips something suitable for "Twin Peaks" while Lykke's voice is a breath. Flashes of light bring to mind "Lost Highways," understandable fragments of a story otherwise difficult to decode.

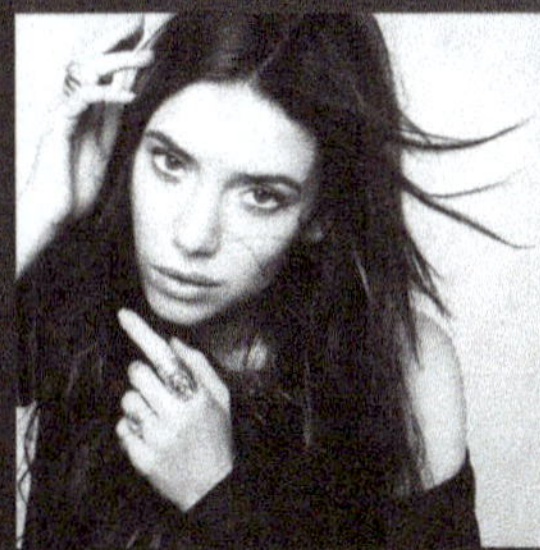

**DAVID LYNCH (ft. LYKKE LI)
THE BIG DREAM
Label: Sacred Bones 2013**

3-SUMMERTIME SADNESS/BURNING DESIRE by Lana Del Rey. Half Femme Fatale, half painful girl, Lana Del Rey drowns excruciating memories, regrets and sorrows in the sepia-like images of "Summertime Sadness." Absolute Lynch-style is also in the (magnificent) fully red interiors of the Rivoli Ballroom in London, the ideal location for a video like this. Huge chandeliers are lit over her, one after the other. The creature, swathed in a white dress, resembles an intrusive thought about Rita Hayworth. Then - finally - she sings "Burning

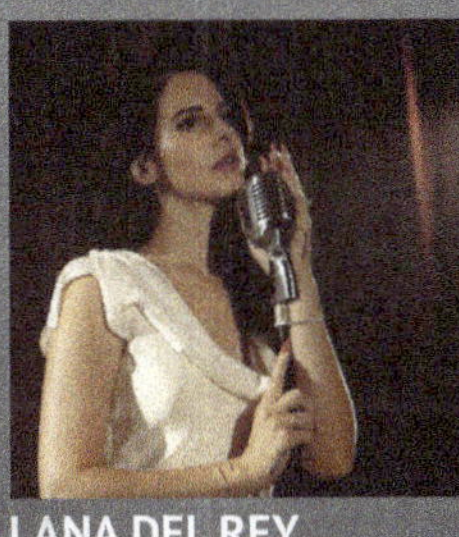

**LANA DEL REY
BURNING DESIRE
Label: Interscope 2013**

Desire." She sways on stage, glittering and sophisticated like a Hollywood star, connecting her hoarse sensual voice to faded images behind her. Postcards of a distant American past, joined with a flaming red Jaguar F-Type, pulverizing the road.

4-JO/LAUREL by Alison Goldfrapp
Elegant steps of high heels, slow and cadenced on the nocturnal pavement... In the living room of her luxurious home, that woman looks for an impossible rest, because something terrible has recently happened and she definitely got to do something about. A car runs in the few nocturnal lights. The melody is slowed, muffled, then the lady runs across a wood. Just a nightmare. Who knows...

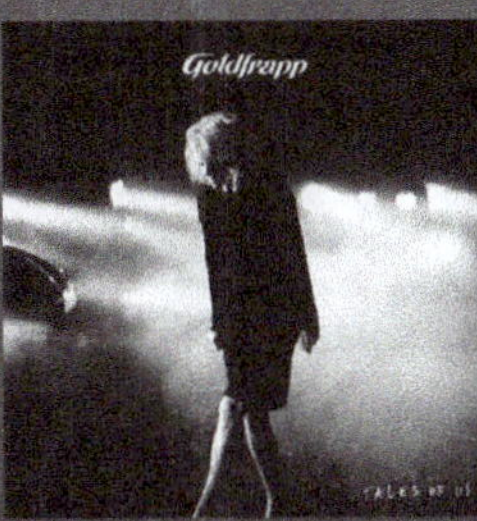

**ALISON GOLDFRAPP
TALES OF US
Label: Mute 2013**

5-FILMNOIR/STARDUST by Inga Liljestrom
"I Don't Know Who I Am," she repeats. Does anyone know who is that woman wandering in the woods? She's disheveled, anguished, dirty of soil and blood, probably in the grip of a strong shock. There are some clues: a motel sign for example. She was driving a car just a moment or a day ago. Maybe she has

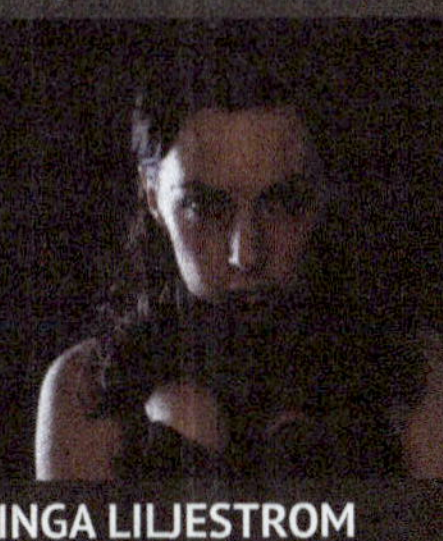

**INGA LILJESTROM
ELK   (r)2005
Label: Groovescooter**

murdered someone. She was on the bed of room. A tap was dripping water and blood was in the sink. Then there were those closed bags, photographs, cigarettes, a mirror, and red lipstick.

Inga is theatrical and mysterious. If "Film Noir" links Lynch to Hitchcock, "Stardust" is totally David Lynch, gathering surreal, grotesque images and fragments of guitar like sounds heard in a dream.

6-SLOW SIN JAZZ by Silencio (Dessa Poljak)
Devoted to the work of Lynch-Badalamenti, Silencio, from Pittsburg, are more than a tribute band or simply followers. This is an amazing project that consists of original songs capturing the true essence of those two masters. The obsession of David Lynch about music, clubs, red curtains, old fashioned microphones, is also an integral part

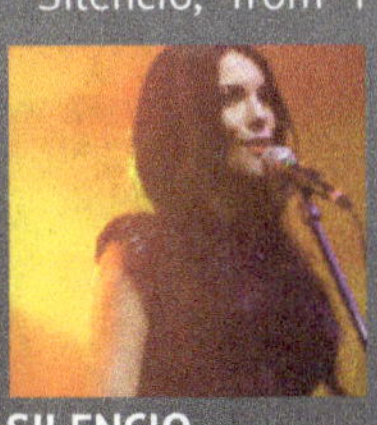

**SILENCIO
MUSIC INSPIRED...
Label: Viking 2012**

of their obscure world. "Slow Sin Jazz" - the video - recalls of The Slow Club in Blue Velvet, Club Silencio in "Mulholland Drive," places of distortions of reality and assorted strangeness. Black hair, red lipstick, black gloves, red dress, Dessa Poljak sensuously performs a high grade atmospheric piece, made of filaments of ambient-jazz focused on light sparks of hi-hat, sax, trumpets bass, piano, and guitar.

7-NIGHTRIDE by Christa Bell
One third thriller, one third Gothic, one third horror, a pinch of sex, like

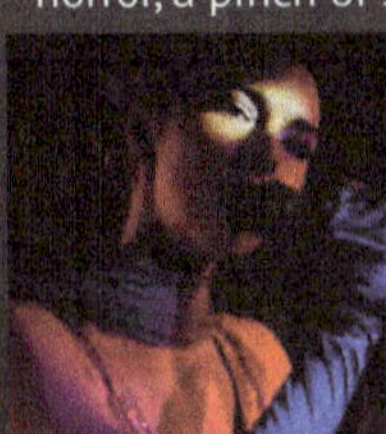

**CHRYSTA BELL
SOMEWHERE IN
THE NOWHERE
Label: Meta Hari 2016**

a cocktail of Lynch/Tarantino served chilled on a tray. It is only a videoclip, after all.

Chrysta Bell is a goddess descended to us - poor mortals - a feeling that walks, rather she glides into the air. A vampire, a dark lady able to steal the scene to everything else around, with her only presence and voice. ■

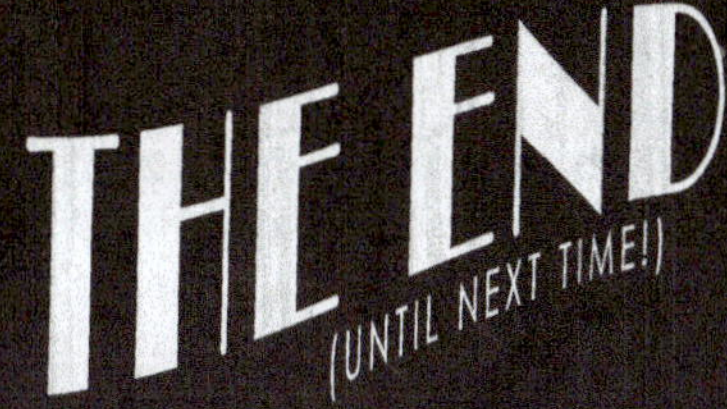

TORN CURTAIN

by Sergio Manghina

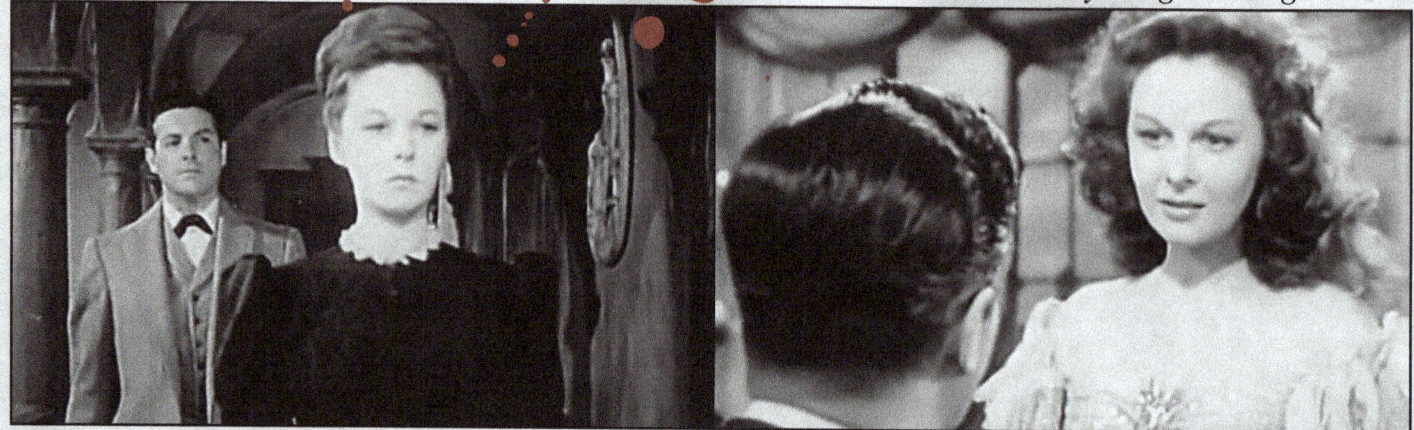

THE LOST MOMENT
Directed By: Martin Gabel
Walter Wanger Productions USA 1947
Studio: Olive Film 2014

Originally, there was a novel written by Henry James - "The Aspern Papers," whose plot inspired, In some ways, the best seller "Possession" by English writer Antonia S. Byatt. The love letters of a vanished Romantic poet of the XIX century are the start point of this story, the reason why Lewis (Robert Cummings) - a New York based publisher - goes to Venice, where those papers could be hidden with an elderly woman. Asking for a room from her, he conceals his identity and true intentions by using a false name. The house is actually a large palace, ancient and gloomy, inhabited by a 105 year old lady called Juliana Bordereau (Agnes Moorehead.) She's the recipient of those letters written by Jeffrey Ashton, the Victorian poet, but she's not alone under that roof. Tina (Susan Haywards), her great-niece, also lives there. She is a very mysterious woman.

Everything is equally played between supernatural, horror, noir and a disturbing psychological aspect. Air is as rarefied, wrapped in a (not only) metaphorical fog. The great mansion seems alive and dead at the same time. So does the people who live inside, with their intrigues, secrets and pains. All things appear contaminated by an invisible patina of haunted dust, that covers each candle or mirror enclosed in the walls of the rooms. The three protagonists fill the space as puppets of fate, bound to each other by those old love letters and that man who wrote them. But, there is another character in this story. It is Venice, magical and disquieting, with its antique gilded stones, elusive, fading, like mist rising from the canals. Only those who have walked at night along certain narrow streets at the risk of icy water fall can understand it. Martin Gabel captures this enchantment, almost making it not visible, hiding it. Actors glide elegantly between the folds of the story. Agnes Moorehead, behind her strong make up of over a hundred years, the gentleman Robert Cummings, and above all the superlative Susan Haywards in the throes of a dangerous split personality. ∎

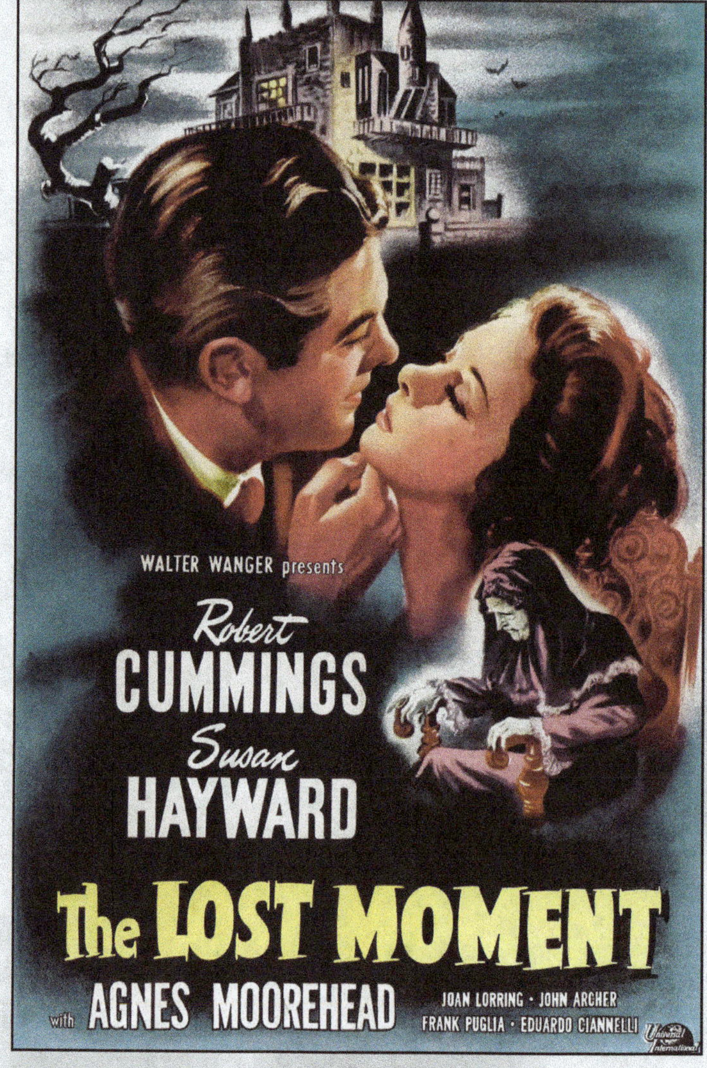

DEARLY DEPARTED

By Ninja

There's never enough to be said about his accomplishments, he was the DNA of Rock and Roll. The origins of Rock and Roll are indeed blurry, some people make the case for different songs and moments. One of the holy trinity along with Ike Turner and Sister Rosetta Thorpe, it all comes back to Chuck Berry. He was the one that gave the world the idea, the style, the energy.... It's soul.

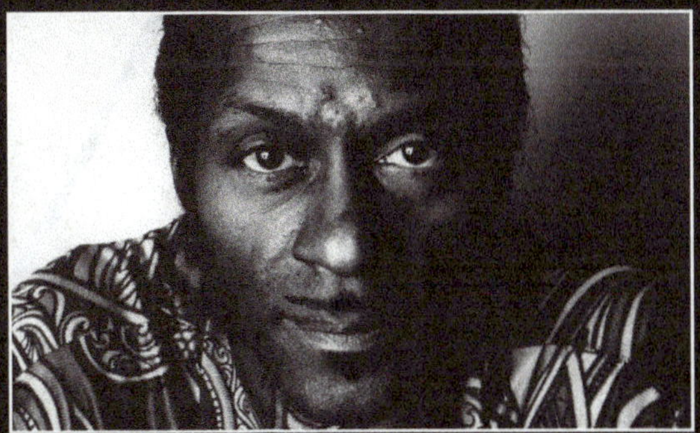

The merger of jazz, blues, country and gospel with a pop edge is an easy way to put it but it's messiness as a metaphor is abstract and unique. Rock and Roll was black music that let whites play in it, spiritual music turned carnal. In post-World War 2 America, the beginnings of the sound was so shaky that only a few could write their own material let alone have it bursting with substance, grace and wit. Chuck Berry's subtext resonates still, he knew he was crafting something big and important while in the moment.

So in tuned with the soul of Rock and Roll, he continued to lick, shuffle and croon until the very end, releasing a final album just before is death at age 90. Born on October 18, 1926, in St. Louis, Missouri, Chuck Berry had early exposure to music at school and church. As a teen, he was sent to prison for three years for armed robbery but was able to become the Father of Rock and Roll before his 30th birthday. Never a stranger to controversy, he was the embodiment of "Sex, Drugs and Rock and Roll" that everyone follows after him. Berry still remains one of the genre's most influential musicians. In 1985, he received the Grammy Lifetime Achievement Award. A year later, in 1986, he became the Rock and Roll Hall of Fame's first inductee.

Keith Richards of the Rolling Stones said, "It's very difficult for me to talk about Chuck Berry 'cause I've lifted every lick he ever played. This is the man that started it all!" The journalist Chuck Klosterman has argued that in 300 years Berry will still be remembered as the rock musician who most closely captured the essence of rock and roll.

by Chirality

What a year 2016 was, and I think 2017 may be no better. We lost George Michael on Christmas Day 2016. George was a singer, songwriter and philanthropist. Michael has sold 100 million records worldwide. His debut album Faith sold 20 million copies worldwide.

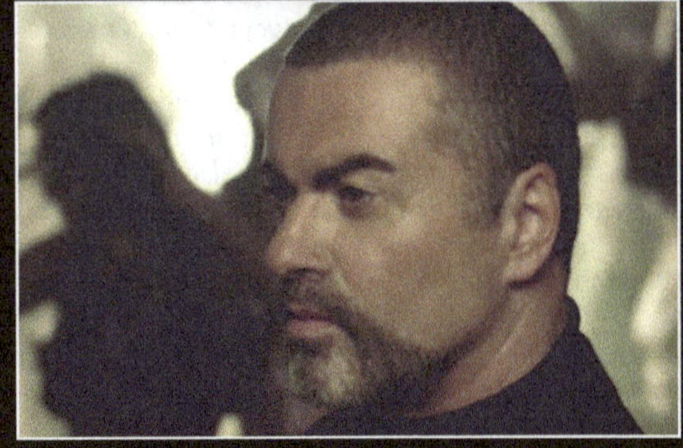

Born Georgios Kyriacos Panayiotou, he was known professionally as George Michael. Michael formed Wham! After meeting Andrew Ridgeley in 1981. The band's first album Fantastic hit No. 1 in the UK in 1983 and produced 10 singles.

In 1987 Michael embarked on a successful solo career. The release of Faith led him down a path of greatness with songs like I Want Your Sex, Freedom, Father Figure, Jesus to a Child and so many more.

Michael was no stranger to controversy. In the beginning of his career, he always thought he was straight. But, he stated at puberty he started to think about men. At age 19 he told his friends he was bi sexual. Later, he was interviewed stating his falling for a man put to rest his bisexuality. In 1998 he was arrested for lewdness in a public bathroom. It led to an onslaught of criticism and led him down a path of drugs. In 2006 he was arrested for possession.

For all the issues that surrounded George Michael, we heard later he was a philanthropist and secretly gave to charity not wanting the people he gave to know it was him. He also inspired Car Pool Karaoke with James Corden.

George Michael passed away beside his partner on Christmas day 2016. Despite his issues, he was a tried and true musician. Not only was he talented, but he gave back when he could. His songs will live on for many years to come, and he will surely be missed. ∎

HOW TO NOT GET EATEN

by Xxx Zombieboy xxX

ZzzzzZZZZZZzzzzzzzzZZZOMBIES!!!

There is an important topic I feel needs to be addressed regarding surviving in a world that has become overrun with the living dead. Ironically, as I write this, it is 4am and I do not foresee any rest in the near future. That topic is SLEEP! Sleep is absolutely vital in survival period. The reason for this heavily relates back to the same thing I always say, and that is to keep your head. A person suffering from sleep deprivation, however, is going to have a very hard time keeping a sound mind. Sleep deprivation not only causes extreme fatigue, but it also make a person delirious. In fact, one can even begin to see things or hear things. Trying to make sound decisions when your machete starts talking to you is going to be problematic! The problem is that nobody wants to shut their eyes and make himself or herself vulnerable to being a human buffet while they try to catch some Z's. And sadly, there is no assured way to make this more comfortable or less nerve wracking. However, here are my suggestions for possible down time napping.

As I list the following, keep in mind that this is based on the Romero type of zombie. A shambling, largely mindless and empty-headed zombie. However, if variables come into play, such as zombies that can smell, see body heat, think at least partially or are only infected (all of these are possibilities) then that changes the game dramatically. And, if you snore well, your team may kill you first.

Trees – This has been used not only in my own writing, but also in a few movies I have seen and barring zombies that can smell you; this seems a pretty sound and abundant option. Get high up into a tree and secure yourself well hidden amongst the leaves and branches. It won't be very comfortable, but at least in rural areas this is plentiful. Make sure all of your belongings are secure as well. Some things to keep in mind are potential defensive birds that may raise a ruckus,

and the fact that you are now cornered. This later, however, is often

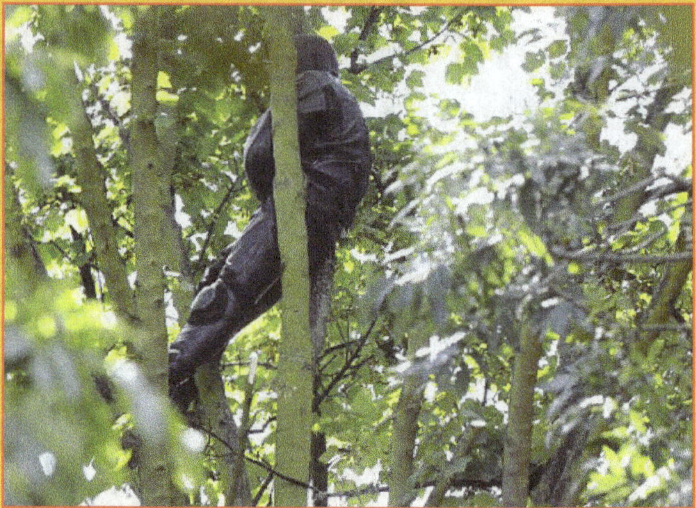

the case when trying to get some sleep. Being out in the open is going to get you eaten. I recommend that if you choose this option, you also devise a way to lure the dead away from under you, should you be discovered.

Rooftops – Particularly flat ones, this is an excellent choice in most circumstances. Get up there and pull the ladder up behind you. Most zombies cannot climb. At least not well. And the ones that could would likely make enough noise to awaken you. If you are discovered, you can always lure the crowds of reaching dead hands away to one far corner of the building (we are thinking one or two story house here) and then drop off the other far corner. Rooftops allow for a good vantage as well, in order to potentially plan your next move. A word about higher buildings; they will offer the same shelter, however, there is likely only one way up which means if the dead get to that one way, then you are trapped up there. Bad scenario that one. Therefore, always have a second way out (or off) of anything, and do not use it unless there is no other choice.

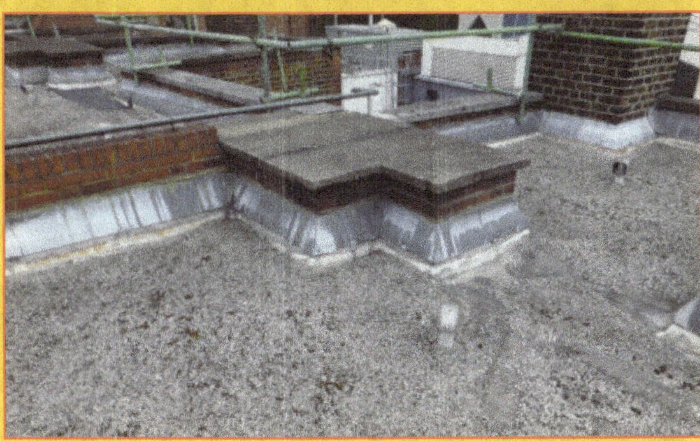

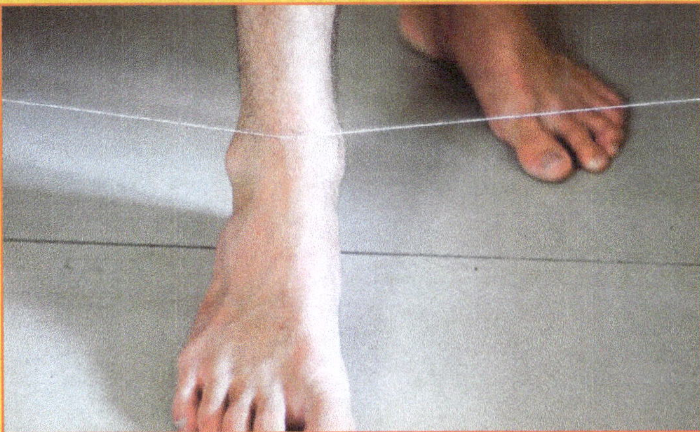

Sewers, coal shoots, cellars and basements – All of these may be an option, but let us not forget the famous argument put forth by Night of the Living Dead. You do not want to put yourself in a hole that you could be cornered in. Again, know of another way out or do not use it unless there is no other choice. I tend to shy away from subterranean scenarios overall in such a world event, simply because they tend to limit your options, unless it is an incredibly armed, fully secure and stocked for years type of bunker. How often do we come upon those however?

The old tin can trap – I have seen it displayed and heard it proposed that lining your camp with sound alarms such as cans attached to a perimeter tripwire would allow you to sleep in open ground such as a field or forest. However, this makes me very nervous. So many things could go wrong. Even if it were loud enough to awaken you (and I guarantee you are going to be tired) then how much warning would you have? Also, would the sound attract even more? However, I feel it is only fair to say that NONE of these options are 100% and that using one of them is better than the alternative. So, if you must use a perimeter alarm to get some rest, then try to make it so that your immediate position is at least somewhat hidden and that the fence is tested for effectiveness.

Stand guard – this is honestly probably the best option. If you are travelling in a group, or there are at least two of you, then take turns sleeping. Be sure though that each of you is capable of remaining frosty and alert or you are both done. One sleepy sentry is all it takes to allow a herd of the dead to walk right over you.

Caffeine and chemicals – The use of alertness aids may assist you briefly but they do not solve the problem at all. For one, they are going to be difficult to procure. For another, they will not stop you from a growing case of delirium brought on by sleep loss. Do not look to these things as a solution.

A raft – This could be a thing, but although zombies may not swim well (and who knows if they can or not) they may float. It is logical to assume that many are going to be very buoyant due to built up gases in their organs. Unless you are laying in a canoe and not visible, I would not resort to this unless you have to.

I know this does not leave you with much. However, it does point out that being unconscious is both necessary and nerve wracking in the zombie apocalypse. The best things to remember are to be totally out of sight, if possible scentless and absolutely no snoring! Unless it is someone you don't like. Then they make great bait! ■

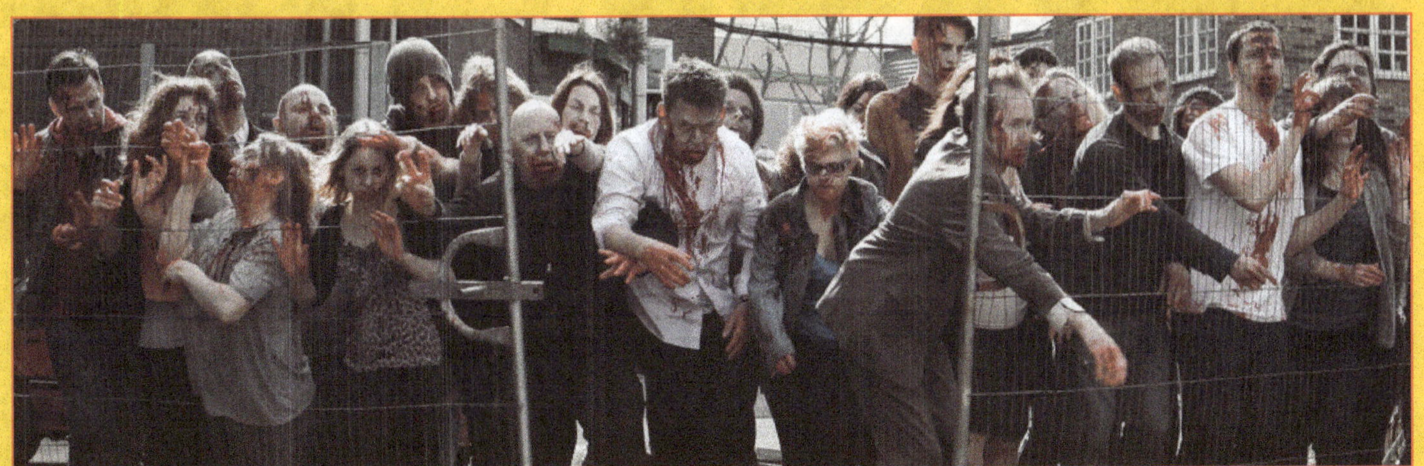

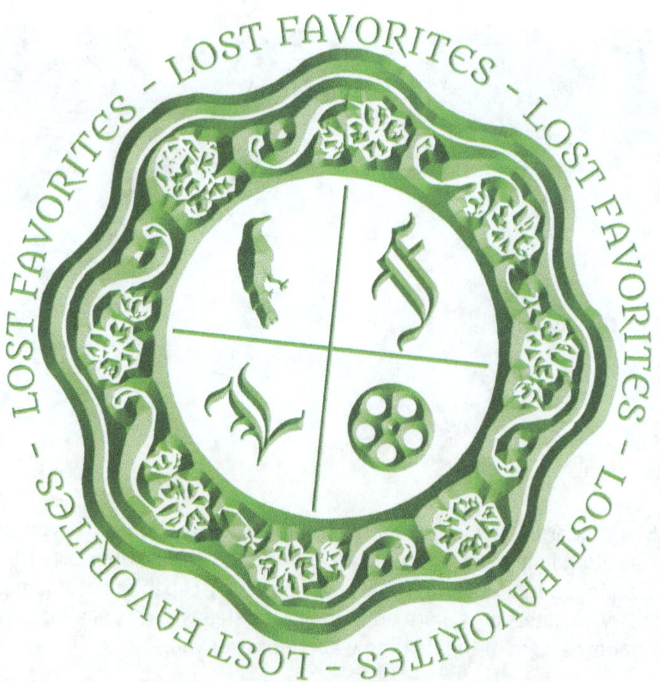

by Xxx Zombieboy xxX

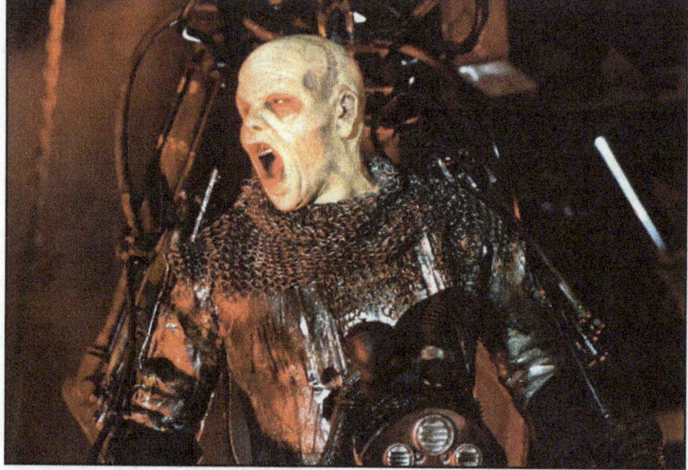

Spacehunter: Adventures in the Forbidden Zone

There were a number of Science Fiction films that I could go into for this column, but one in particular always stands out first for me. That is the excellent Lamont Johnson directed vehicle, Spacehunter: Adventures in the Forbidden Zone. This film winds up on so many bargain DVD collections, and it is largely overlooked by all but those that love cheesy science fiction B-Movie films. Starring Peter Strauss, Ernie Hudson and a young Mollie Ringwald, this film is just too much damn fun!

The plot is fairly standard rescue mission fare. Three women escaping a doomed space liner crash on an alien world and are quickly captured and taken to first a scavenger ship and then to an overlord's complex. Answering the possibility of reward, a scruffy anti-hero goes in search of them, eventually joining forces with a local scavenger and a former fellow soldier.

What makes the movie great is its buffet of weird encounters and misadventures. Our hero Wolff and his new "partner" Niki must face mutant blobs, bomb dropping mutant children, siren like amazons, broad waterless wastes and even a weird water dragon. One odd and freakish encounter after another befalls them until they finally reach "The Zone" where the villain Overdog (played by the ever wonderful Michael Ironside) captures Niki and throws her into a maze of obstacles and death traps. Will she make it through? Will Wolff save the girls? How spectacular will Ernie Hudson's fireworks be? The film was one of the many during the 80's that tried to cash in on the resurgence of 3-D and thus we are treated to a number of silly scenes designed to jump out at the audience. The musical score is an adventurous classic 80's theme by Elmer Bernstein of Ghostbusters fame. The effects are all practical and though professional, they are so over the top silly that it is entertaining!

A classic late night treat to share with friends that enjoy making fun of it the whole time!

Release: 1983, Columbia Pictures
Starring: Peter Strauss, Molly Ringwald, Ernie Hudson, Michael Ironside
Music by: Elmer Bernstein ◼

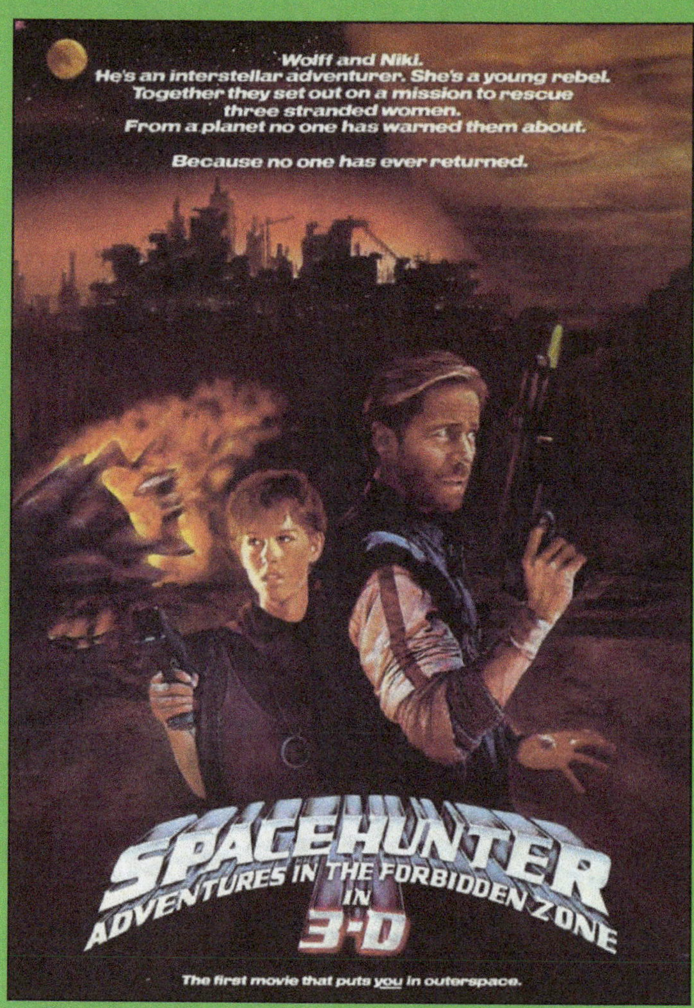

NIGHTMARE WORLD
Vols. 1 - 3 by Dirk Manning

by Noel Rivera

Lucifer has finally concocted a way to win the eternal chess match against his Creator. For centuries, he has failed to gain a foothold on Earth, but with the shifting of a few formerly untapped pawns and the assistance of powerful immortals that, until now, have been asleep or in hiding, Lucifer stacks the odds in his favor and waits for the results to play out according to his plan.

In this anthology of interconnected visual short stories, author Dirk Manning tells tales that rarely go where expected, usually addressing the darkest possible outcome rather than softening the blow for the reader. Manning pulls no punches, tackling disturbing and taboo topics and concepts that other writers might shy away from and, in doing so, telling a series of unsettling stories that pulls the reader into the nightmarish world he has created.

Each volume of the comic anthology employs myriad artists with a variety of styles, yet each style manages to capture the feeling of the story it tells. Whether it's an atmospheric and psychological Sherlock Holmes period piece, a werewolf's night out drawn entirely in stick figures and pictorial dialogue, or a classic summoning of Old Ones rendered in horrifying detail, each artist uses his or her style to great effect.

The overarching storyline may not be evident to everyone at first glance, but savvy readers will pick up on the nuanced elements and characters as the series progresses. The details make these comics entertaining to read time and again, both for the individual stories and as a complete work, but those who particularly like picking out Easter eggs will find Nightmare World eminently enjoyable.

The fourth volume of Nightmare World completed a successful Kickstarter campaign at the end of 2016, delivering still more terrifying delight to fans of the series. ■

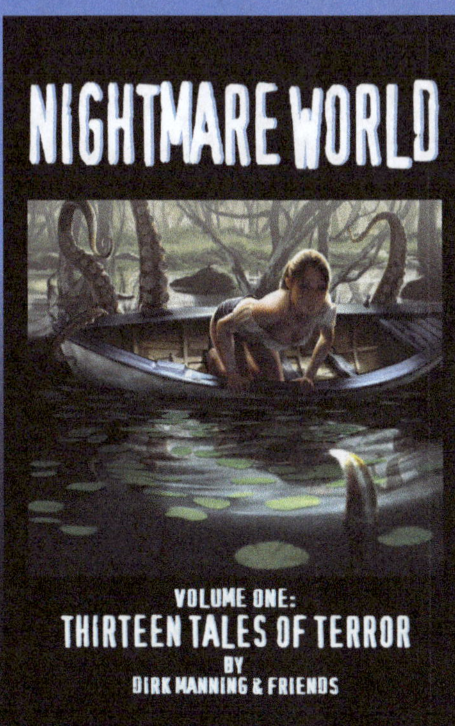

VOLUME ONE:
THIRTEEN TALES OF TERROR
BY
DIRK MANNING & FRIENDS

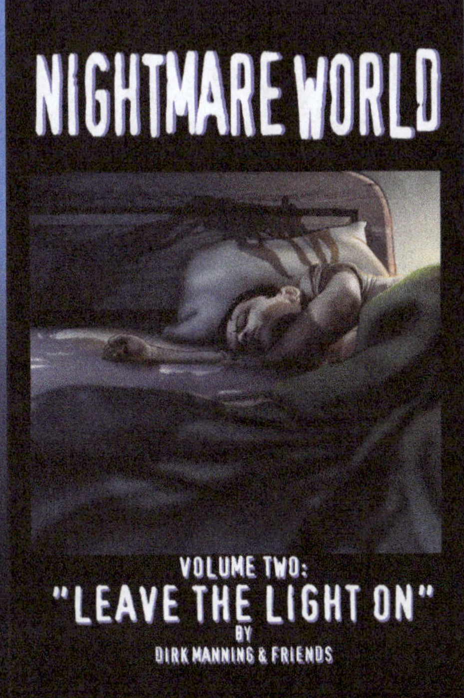

VOLUME TWO:
"LEAVE THE LIGHT ON"
BY
DIRK MANNING & FRIENDS

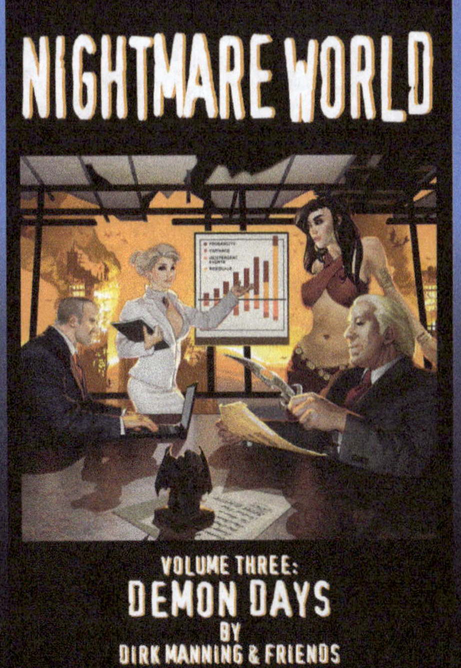

VOLUME THREE:
DEMON DAYS
BY
DIRK MANNING & FRIENDS

SOUNDS OF THE LIVING DEAD

ALBUM REVIEWS

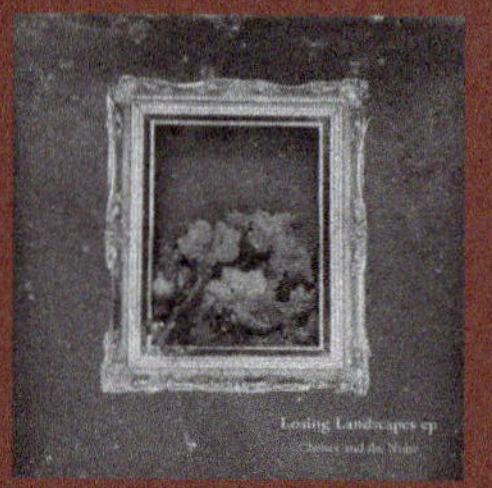

Artist: Chelsey and the Noise
Album:
Losing Landscapes EP

By Asylum Attendant

The first time I listened to Chelsey and the Noise they reminded me of a gothier, more haunting version of Sleigh Bells. Turns out Sleigh Bells is one of their biggest influences. This dark electronic pop group hails from California, but members Chelsey Hice and Brent "the Noise" Watters create music better fit for the Transylvanian crowd. Their first EP Losing Landscapes is full of shadowy themes, dreamy vocals, guitar shredding and industrial synths. Add in a healthy dose of glitch, too.

"Graveyard", the first track on the EP, is probably most my style. It has a sinister theme with a pop production format. Ghostly bells open the song, leading into powerful guitar riffs. I love the lyrics, comparing a bed to a graveyard with bones beneath the sheets. What an evocative image! Next, we are pushed to the "Edge of Infinity" with frenetic hip hop beats and vocals that ricochet off of one another.

"Parish" displays Chelsey's mysterious singing accent and vocal distortions, which urge the listener to pay close attention to the religious lyrics. The chiptune synths at the end of the vocal phrases are a nice touch. The EP concludes with "Cavern", which implements reverberating, fat synths, cleverly placed guitars and transformative vocals. The personification of a crying cavern is just one of the intriguing lyrics that this band showcases on Losing Landscapes.

Chelsey and the Noise cover many genres with ease. They are unafraid to forge their own musical lane of somber electrogaze tunes. I look forward to a full-length release!

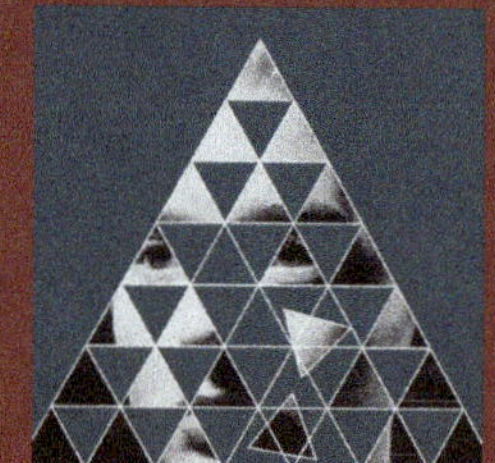

Artist: Private Pact
Album: Perfect People

By Sergio Manghina

Private Pact are a Danish-Russian group based in Copenhagen. Their first album "Purity" - released in 2014 - was a more than good example of New Wave/Synth-Cold Wave, tending towards Industrial music, harsh but not so corrosive. It contained a mysterious patina, arcane and enigmatic, even with a mood of apocalyptic-folk, cadenced by a martial beat of the drums. As after a bath in a glass bowl, "Purity" has now become "Perfect People", the continuation in another direction. The overall tone is, in fact, softened and the flint-paper soaked by coloured water.

Everything is vaguely lighter and danceable, but without ever being frivolous. On the contrary, among these electronic tracks there are some very nice things and also several sparkling aromas. An eclectic sound that often recalls (consciously or unconsciously, who cares?) of different kinds of eighties music; from Gary Numan ("We Were Young") to Siouxsie ("Lost in Favours" has something of "Arabian Knights") and more ancient stuff ("Perfect Love") dating back to the seventies. "The Great Display", just to say, suggests the name of Alan Parsons. "Better Days" draws a magnificent melody, while "Diving Down" grinds pulsations of psychedelic darkness. "Lost in Favours" and "Divine" show – instead - a stronger temptation oriented to the dance floor.

Julia Popova gives a dreamy touch to each song with her ethereal voice, as opposed to the composed solemnity of the lead singer Jonathan Pedersen, accentuating the Gothic aspect.

Private Pact are a band that start quietly, in the manner of the cyclists in the bunch, before the final sprint. The surprising fact is that they could really finish in the top. ■

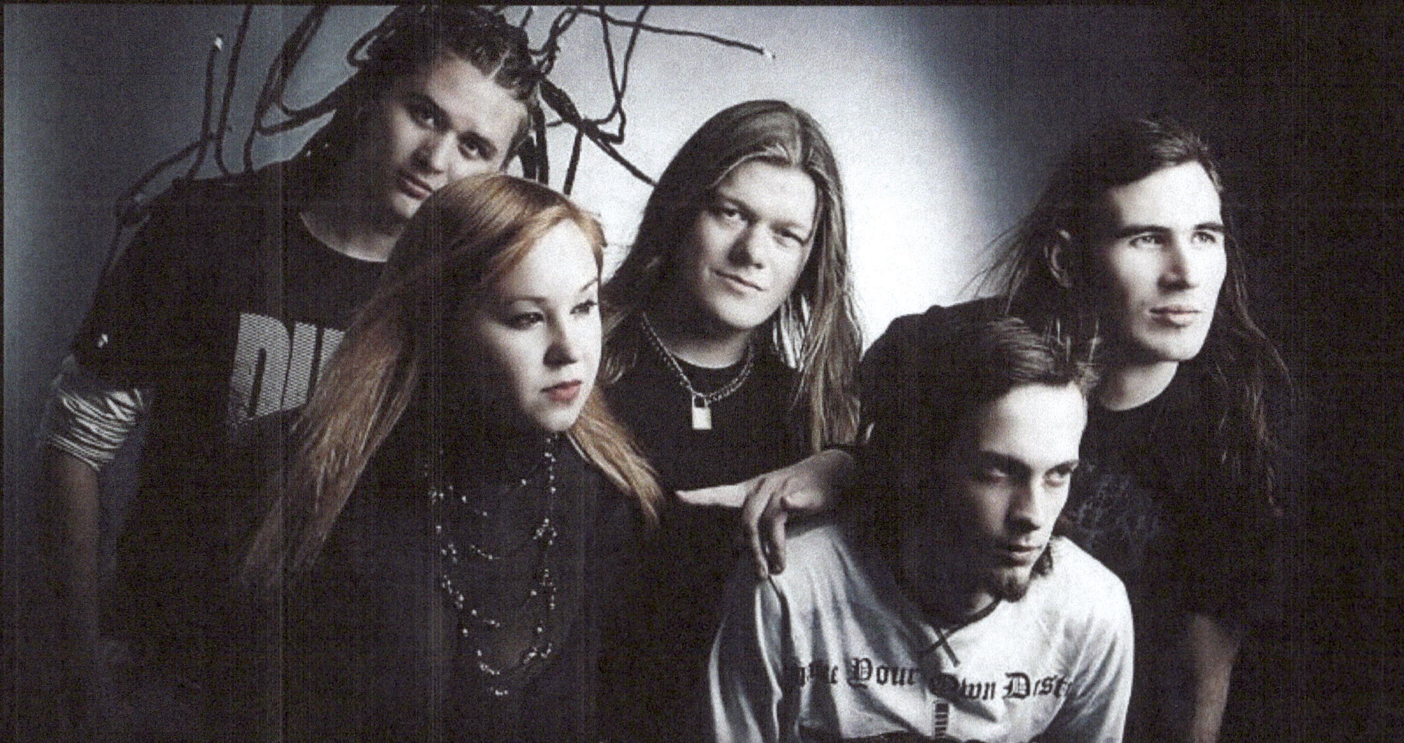

XE-NONE

by Chirality

Xe-None are a Russian band from Kirov. They emerged in 2004 when Lexy Dance (who does vocals and programming) and Newman (who does synths) worked on crossing modern metal with electronic dance.

The band was formed by Lexy Dance and Newman in the summer of 2004. They added EvilAnn who did vocals, Schultz on bass, Max on guitar and P2D2 on drums. The name Xe-None is a hybrid of aliens (Greek) and of course none, or nothing in English.

In October 2004 they released their first album Digital Fucker. The underground was soon abuzz with this band and local word of mouth quickly made them a nice following. In 2005 a new drummer Watson was added to the line-up. Blood Rave was also released that year which was a mini album and was compiled of 5 songs.

During the next few years the band saw numerous member changes. Max left the band and was replaced by Fucker. Soon after Schultz left the band and was replaced by Andrew Rex. It was during this time that the band had started to play various festivals and get a more solid following.

In May of 2007 they released a full length album Dance Metal [RAVE]olution. In 2008 Watson decided to leave the band and was replaced by Push but due to medical issues, Push had to take some time off. The band did however start working on the second album and a Eurodance mini cover album.

Dance Inferno Resurrection was released in 2009 and contained seven classic 90's songs. It was released on the internet for free. In 2011 Dancefloration was released.

We are curious to see what has been going on with the band as it seems there has not been much since 2012. Their Facebook page is active and you should definitely go and check them out. They also have a BandCamp set up and it seems they have been playing small shows in their country.

Hoping 2017 will be a good year for them so we can see what is next. Check them out! ∎

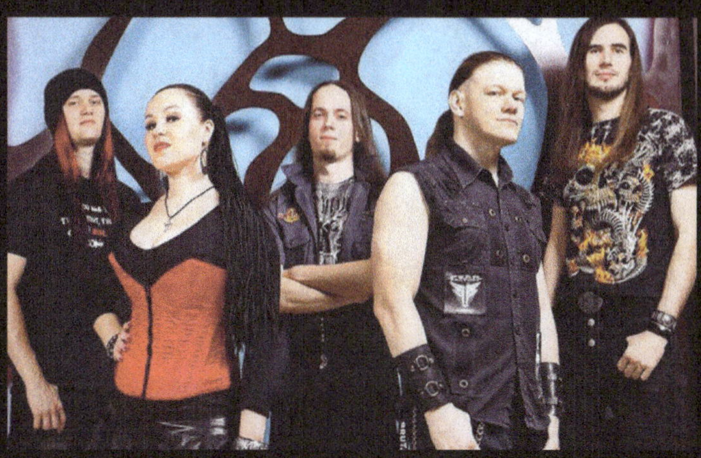

by Asylum Attendant

Physical disabilities have the potential to hold a person back from going for their dreams. However, they can also motivate an individual to work even harder at their craft and pave a new path to success. Society may not believe that a person missing one leg could become a model, fashionista, artist and musician. These people obviously haven't met Viktoria Modesta. She may use a prosthetic limb, but that has not kept her from becoming the world's first bionic pop star. Viktoria can slay a stage just as hard as your favorite able-bodied diva.

Viktoria was born in Latvia under the USSR regime. She was a victim of doctor negligence during her own birth, causing the dislocation of her leg and hip. Unfortunately, Viktoria's leg never became fully functional, even after many surgeries throughout her childhood. She and her family moved to the UK when she was twelve and the bullying was so severe at school that Viktoria stopped attending. Viktoria wanted to get her useless leg amputated, but many surgeons refused to do it. She finally found a doctor that would perform the surgery and a whole new world of possibilities opened up for this beautiful woman.

THE WORLD'S FIRST BIONIC POP STAR

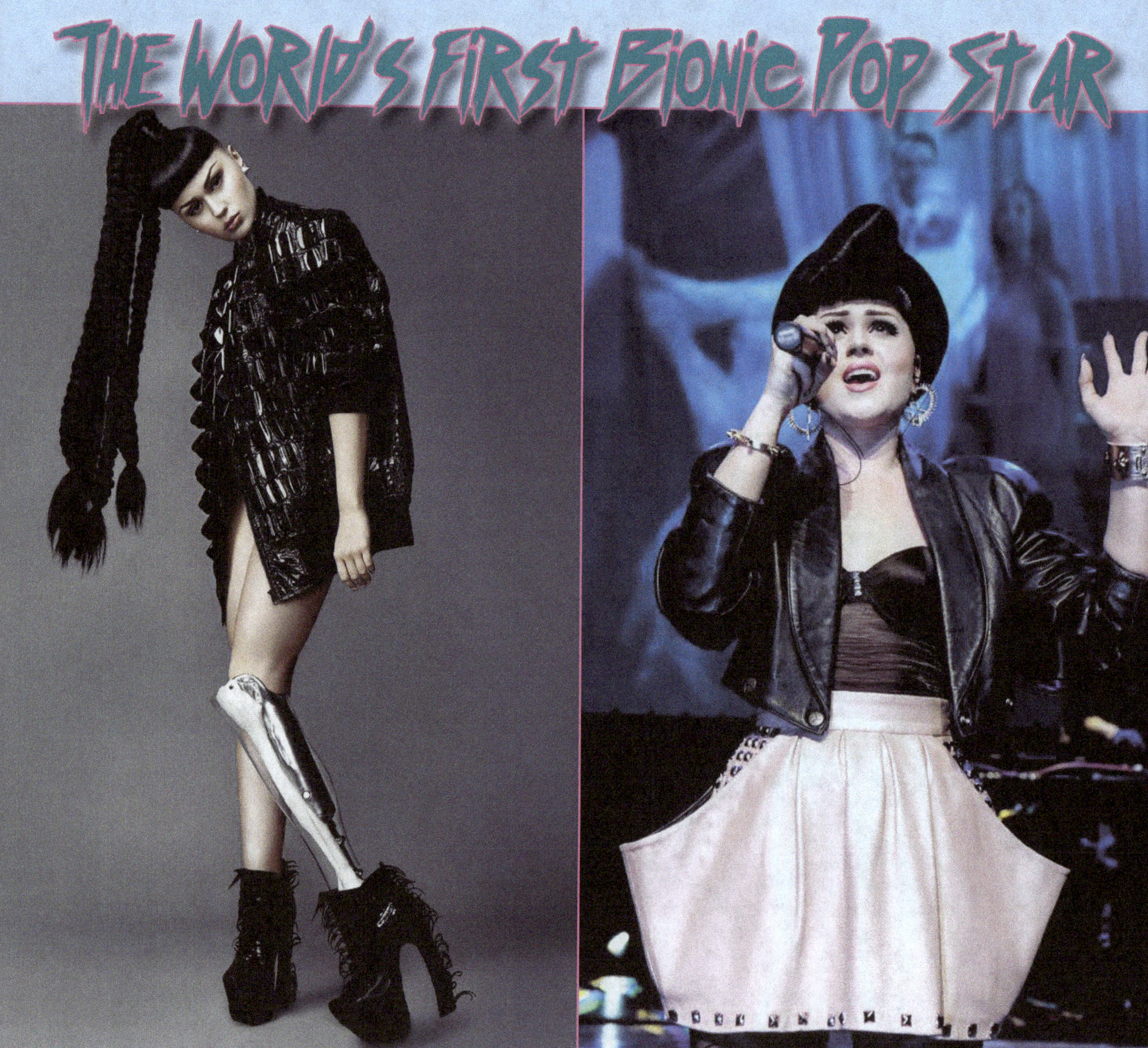

Music was always a large component of Viktoria's life. She attended a performance art school as a child and learned vocal techniques, dance and how to play the piano. Viktoria released her debut single "Only You" in 2012, a sultry number worthy of being in a James Bond film. Her big break came in 2014 with the release of the song "Prototype", with the accompanying music video premiering during The X Factor finale to millions of viewers. The video is a work of art, showing the strength behind a disability with Viktoria using a metal spike as a prosthetic leg. The song itself is super empowering, urging the listener to break boundaries and create their own identity. The response to the video was positive and it normalized disabilities to the general public, which is exactly what Viktoria had hoped for.

Viktoria released her EP titled Counterflow in 2016. The EP is electronic and futuristic, with vocals that remind me of dark pop artist Natalia Kills. Her live performances do not disappoint either.

She closed the 2012 Paralympics as a Snow Queen complete with a bedazzled prosthetic. Viktoria is a mainstay performer at cutting edge fashion, tech and art shows. Viktoria's prosthetics are created by The Alternative Limb Project, a company that specializes in constructing original limbs that reflect the personality of the wearer. Their creations include porcelain floral, droid and light up limbs. Wouldn't you want your prosthetic arm to be made out of feathers, too?

Viktoria is the perfect example of rising above adversity and not falling into being a victim of one's own hardships. She is fighting to shatter stereotypes against people with disabilities and turn something negative into something to be proud of. You can keep up with this bionic beauty at www.vikoriamodesta.com. The future is transcending the human body. Viktoria is doing just that. ∎

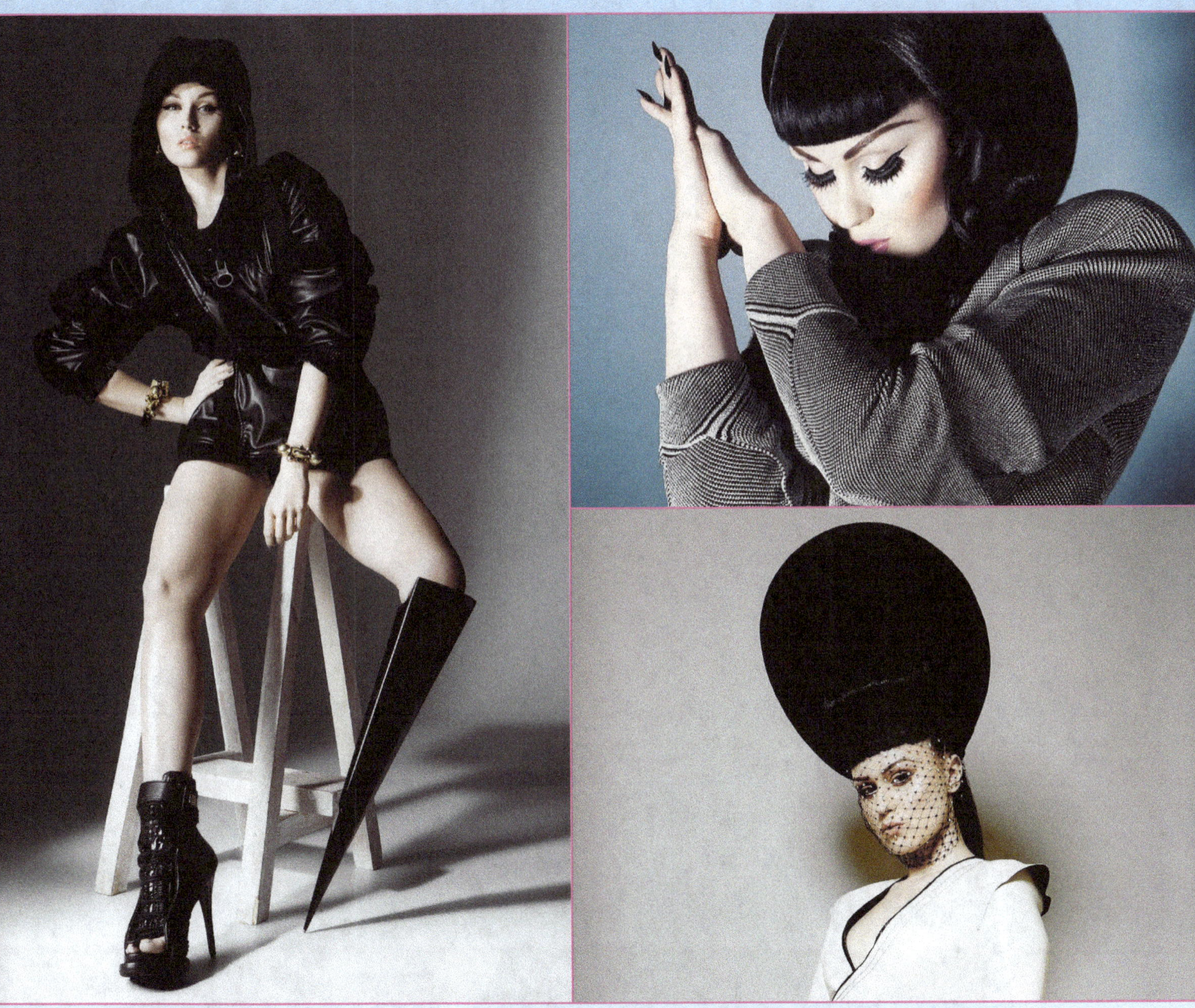

Interview with Michale Graves

by Dawn Wood

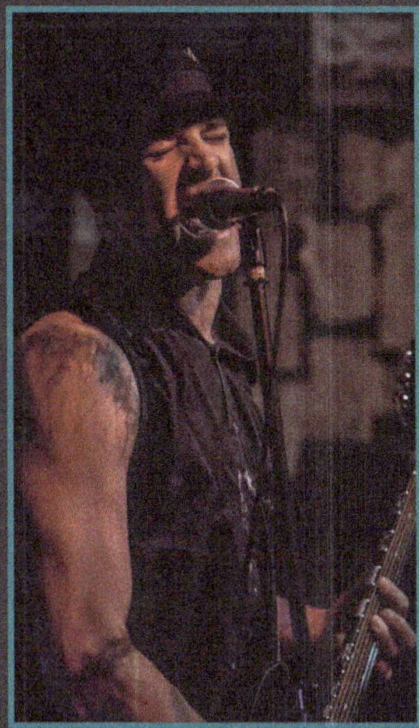

The first time I heard of Michale Graves was in relation to the 1990s re-emergence of the Misfits. My brothers were fans of the Misfits growing up, but I liked the Michale Graves version much better. Michale Graves was the vocalist on the Misfits albums American Psycho (1997) and Famous Monsters (1999). In my opinion, he wrote some of the best Misfits songs of that era, like "Dig Up Her Bones" and "American Psycho." Michale showed passion, and there was something about him that was not the normal dude "trying to be a Rockstar." When I heard he was doing a horror project called "Graves," I was excited to hear the music.

The band recorded a demo before "Web of Dharma," which was never officially released. Graves recorded and released one album with Graves, "Web of Dharma," that was produced by Dr. Chud. Alas, in 2002, the band broke up. Graves then formed Gotham Rd shortly after with Loki, JV Bastard and Paul Lifeless. Under the assumed name of Graves, they recorded a five-song demo of redone Graves songs, three which were released on "Web of Dharma" and two other songs which had been written and demoed with the original Graves lineup, but not officially released. Around this time is also when Graves announced via his website that he would also begin producing some other bands albums during his off time. After a few months of the band practicing, they decided to change the band's name to Gotham Rd. They released one album before going on hiatus, so Michale could join the U.S. Marines. His last show ever was to be on December 31, 2004.

Since that time, we have seen him partnering up with Marky Ramone, and since 2012, soloing his own music path. He has an impressive discography of songs and his voice speaks to the soul. For me, this interview was important because it was one that inspired me of my own true feelings about not only music, but also about where we stand today as Americans and how fragile we have become. Only one other interview I have done for Carpe Nocturne has inspired me in this particular way, and that was Henry Rollins. And so.... readers, it is with great pleasure I give to you my interview with Michale Graves. If you haven't yet familiarized

yourself with his music, please jump on YouTube and check him out. He's also on Facebook.

[Dawn]: Michale, a lot of people are familiar with you in the Misfits, but you have been an accomplished musician far prior to and have won over many fans since. When did you start your career in music?

[Michale Graves]: I loved music from a very early age. Music has always stirred my soul in a profound way and I have found it to be most effective way of communication. As a teenager, my Mom has to be given the credit for constantly pushing me and getting me involved in theatre programs, music programs that were preparing me for opportunities to come and developing my natural talent as an artist. My big break came when I joined The Misfits in 1994. I have been writing and performing music for two decades. I am still waiting to be discovered...(laughing)!

[Dawn]: You have your own band now, and have been successfully touring this past year. What/when are your next tour plans?

[Michale Graves]: I start out in February with some shows in Brooklyn, Delaware, I will be in a few other spots as well before really getting going in March. I begin in Canada with the full band. I then transition to my acoustic tour in support of a brand new acoustic record called "Backroads." The "Backroads" American Tour will take me from coast to coast ending sometime in May.

[Dawn]: I heard about you all having your gear stolen. This is terrible! Did this force an end to the 2016 tour? Any leads on the perpetrators?

[Michale Graves]: That situation indeed forced an end to a tour that for sure had been hexed. No leads, no suspects, game over, man. That tour aged me a few years to say the least.

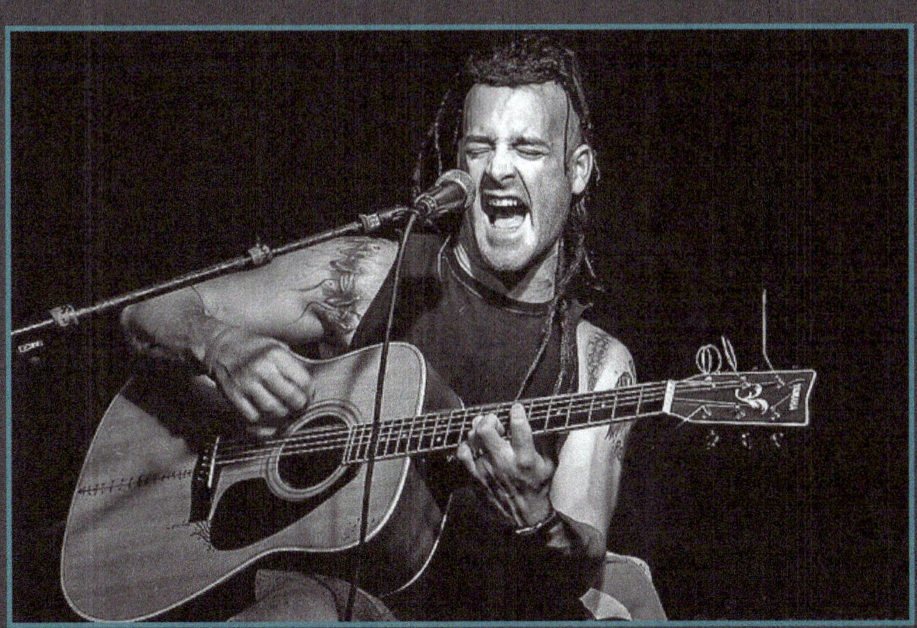

[Dawn]: We are so sorry to hear this and hope that whomever did this is brought to justice.

[Dawn]: Tell us about your Kickstarter campaign?

[Michale Graves]: The Kickstarter campaign for 'Backroads' runs from January 26th until February 2nd. There are reward pledges with different value. You can simply pre-order the album or check out the other pledge levels that are offered for a short time. There are private performances, original paintings, memorabilia from the studio sessions and from my collections. Like everything Hydraulic Entertainment does, we add an experiential element in everything we do. The fans have access to things and have opportunities to be a part of the story and the music in innovative ways.

[Dawn]: What are your feelings on the music business? Obviously, it has gone through changes since you first broke into the business. Where do you see it going?

[Michale Graves]: I love the business of music. I detest the "music business" and the culture it has created. I reject the values and the principals of a super large majority of artists and entertainers across the boards. It is a sewer pipe of sludge and ugly fake culture and dead music that further isolates, strains and confuses the minds of young people. Drooling fools and ignorant brats, and there is a long list of them from Bruce Springsteen to Madonna....butthurt pansy boys like Billy Joe from Green Day squawk there nonsense and go unchallenged by anyone considered peers. The business has changed because of the massive machine that the business has become and the worldview and program that it has signed on to. I just don't want any part in any of it actually....(laughing).

[Dawn]: Where is home for Michale Graves and what inspires you when you are not on the road?

[Michale Graves]: I live in the mid Hudson Valley of New York. Not far from where I live is where Rip Van Winkle fell asleep. I live in a small rural town that doesn't even have cell phone service. My home is an old 1800s farmhouse that is situated on what once was an old goat farm. The Catskill Creek borders the land I am on, and there is an apple orchard that was planted by a band of gypsies that came by hundreds of years ago. This place inspires me. Life inspires me....my children inspire me.

[Dawn]: I understand you have some political leanings. I also read your inspiring blog: "MTV Hates White People." Thank you for writing something so poignant to identify the hatred going on in our country today, and how it is misdirected and just causes more hatred and alienation. What inspired you to write this, and do you have any additional thoughts/suggestions for us coming together instead of being so divided and blaming each other?

[Michale Graves]: We are in a bad place. People like me, other musicians that hold the same value set, world view and ideas as I do, do not behave...and are not behaving, or saying things like we see coming from those who oppose people like me. We are two minutes from civil war in this country if we don't keep pushing back and reaching out. I fear, in ways, it's too late and we are beyond event horizon. What will set us free and bring us together, as it always has and always will, is the truth. We are in an information war and it's important to contribute to the fight, especially in the many battles of the culture war. It's a 'David and Goliath' kind of a thing when it comes to music and pop culture because the machine is so big and the mindset is so pervasive and deeply ingrained, not to mention well funded. So, voices like mine...artists like me, are not top of the list folks given opportunity to VOICE a counter point of view. I know what it is liked to be blacklisted. It happened to me. I, however, do my best to resist and counter that worldview at every chance I am given and will do so until my last breath.

[Dawn]: What is your favorite time: Studio or Touring?

[Michale Graves}: Studio. I look forward to a time I don't have to tour anymore.

[Dawn]: I noticed much of your video is live footage or song videos fans have made on Youtube. How do you feel about videos? Any plans to make a video soon?

[Michale Graves]: I love working with video. I have a ton of editing experience and have a passion for photography. The films are coming.... the videos are coming....I am pivoting as we speak!

[Dawn]: What is one thing you would love to do that you haven't done yet?

[Michale Graves]: I would love to be able to make a living that doesn't take me away from home anymore so I can spend more time with my children and become more active in other things I have a passion for. I am not in this thing to be famous, I don't need recognition to be ok and I certainly don't need to be applauded to feel worth. I am everything the music industry isn't and is against.

[Dawn]: Anything else you would like to promote?

[Michale Graves]: Go to http://hydraulic-entertainment.com/ for all things Michale Graves. For a short time, you can go to the Kickstarter and also other links.

Facebook: www.facebook.com/michale.graves.771 ∎

Nine years ago this August I was lucky enough to get to meet two amazing artists while I was at GenCon in Indianapolis. They were there to do a preview showing of The Dead Matter, a movie created by Edward Douglas in 1996. I will freely admit that up until that point I had always thought that Midnight Syndicate was a musical compilation and not a band. I had heard their music during many of the games I had played over the years but I had never dug into the depths of that music until I picked up Out Of Darkness at their booth that fateful day. I will not make that same mistake again.

It is hard to understand how amazingly Midnight Syndicate can create a setting unless you have heard their music. No lyrics to ensnare your memory, instead they use the emotive power of music and create artificial recollections of daydreams, on the verge of waking where the darkness still haunts our mind and reality and fantasy are drawn by a dim line. Over the last twenty years Midnight Syndicate has been the background music to our darkest fantasies, the theme songs to horror nights and the unofficial soundtrack to Halloween. It was my good fortune to catch up with Midnight Syndicate and get to talk with them, informally.

Carpe Nocturne: First could you introduce yourselves to our readers?

Edward Douglas: This is Edward Douglas. I began Midnight Syndicate back in 1996. The idea behind the project was to create "soundtracks to imaginary films" - albums that blended music and sound effects designed to transport the listener to a world or movie of their own creation. Our predominantly gothic, horror, and fantasy themes and instrumental style have resonated with people in the Halloween, haunted house, gothic music, film, and gaming industries as well as with artists and people with active imaginations that like to use the music for inspiration or background while creating their own art. While, the first Midnight Syndicate album was more of a solo project for me, I began working with Gavin immediately afterwards and have been ever since.

Gavin Goszka: Gavin Goszka here. I share songwriting and mixing duties with Ed and also handle most of the audio mastering for our releases.

CN: How did you first meet?

G: Ed had asked me to give him some feedback regarding the songs on the first (self-titled) Midnight Syndicate release. Although it incorporated a wide range of musical styles, I was particularly drawn to the darker, atmospheric tracks. I went to the multimedia concert that Ed had put together in support of that first CD and after seeing these darker elements brought to life in a live setting, suggested the idea of possibly working together in the future on a horror-related musical project. I think it was only a few short months later that I

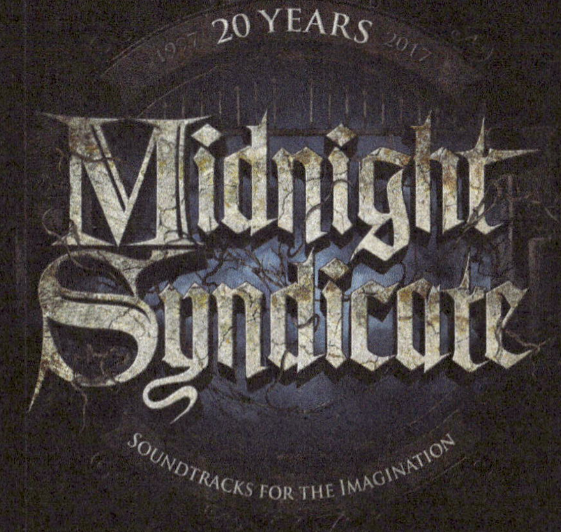

by Kathleen Sharkey

got a call from him about the idea for "Born of the Night". Doing an exclusively-instrumental CD of atmospherically dark music was something that I could immediately get behind. There really wasn't anything else quite like it out there at the time, and although it was difficult to predict exactly how well it might be received, I think it was something that I simply felt I wanted to be a part of right from the start.

E: I first met Gavin when he was working at my local music store, Sodja's. He helped me equip my first studio. I was always in awe of him as a musician (both on keys and drums). However, I remember going to a coffee shop to hear him perform. He played this one song entitled "Sleepless" that grabbed me immediately. It was so cool, atmospheric, and had a ghost story theme to it. I just remember hearing that song and thinking "I have to find out who wrote that because that's the perfect example of the direction I want to take Midnight Syndicate in". I thought it was an obscure Alice Cooper or Genesis tune or something. Turns out it was an original that Gavin had wrote. Upon hearing that, there was no doubt that I had to do whatever it took to get him on board. Fortunately it wasn't difficult because he had enjoyed the darker material I had written on the first Midnight Syndicate self-titled CD and liked the direction of the material I had already written for the next album. We had a lot in common and always seem to be on the same page creatively. It's been an amazing ride.

CN: You have created music for games, music for movies and your music is used in a variety of haunted houses across the country. How does preparation for creating these specialty sound tracks differ? Are there any similarities?

E: Our main gig has always been creating stand-alone Midnight Syndicate albums. We find a theme like a haunted Victorian asylum, a mysterious turn-of-the-century carnival, vampire's crypt, dragon's lair, etc. and then we build this world around it through music and sound effects. Right from the get go, we knew that our albums would be perfect for professional haunted attractions and amusement parks. There just wasn't any kind of music albums like ours out there at the time and a real need for professional-grade, non-cheesy horror-themed atmosphere. So we kept them in mind while we created our discs. The same goes for our albums' applications as background for other Halloween-related activities and roleplaying games. After being in the business for a while, new opportunities presented themselves, like scoring films and writing soundtracks to specific roleplaying games like Dungeons & Dragons. In those instances, we did need to adjust our preparation. Those albums or soundtracks weren't just coming from our imagination, they were designed around worlds or movies created by others. Getting ideas and feedback from our partners (directors, game designers) as we went was critical to make sure that the end product was something that matched their vision as well as ours. It's more of a collaborative process because there's more folks involved.

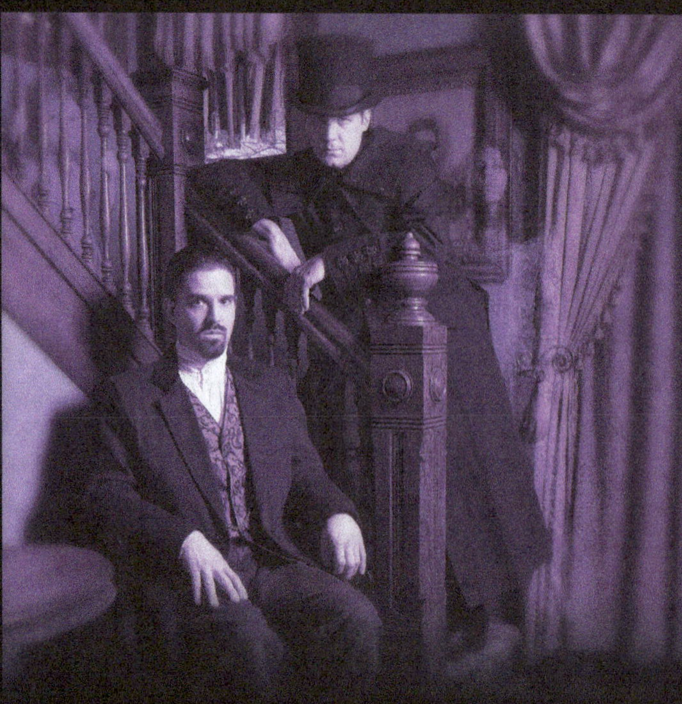

CN: I know that The Dead Matter was directed by you Mr. Douglas, how does creating a soundtrack for your own movie compare to other creations?

E: Scoring a film is very different from writing for a Midnight Syndicate album. On a Midnight Syndicate album, the music and sounds are everything. They must be compelling enough to take you on a journey without the aid of any visuals, narration, or anything else. In a film, the score is just one cog in the machinery. It is a very, very critical cog, but still just a part of the whole (which is the film). Everything you do as a movie composer has to serve the movie, the characters, the story, and the director's vision. There's plenty of room to be creative, but you have to be mindful that what you are creating is always elevating what people are seeing on the screen and not taking away from it in any way. My approach to writing the score to my own film, "The Dead Matter", was no different from the others I've scored. I remember wanting a few more outside "ears" on that particular score. When it's your own film, I think you tend to get really close to the material and can lose some objectivity. Getting trusted team members' feedback was critical.

CN: Each one of your songs has a life unto itself. Where do you come up with your ideas?

G: We both draw inspiration from a range of horror movies, artwork, literature, etc. Sometimes a setting, theme, or character might suggest a particular musical treatment, but sometimes it's the other way around, where we'll come up with a melody or a chord progression and then see what images or ideas that seems to

suggest. Deciding on a theme or rough story is typically one of the first things we do when starting to write. Beyond getting the creative fires burning, I think it also serves as a guide when we get to the stage where we're deciding which songs to keep or set aside for a particular project. There have been many times when a particular song may be fine on its own, but not quite as effective when we hear it within the context of the rest of the material.

CN: Do you come up with a story line for each song?

E: Not for every song but we have rough ideas about the story that's being told on each album. At the very least, we each have some details on the scenes and inhabitants (both present and past) that are a part of the world we are creating.

G: One of our ongoing goals has been to leave a lot of the details up to the imagination of the listener, so that they can take the album's story in whatever direction they choose. It's always interesting to hear how different people can imagine different things when they listen to our music. I think trying to tell a very specific story via instrumental music would be inherently difficult anyway, especially when it comes to conveying visual or tactile details, plot points, etc. Song lyrics can allow a writer to spell things out to the degree that they wish to do so, but with instrumental music, you have to rely solely on the music's ability to evoke emotions or establish a particular mood or atmosphere indirectly.

CN: Your music inspires a great deal of people. What or who inspires you when working on an album?

E: I love immersing myself in the world we are creating before beginning the writing process. A lot of times that means locking myself up in my studio and watching a ton of horror movies. I also get a lot of inspiration through doing historical research. Researching the history of traveling carnivals and circuses for our Carnival Arcane album was an extremely rewarding process that yielded a ton of material for that album (both musically and sound effects-wise). The same goes for our Christmas: A Ghostly Gathering album. Learning more about the history of Christmas and the celebrations tied to that time of year from around the world throughout history gave me a lot of stories, characters, and ideas to pull from. I love reading (and re-reading) Stephen King short stories and Tales from the Crypt comic books. They are always a source of inspiration. I think artwork and photography too can be a great spark. I remember spreading out all of the artwork and covers to my Dungeons & Dragons modules on the studio floor while writing for that album. Viewing images that are reminiscent of the world I am trying to create not only provide me with inspiration but also help me keep the material focused.

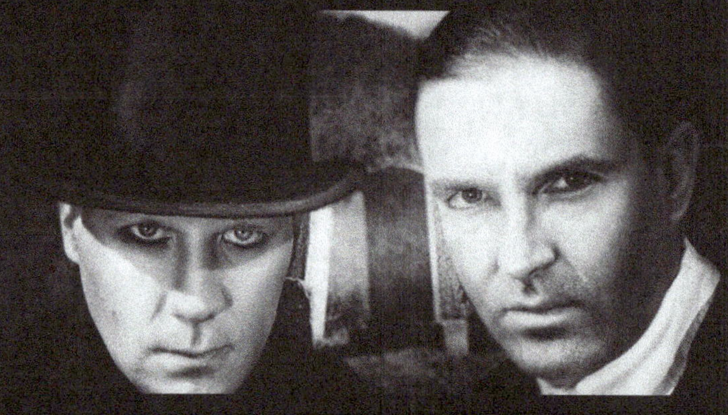

G: For me, I think it's more of a desire to push and challenge myself to do something I haven't done before. I remember Gates of Delirium being one of those defining moments when we really took a step forward in terms of being able to create a truly immersive sonic landscape

The 13th Hour was another one of those moments. Christmas: A Ghostly Gathering allowed us to not only explore a different sonic palette but also offer up our own unique treatment of songs that were already very familiar to our audience. I would say that being able to continue to improve my skills as a songwriter as well as helping to create our own variety of musical soundscapes are the two biggest factors driving me forward.

CN: You have recently started doing a live performance for Cedar Point. After so many years of doing only studio albums what inspired you to do live performances?

G: We had been toying with the idea of doing a live show for a long time, but between our constant production schedule and the requirements of putting together the kind of fully immersive experience that we had in mind, it just never seemed to be a realistic option. The Cedar Point show was the perfect opportunity in that it allowed us to test the waters in a much more contained, consistent setting and on a smaller, more manageable scale than what we had been considering. I think it was definitely a case of all the right factors being in play, from the venue to the amazing staff, cast, and crew. When I look back on that time, I remember the entire experience being one of the most rewarding and enjoyable things I've done with Midnight Syndicate to date.

E: It was an absolutely amazing experience and a very positive one for everyone involved. The success of that show has made performing live a permanent part of our plans for Midnight Syndicate going forward which is exciting for us.

CN: Is there anything you would like to share with composers just starting out?

G: The whole music industry has changed so much since we started doing this. I think some of those changes are definitely for the better, but as with so many things, there are usually trade-offs involved as well. Beyond the many technological improvements that have made the creation and recording of music so much easier and less costly, artists and composers are now able to get their music out to the public in ways that simply were not available 20 or 30 years ago. YouTube has proven to be a powerful tool for discovering and promoting music, and social media allows people to communicate directly with fans that live practically anywhere in the world. The downside to all this freedom, however, has been the diminishment of music's value as a tangible, monetizable product. There are so many artists out there now, and so many ways to easily consume and enjoy their music, that it can almost seem like an inexhaustible resource. I think one of the biggest challenges today can be getting your music heard, considering the vast pool of entertainment choices that audiences currently have available to them. That being said, I certainly wouldn't want to discourage anyone from pursuing their dreams – I would simply advise being as aware and educated as possible so that you know what to expect going in.

E: The world is your oyster sonically. The music technology that is available today blows my mind. When I think back to what we were using back when we started, the quality we could get, the astronomical cost in equipment by comparison, I just feel like composers today have unprecedented opportunities to take what they hear in their head and make it a reality. My advice would be to take advantage of the technology but be aware that everyone else

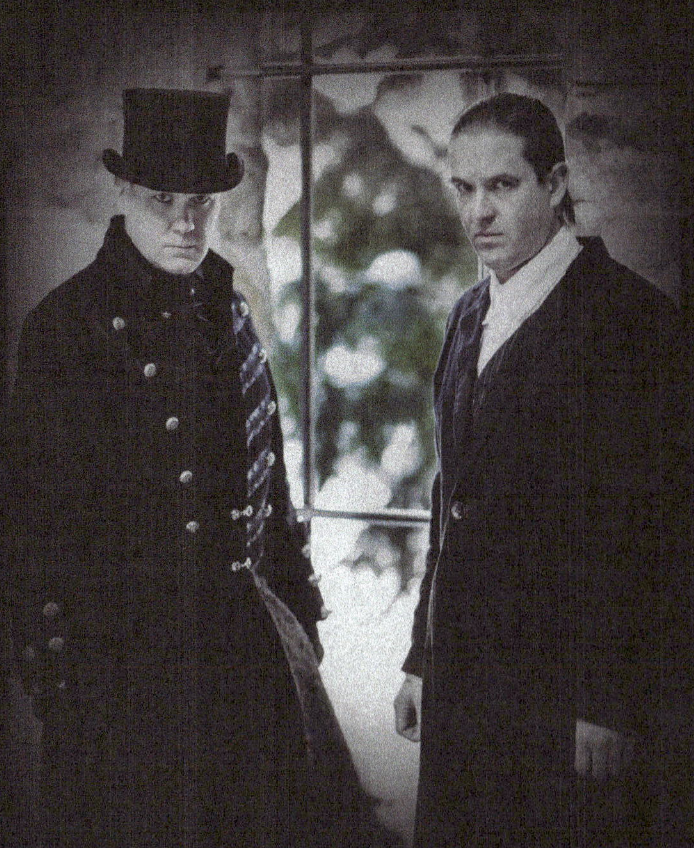

has access to that same technology. To stand out you're going to have to work at developing your craft. You do that by continuing to compose. My idol, composer John Williams, once said that you should spend time composing every single day. While I haven't been able to stick to that schedule, it's advice that I always keep in the back of my mind. The best way to learn is by doing.

CN: Twenty years and twenty albums, we are looking forward to the next decade. Can you share anything you are currently working on with our readers?

E: We do. Both Gavin and I are thrilled to announce that, after three years, we will once again be returning to Cedar Point's HalloWeekends in Sandusky, Ohio every weekend from September 15th through October 29th. Our show, Midnight Syndicate Live! is a horror-themed multimedia concert experience designed to both entertain and thrill audiences. It's as much a visual experience as a musical one and we can't wait to unleash this new version of the show. If you enjoy Midnight Syndicate's music, the supernatural, haunted houses, and horror films, you'll enjoy what we have in store for you. What's best is that once you leave our show, you're at Cedar Point which is regarded as the roller coaster capital of the world. If coasters aren't your thing, there are a ton of haunted houses and scare zones throughout the park as well as other live entertainment. We already have a lot of ideas for the next Midnight Syndicate album although that probably won't be in the works till after this show's run. People can find out what we're up to, connect with us, and preview our music through our social media pages (Facebook, Twitter, and Instagram) and our website, www.MidnightSyndicate.com! ■

MADVILLAINY:
THE SCI-FI WORLD OF
SPLIT

by Bryan Akerley

Blumhouse Productions has wrangled the scattered brilliance of M. Night Shyamalan, who in the last couple of years has turned in two excellent creepy-fun thrillers in 2015's The Visit and this year's Split. It's a comeback story, like a once-great musical artist signing to a new label and it becoming a perfect marriage. The Visit is touted as a true return to form, but with Split, it seems this new stride has got Shyamalan thinking of the big picture.

See, for the man known for his twist endings, this movie is a bit more straightforward. The twists are there, but nothing so mind-bending as a character realizing he's been dead the entire time we've been watching him. In fact, the ending is hinted at, and it feels natural as we watch it, but by the end Shyamalan has changed the genre of the movie we're watching. The film we thought was a horror-thriller is actually a sci-fi thriller. Then, to eliminate any doubts about this genre bend, the last scene hammers in the nail: Split is a super villain origin story.

A man with Dissociative Identity Disorder named Kevin (James McAvoy) kidnaps three girls and keeps them trapped in a room underground. Kevin has 23 personalities—the aggressive leader Dennis, nine-year-old boy Hedwig, rational Patricia, among others. The girls meet these different versions and soon realize they are being kept as "food" for a new personality: the Beast. Meanwhile, Kevin's therapist Dr. Fletcher (Betty Buckley) deals with his personalities and the burgeoning threat of the Beast. She discusses the potential of humans with such a disorder, the possibility to become more powerful.

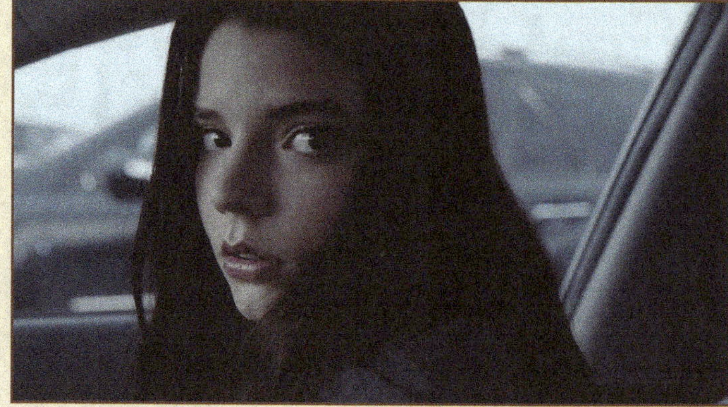

In a way she's right, and the Beast reveals itself as a superhuman form of Kevin's body that feeds on two of the girls and kills Dr. Fletcher before sparing Casey (Anya Taylor-Joy), because like Kevin, she was abused as a child.

The final scene reveals that Split takes place in the universe of Shyamalan's Unbreakable (2000) with David Dunn (Bruce Willis) realizing the threat of the Horde, a name given to Kevin's collective personalities.

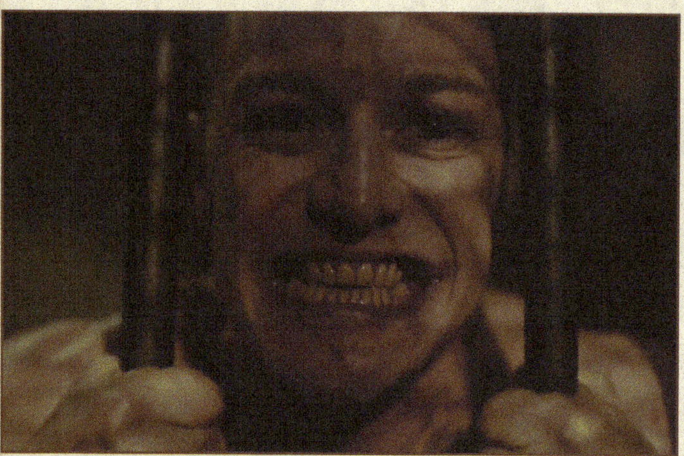

genres reflect the world of the character. Unbreakable is mystery sci-fi, a noir-ish and atmospheric family drama until the audience realizes Dunn is becoming a straight-up superhero. By contrast then, it makes sense that Split throws its audience into a tense horror setting as it reflects the chaos of Kevin's head, until the worst-case scenario gives birth to a formidable villain in the Horde, and a sci-fi counterpart to Dunn's story.

It works so well simply because of the time that's given to developing these two characters in their respective movies. Marvel's powerhouse franchises are often criticized for their one-off villains only because so much screen time is dedicated to building the heroes. But what if the villain had his own movie, where the audience hadn't even yet realized that this tortured, conflicted character would grow up to fight the Avengers?

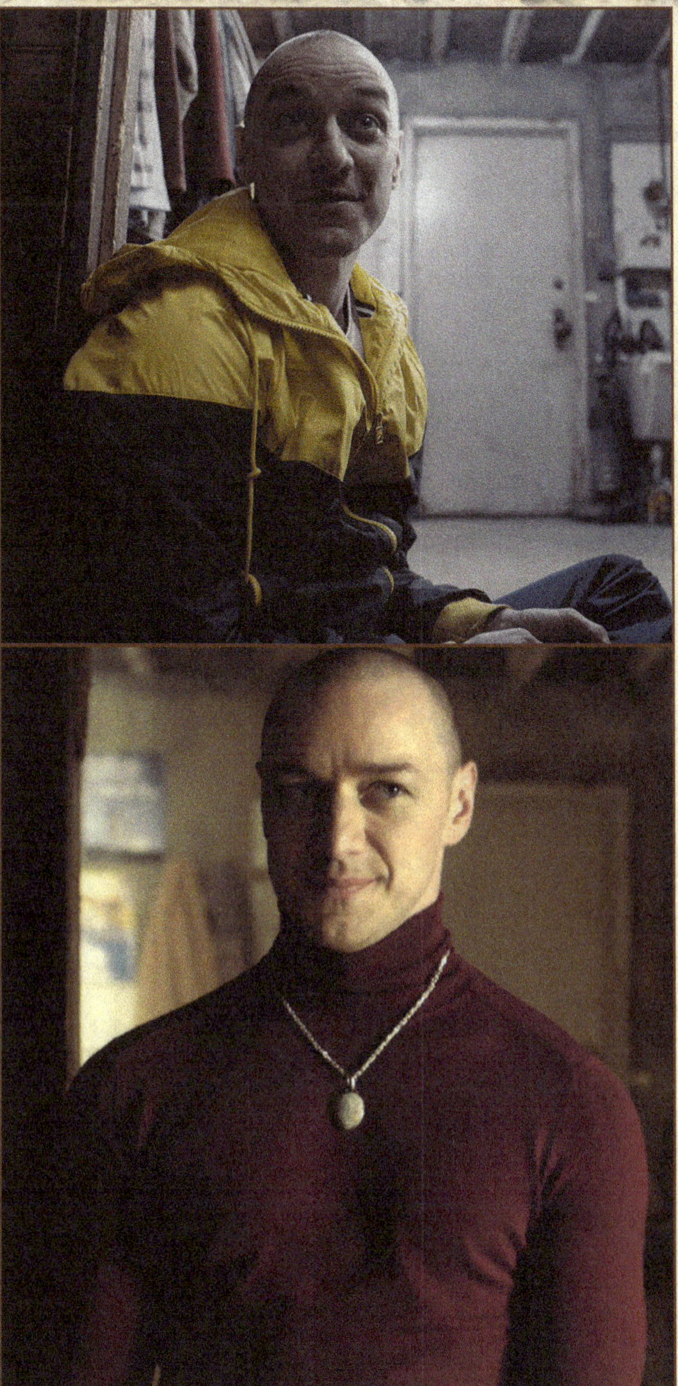

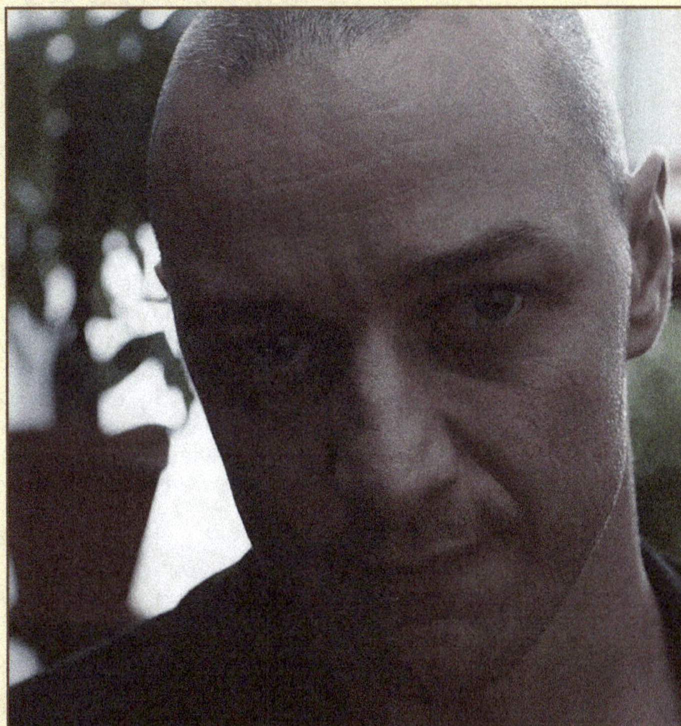

The nature of Kevin's disease and Shyamalan's use of flashbacks where the child Kevin is hiding from his abusive mother make us sympathetic toward this character. He himself has no control over the personalities fighting for the spotlight, even telling Casey in a moment of lucidity to shoot him with a shotgun. But the Beast assumes power, and the Horde's path of destruction is just beginning by the end of the movie. We're left conflicted about this villain; we don't want to hate him, like many sci-fi films angle their villains. We want him to overcome these sinister personalities.

The confrontation of Dunn and the Horde may come, as Shyamalan has started early work on a third movie. And when it does, it won't be a battle of explosions without a stake in any one side. We know these characters now. The fight will be intimate, complicated for us as the audience and full of depth, uncharacteristically sci-fi, but sci-fi nonetheless. ∎

Dunn, in the events of Unbreakable, realizes he is superhuman as well—a supremely strong and, well, unbreakable man. The film plays as a slow-burning superhero origin story where Dunn must contend with the adage Spider-Man's Uncle Ben put so well: "With great power comes great responsibility."

Years later, in the same universe, we have the uncontrolled menace of the Horde finally doing away with its benign personalities and becoming, throughout Split, the super villain complement to Dunn's hero. The films mirror each other in a stroke of genius: the films'

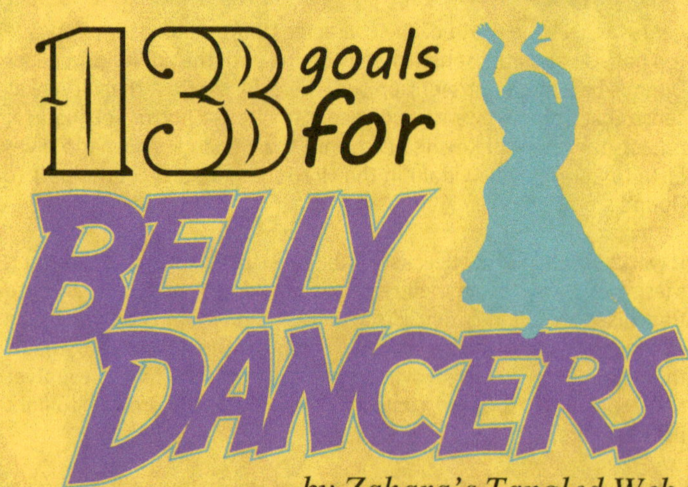

13 goals for BELLY DANCERS

by Zahara's Tangled Web

Spring is a time of rejuvenation and growth. We emerge from our wintery caves with renewed energy and optimism for what the world has to offer. As belly dancers, this is a great time to take stock of where we'd like to invest our precious creative energy in the coming months. Setting goals provides focus and pushes your skill set forward as a dancer. My successful artist friends, whether they are writers, painters, or dancers, all occasionally review their past efforts, then plan ahead for what's next. Without a game plan (even an informal one), you may find yourself spinning your wheels doing the same thing over and over again. A short list of goals can help you limit expenditures of money and time to only those activities that align with your personal aspirations. Take some time to look over your activities (classes, performances, etc.), and think about what you would like to accomplish as a belly dancer by the end of this year. Then, come up with three goals to work towards. Here are 13 ideas to get you started.

1. Specialty Middle Eastern Dance Classes - Shake up your status quo by studying a new style of Middle Eastern dance. If you're an Improvisational Tribal Style dancer, take some Egyptian belly dance classes. This could give you new insights on musicality, teach you accent moves you've not considered, and give you valuable history about our dance form. If doing drum solos happens to be your specialty, try taking Persian dance, which could introduce you to some interesting dance combinations, taking you into more sweeping movements and away from heavy hip work. If nothing else, you'll gain an appreciation for various Middle Eastern dance genres you may not otherwise have without physically doing the dances yourself.

2. Videos - If you're like most of my belly dancer friends, you probably have a DVD or two that you consistently watch for performance techniques or drills/combinations. You can get belly dance instructional videos through Netflix and Amazon, as well as through your local library (although they may need to be ordered). Find something new, and use that for your at-home instruction for the next 30 to 60 days to build muscle memory for different combinations to add to your dance vocabulary.

3. New Rhythms - If you've never drummed before, this might be the new learning experience that truly pushes you out of your comfort zone. Try starting with a commonly used rhythm, such as chiftitelli or baladi. If you're more proficient at drumming (or even using zils), select a really intricate rhythm or try switching between two rhythms. Some drummers offer lessons, and there are wonderful tutorials on YouTube. Visit Karim Nagi (karimnagi.com), Jeremiah Soto (soundsofsolace.com), Issam Houshan (tablabyissam.com), and Raquy Danziger (raquy.com) for information about their workshops and online drum lessons.

4. Change Your Look - Have you ever watched your performances over a span of years and realized you look the same in most (if not all) of the shots? If so, then it's time for a make-over! This doesn't necessarily mean purchasing a brand new, expensive costume. It could be something as simple as trying different makeup, adding false eyelashes, styling your hair differently, or using gold (not silver) accents. Remember - never sacrifice proper fit for the sake of changing your look! If you're really happy with your favorite costume, try layering a veil or wearing different harem pants to update it. If you're crafty, make your own bra & belt set or other new performance outfit for this year. If you're not crafty, this could be your chance to try sewing for the first time, perhaps a skirt or some pretty tribal fusion panels to wear over your harem pants.

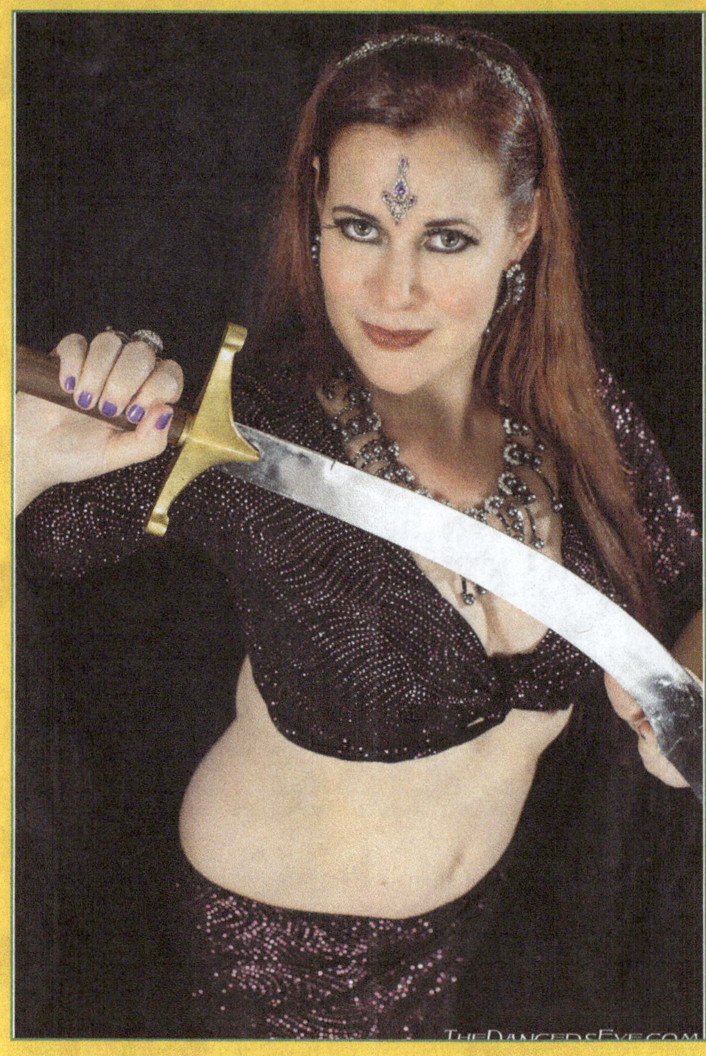

5. Cross-Train - It's important to build upon certain skill sets by studying complimentary dance styles. If you have a goal to improve your spins over the next several months, consider taking a ballet

class. Or if you prefer belly dance fusion, you may enjoy strengthening your body during a vigorous hip-hop class.

6. Private Lesson - If you have the opportunity and it's in your budget, try spending some one-on-one time with a local instructor you admire, or through a Skype lesson with one of your professional belly dance favorites. Keep in mind that the instructor's job is to give you constructive criticism and to push you out of your comfort zone. Remain open to their suggestions, because this personalized feedback is invaluable.

7. Observe - I know this sounds counter-productive if you're trying to improve your belly dancing, but it's a great way to gain inspiration. Simply enjoy the show and really concentrate on the other dancers' performances. You could hear a great piece of music, see unique prop work, watch some difficult layering techniques... who knows. But if you're performing in the same show, you may miss those subtle ideas because you're backstage, worrying about your choreography, or fixing a wardrobe mishap. Take a break every so often to simply observe and soak up ideas.

8. Document Your Belly Dance Journey - Start a journal, blog, or photo album. One thing I've noticed after belly dancing for over fifteen years is that I have very few photographs of my friends... which is ridiculous! I have some beautiful performance pictures of myself, but what about the students I've taught over the years, or how happy their families were during their first moments onstage? What about my own teachers and how they've continued to gain mastery over the years? This is one area I'm concentrating on correcting for 2017. Your personal journal or blog will prove to be a valuable resource in the future, especially when you're trying to remember the notes from that choreography workshop you took six years ago, or the names of the shows you've attended.

9. Clear Belly Dance Clutter - Clutter has been referred to as "visual noise", and I couldn't agree more. It's easy to let your belly dance possessions overwhelm you at times, whether it's fabric, makeup, hip scarves, or whatever you just can't seem to let go. One resource that's been extremely helpful to me is "The Life-Changing Magic of Tidying Up" by Marie Kondo. She details how to purge and organize different classifications of belongings. She even explains why we keep things (even items we dislike). Sell costumes that don't fit well, put your show programs and flyers into a binder, and roll up your favorite veils. Soon, you'll have a clearer space... and peace of mind.

10. Organize a Show - Maybe your goal is to find another performance opportunity for yourself or your students, or to host a community-building event. You could sponsor a formal belly dance show or a more informal student hafla. If you've never hosted anything before, try starting small and growing your event over the years. There are expenses involved (venue, insurance, sound system, etc.), so prepare a budget and don't overextend yourself financially! Managing an event is great experience, and you'll learn a lot about your fellow teachers and dancers.

11. Choreograph a Three-Minute Song - Sounds easy, right? Especially if you're really great at creating choreographies. But if you're always "winging it" during your performances, then the idea of choreographing a dance, remembering it, and executing it will seem daunting. It uses a different part of your brain when you create a choreography, so give it a try! If you're comfortable with choreographies, then try mixing up

things a bit by venturing into a different genre of music.

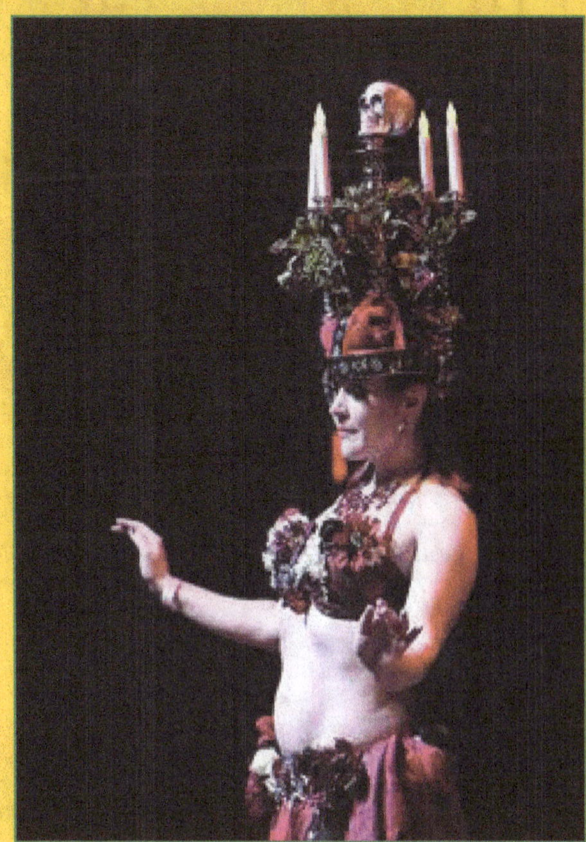

12. New Prop - If you've watched routines and admired the prop being used, then begin incorporating one into your own dances. Examples of popular props include swords, trays, candles, and shamadans. You may be able to borrow one, if you're not ready to purchase it. Benefits of using props are increased balance and fluidity, as well as gaining some cultural insight regarding the use of that prop (especially the shamadan).

13. Collaborate - It's easy to get comfortable dancing by yourself or just working with your own troupe/students. Reach out to other dancers, and try collaborating on something new. This could mean working with new dance partners, co-sponsoring an event with another troupe, or finding some musicians to join. Discussing new ideas, working together for a good cause, sharing different ways of incorporating dance combinations, and meeting like-minded people could really inspire you.

Setting a few goals for yourself on an artistic level is vital to continue growing and creating. It helps prevent burnout and keeps you from getting bored or too comfortable. What goals have you set for yourself for 2017? I'd love to hear from you, so drop me a line (zahara@carpenocturne.net).
Links
www.ZaharasTangledWeb.com
Photo Credits:
Zahara with Sword (Dancer's Eye Photography)
Mayan Ruins Collaboration (by Eric Greiner)
Zahara Shamadan (by David Sorcher) ∎

an afternoon with

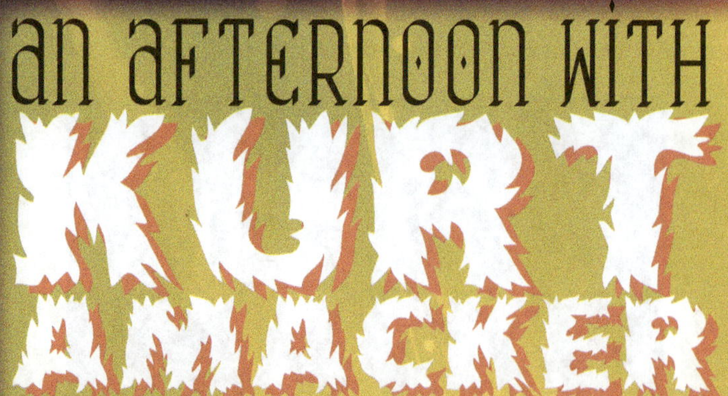

KURT AMACKER

by Xxx Zombieboy xxX

The sudden burst of wind nearly liberated the hat from my head as I hurried down Saint Charles Avenue towards my appointment. The storm had only just dropped another tornado on New Orleans earlier that morning. I take one glance over my shoulder to make sure another is not coming. The Avenue Pub loomed in front of me, with its doors ajar, and welcoming any and all lost souls to adjourn within to drown their sorrows and dreams alike in a river of potent amber intoxications.

Entering the neighborhood public house, my nose is assaulted by the familiar scents of whiskey, beer and frying food. I cast my eyes around and find my friend Kurt has already arrived. A glass of half empty Maker's Mark whiskey and a copy of Ernest Hemingway's The Sun Also Rises sat open upon the table. He sees me and waves me over. Weaving my way through tourists and sassier locals, I take an empty seat.

Kurt Amacker is one of those people with whom your path will always eventually cross if you are a writer, a comic enthusiast or a "Goth" in New Orleans. The son of a Naval officer, he first "arrived" in 1980 and would begin leaving his mark like a brand woven through the hidden history of the scene here. Dissatisfied with college life and torn over a bad relationship, Kurt joined the Marine Corps Reserves. Fate would intervene in his world when his unit was activated in March of 2003 in support of Operation Iraqi Freedom.

"I had an idea for a comic during a Marvel call for open submissions and had begun working on it when my unit was activated, and it had to be shelved," he told me. Then, while training in Camp Pendleton, he suffered a severe knee injury, which left him stationed in California. With a year of surgery, physical therapy and down time ahead of him, he picked up the comic idea once more. This was the beginning of the series that would gain Kurt the international attention and a slew of comic fans. Dead Souls was born upon the humble pages of a legal pad.

"While I was in college, a friend introduced me to Cradle of Filth. I was more into traditional Gothic music at the time, and not as much into metal, but the lyrics really pulled me in. With the sensibility of a poet, Dani inspired me to begin reading more history and 'literature' with a capital 'L.' This gave me the idea of historical figures such as Vlad Tepes and Elizabeth Bathory interacting and doing what they do. The idea was for them to be slaughtering criminals in modern New Orleans. The idea sounds outlandish now, but I was young."

Upon returning to New Orleans, Kurt married his wife Sabrina, and did various projects while working on Dead Souls. One of these jobs was for the entertainment website Cinescape (later, Mania). Kurt also picked up DJing and promoting almost by accident, which coupled with his media credentials, would open doors for him. In 2008, Kurt met another promoter and comic publisher named Marc Moorash of Seraphemera Books. With Marc's help, Dead Souls finally saw print, and three important people in turn saw Dead Souls.

"There were three really talented creators who saw my work early on and vouched for me. They were Alan Moore, Dani Filth (Cradle)and Jyrki 69 of the 69 Eyes," Kurt told me. "I don't want to go down as some kind of coat-rider," he said, "but I'd be wrong not to thank those guys every chance I get."

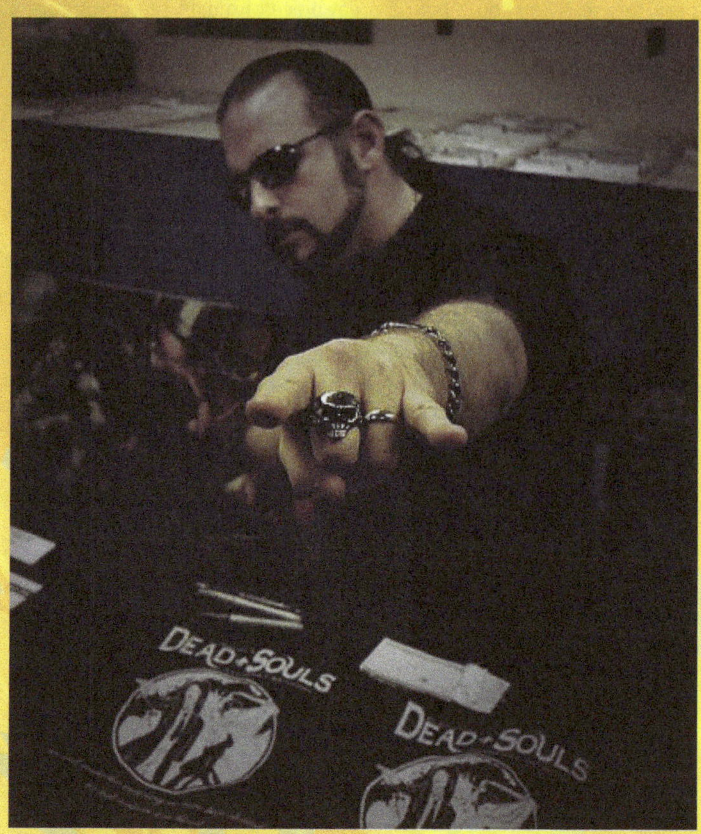

I offered then to refill his glass and procure my own. I walked over to the bar and ordered a pint of the black stuff and a glass of Angel's Envy. Looking back, I saw Kurt once more immersed in the Hemingway novel. I flash back in my mind to one of the first interactions I had with him.

Back in October, running from my own nightmares, my friend Carlos handed me a flier for an event at Bar Redux called Loupgarou. It was a science fiction and horror film festival. The tiny bar was at the far end of Poland Avenue and in its own strange pool of light surrounded by darkened buildings and shady Nola night streets. I had read Dead Souls, having purchased it long ago at a now-defunct Gothic boutique called Wicked Orleans. That night at Bar Redux, I saw Kurt sitting at his table. He had been reading a book then as well. It was easy for me to imagine him working through the plot ideas for Dead Souls and for the further works he would eventually accomplish.

I walked up to his table and immediately noticed a Cradle of Filth shirt upon it I had not seen before. I was intrigued when I noticed that he had a comic in his selection that matched it. The graphic novel was titled Cradle of Filth: The Curse of Venus Aversa. Taking place in Victorian England, it follows the story of a controversial poet named Lord Daniel Impudicus, who is forced to confront vampires, ancient goddesses and local authorities after the murder of his lover Gabrielle.

Kurt had put his book down and stood up. He is an imposing figure at first glance. Some of that warrior is still in his stance. Then he broke out in a smile and his demeanor was friendly and welcoming. Something that sold me on him more than even his intriguing connection to one of my old favorite bands. I would end up buying up everything I could afford that evening.

Returning with the drinks at the Avenue Pub that afternoon, I suggest the upper balcony and we make our way outside. It is still windy as I light a clove cigarette and hear the street cars rumble by. It is a moment I would recall when I later picked up Kurt's vampire-noir novel, Bloody October.

Reseated and settled, I asked Kurt to recall once more the story he had told me that last October. The story of how he got involved with Dani Filth.

"I had basically written Dani a fan letter, telling him how I had become a better artist because of him, and I gave it to him at a VIP meet and greet. Then Amy at Roadrunner Records helped me get a PDF of Dead Souls into his hands. I requested to do an interview with him as a supplementary feature to the first issue. He and I discovered a common ground in literature and history. I would eventually build a friendship through back stage visits and online. We kept in touch and then in the spring of 2013, I got a message asking me if I would like to spearhead a Cradle of Filth graphic novel."

After a wildly successful Kickstarter campaign, and procuring the talents of artists Montgomery Borror, Jamie Huntley and Tim Lattie, The Curse of Venus Aversa was unleashed into the

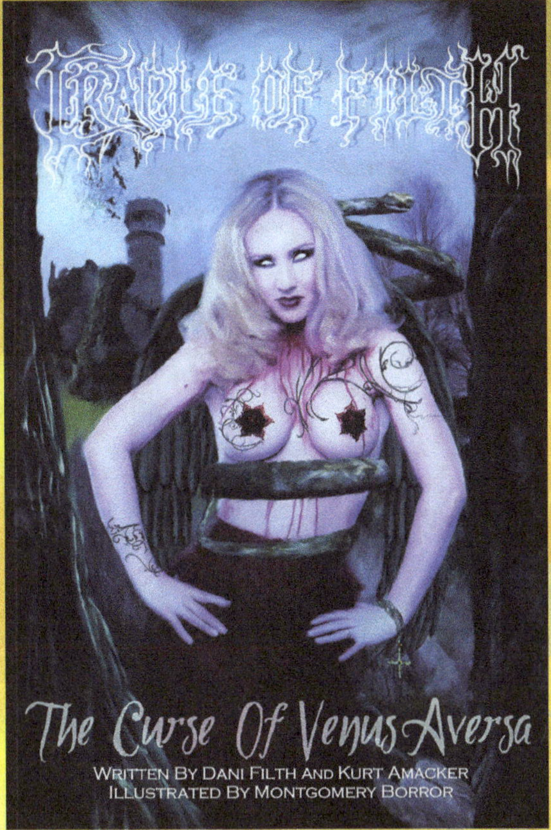

world in April of 2014. Kurt was able to focus his attentions on his craft full-time. But in the intervening years, Kurt had already caught the attention of Jyrki 69 of the 69 Eyes.

"We met while I was DJing. I was with a small production group and we had booked them, and at a big after party at the Whirling Dervish, Jyrki and I hit it off. We created the idea of doing a whole "true back story" of the 69 Eyes in a comic series. It was a big honor for me, and he is still one of my best friends."

The premise for the series is that the secret history of the 69 Eyes is pieced together from a story hidden in six of the band's songs. A story that traverses from the Hundred Years War, into 1970's Europe and into the early Goth scene of the 1980's. Jyrki is a vampire in search of the witch Christina Death, who he hopes can reverse his condition.

"And Alan Moore?" I ask him.

"I connected with him when he was doing Lost Girls. That was a kind of tasteful literary porn pastiche take on The League of Extraordinary Gentlemen. It's a truly beautiful, sublime book about Alice Farechild, Dorothy Gale and Wendy Darling having sex all over a hotel and telling their life stories. I was working for Cinescape at the time and did a long interview with him about it. We kept in touch and I wrote once for his magazine, Dodgem Logic. I still talk to him regularly. I called him a few weeks ago to tell him I'd picked up his new novel, Jerusalem."

Another streetcar rumbles by and far off, one of the countless churches in the Garden District begins tolling its bell. You can always count on New Orleans to set the scene. I segue momentarily away from comics to ask Kurt about DJing and why he largely excused himself from the Goth scene. Kurt looks down and I see memories pass through his mind in his shifting expression. I immediately gather that the story is less positive than all he has told me thus far.

"I had a friend living in my guest room after Hurricane Katrina in 2006. He had this idea that we would do a Goth night that was all-ages and really artsy, old school, and serene. That transitioned into doing a monthly night at the Dragon's Den and really going out of our way to decorate

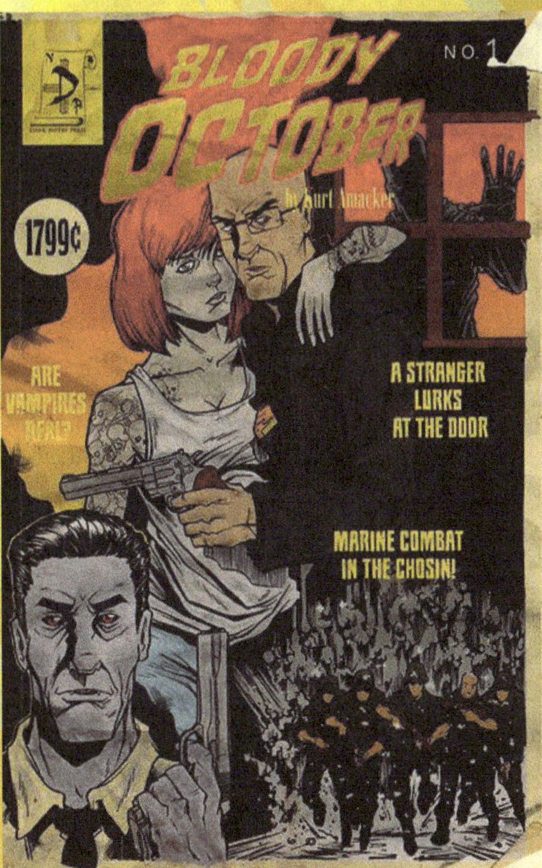

it and make it something special. I love the Goth scene, but we wound up in turmoil with other nights. It became this really tedious scene fight—one of many I'm sorry to say I participated in, in the ensuing years. The short version is that I walked away from it because of the drama and the insularity of the whole thing. When you do that—when you step outside and look inside—it is a bit of a snow globe. Seeing even just the rest of New Orleans society outside of that clique is like getting out of a fishbowl to find you've been in the ocean the entire time. I was born here and it took me 17 years to disentangle myself and see the rest of the city. Why stay at a place when it becomes nothing but feuds and drama? I very publicly walked away a couple of years ago. I still do a guest appearance as a DJ every so often. I enjoy [local promoter and DJ] Mange Vorhees's events, but I don't make any regular thing of it. I wish all of those guys and their nights well. I really, truly do. I love Gothic art, literature and music—and I suppose the idea of the subculture. But, it just wasn't for me anymore."

There is a long pause and I put my pen down a moment to take a drink and light another smoke. I look at Kurt and I can see some of those old days rolling through his mind. I admit to myself a moment of guilt for bringing up bad memories, but then he looks up again and grins, bringing up mutual friends and our plans to engage in a future round of whiskey and cigars with them. I am relieved that the moment has passed. Familiar all too well with the drama that can sprout from the Goth scene (or any other scene for that matter), I am happy to leave the subject behind.

Picking up my pen again, I reflect upon the latest of his works that I had purchased. It's one I intend to review at a later date. That being Kurt's first novel Bloody October. The cover immediately grabbed my attention, being a mix of comic book flare, pulp noir aesthetics, and a title worthy of 42nd Street in its heyday.

As of this writing I am only half way through, but I found it immediately delightful. It's the kind of tale you expect when set in New Orleans and involving vampires and the Goth scene.

"I started writing it in between comics and had to keep setting it aside because of life. I sought to create a semi-comedic novel from the POV of a vampire's best (human) friend in the line of Rhenfield. The idea stayed with me and I initially wrote it from the gut, with no outline. It starts off as two guys having coffee. It's a barebones slice of life that suddenly becomes a murder mystery. It is a more grounded and realistic take on vampires (and their own corresponding club scene), pulling from less romantic visions and more from Eastern European folklore," Kurt told me.

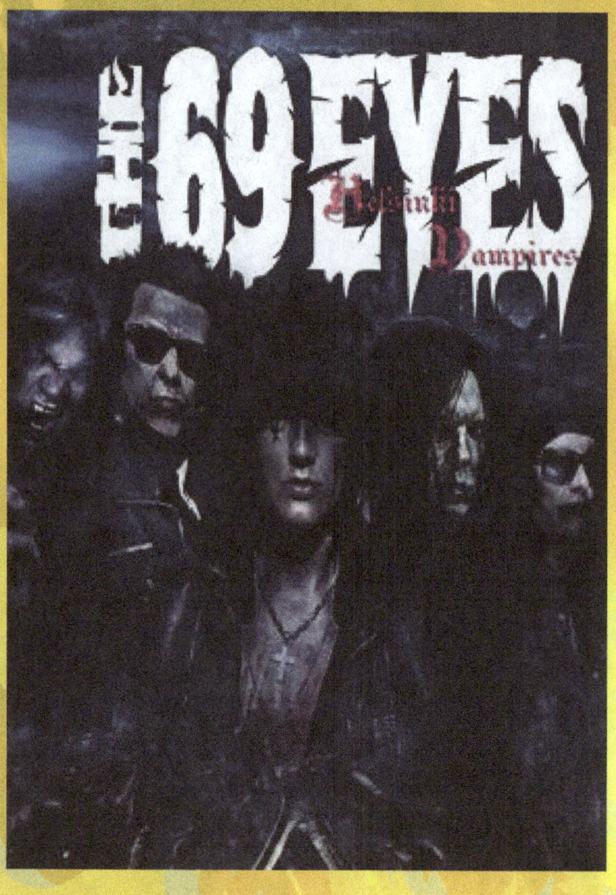

"It is also kind of a love letter to the late 90's Goth scene, which I see as its crescendo. What I tried to do, in the vein, again, of Hemingway, is to put the reader in a time and place of interesting historical moments that I am very grateful to have been a part of. I really wanted to dedicate a story to that period with a nostalgic, but kind of reflective look at that time. I used real folks in it like the tour guide (and a good friend of mine) Lord Chaz to give a wink and a nod, thus adding grains of truth to a fiction."

"You know," he says, "I try to work without pretention or politics and more in the vein of broad and universal life experience, rather than what I think of Clinton or Trump, for example. You don't win people over by insulting them or calling them out."

I asked Kurt what currently had his attentions and he told me that he would love to do a prequel and a sequel to Bloody October, but that Dead Souls is in the middle of a reboot. I put out my smoke and look out over the overcast rooftops of the city we share, and I make some comment about the difficulties of making it by as an artist. That sparked something in him.

"What the world needs is more hobby artists, because the real world gets in the way. Even successful artists like us still have to make our way with regular jobs most of the time. We use day jobs to finance what we truly love. You often wind up getting something more experimental and interesting that way, when you're not trying to make something that must, by necessity, be commercial."

I cannot disagree with his outlook, though I have been a fan of many artists who have found lavish success. It has always been those artists that still struggle to support their craft that I tend to love the most. There is honesty in it somehow. We begin gathering our things to go our separate ways. I ask Kurt how he feels about his work and if at times he considers it a statement on the climate we live in.

"My thoughts are this. An artist may not be an authority on a given subject, but you are always, of course, always allowed to have an opinion. For example, I am not qualified to discuss brain surgery or pottery... but we all live life. We've all been in love. We've both walked around this city. And I can talk about those things."

https://www.facebook.com/events/348117795550306/

Kurt Amacker will be appearing as a guest DJ at the Black Syndicate's A Night of Ritual with DJ Mod Escher and PAPArazzi in Pensacola, Florida March 31 ∎

The End of BLOOD ON THE DANCE FLOOR

by Samm Sanity

You just cringed or grinned. After ten years of music, Blood on the Dance Floor have broken up. The electronic duo consisting of Dahvie Vanity and Jayy Von Monroe parted ways nearing the end of 2016, after six of the ten years together.

Dahvie Vanity began the electronic/dance/crunkcore band in 2007, originally under the name of Love the Fashion with Christopher Mongillo and Rebecca Fugate. Ultimately nothing but a joke in the beginning soon became Blood on the Dance Floor and they released their first album "Let's Start a Riot" then their second "It's Hard to be a Diamond in a Rhinestone World". Christopher and Rebecca left the band when the touring began as they were unable to.

Shortly after, in 2008 Garrett Ecstasy joined Dahvie while he was touring. They recorded and released three songs in 2009. Garrett's spot in the band was short-lived, he left in 2009. There were rumors that he was stealing from Dahvie and other rude behaviors.

Enter Jayy Von Monroe.

Jayy Von Monroe and rapper Matty M. joined Dahvie in 2009. Matty M.'s time in the band was also short-lived since Jayy took over the rapping. The duo finished out the last years of the band together. The band is infamous for their offensive and sexual lyrics, and offbeat style and performances, along with Dahvie's numerous rape allegations. These I dismiss, as the first girl refused a test and another admitted it was all fabricated. No one really knows except the people involved.

Now that the backstory is out of the way, let's get into the break up. Dahvie announced the end of the band on September 14th of 2016. It was originally going to be a hiatus, but Jayy announced he was leaving the band, so Dahvie "only thought it right that he started the band, so he would be the one to end it".

Fans were distraught and heartbroken about the disbandment of the band. Yours truly included. Nothing more about the subject was said, until Jayy posted about the break up on his Facebook on November 16th. It shocked and saddened the fans to hear his story. "With respect, and all honestly, I feel that it is only the right of any fan out there to know why I left Blood on the Dance Floor a few months ago..." is how the post began. He goes on to write about how

he has grown and changed as an artist, and the constriction he felt "from the other half of the band". He says it started in 2014, around the time when the band had started to mature in their sound and lyrics, making more inspirational songs instead of the overly explicit stuff in the beginning. Jayy says Dahvie panicked when streaming became more popular, so he insisted on returning to the old sound. It's well known that the fanbase is mostly young teens, and Jayy felt wrong singing the sexual lyrics to these now younger than him fans. Jayy joined the band when he was 18, at the time he didn't feel like it was weird when he was more their age, but he says it now feels "perverted" to do so.

Jayy then goes on to say Dahvie refused to pay him. Instead, Dahvie paid for his bills and necessities, like a caretaker instead of a partner. When he was younger, he allowed it because he was just 18 and afraid of Dahvie's temper. Later he had a long talk with Dahvie about just paying him, he did but it was usually late or incomplete. In late 2014, Jayy began working on a side project, which is how he kept himself afloat.

The next thing he talks about is his sickness and getting diagnosed with HIV. He justly assumed, because he needed medical attention and would be unable to tour, that the tour would be cancelled. Unfortunately, he thought wrong. He says Dahvie said they couldn't afford to cancel the tour, and he would have to wait for medical

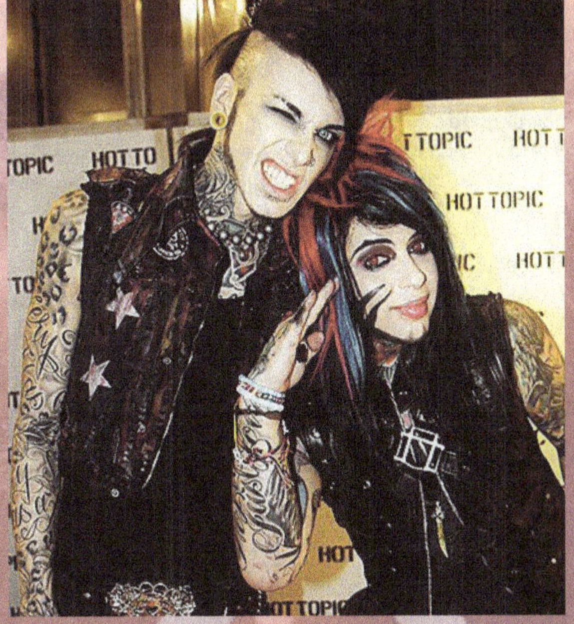

treatment until they returned from tour. By this, Dahvie meant he, himself, couldn't afford not to tour as he had racked up quite a lot of debt. Jayy reluctantly went on a tour that was ultimately a bust anyway, sick as hell. Jayys says he did eventually get treatment and is back to good health.

Jayy goes on to write about being paid $1,000 to write the entire, save for two songs, final album "Scissors". All within a two-week time limit. This and the feeling of being taken advantage of resulted in Jayy's decision to leave the band.

A little while later, Dahvie stated on his Facebook and Instagram, that after the final tour, he would post his "side of the story". He has yet to, or comment on anything really.

So what does this fan think? I think Jayy has no reason to slander Dahvie or make up wild stories, so I believe him. He's a good guy and it's a total shame that he was taken advantage of. I still love the music, and I really enjoy Jayy's new music and drag projects. I wish him all the best in his new path. As for Dahvie, I'm not sure what to really say. I'm just really disappointed and, honestly, not all that surprised with his behavior. While I would like to give him the benefit of a doubt, I just don't see how. His lack of comment on the whole thing leads me to suspect that Jayy is indeed right, or he is trying to find a way to twist around what Jayy has said to make himself look good. Either way, I think there was some sketchy shit going on behind the scenes and Dahvie is not as innocent as he tries to appear. ∎

The 10 Most Disturbing Films I've Ever Seen

by James Donnelly

Cinema has so much power; more power than some people care to admit. It can change the way we view things; from interpersonal relationships, to the way we view ourselves to the way we view historical events and/or socio-political perspectives. The most obvious power that any form of art has is the power to make us feel something, and cinema can really show the great pantheon of the human experience. It can make us laugh, cry, and hope. It can inspire and it can enrich. But not every film wants to make you feel good. Some films are interested in the long dark night of the soul and forcing you to stare into the abyss. In the forty-two years that I've been alive, I've seen all manner of films, and have not only been shocked to the core, but shaken to my very foundation as I questioned human nature, reality, and the basic meanings of good and evil. The following is a list of the ten films that, over the years, have left me with gaping wounds in my soul and still make me cringe when my mind recalls them.

Bear in mind that there are Spoilers aplenty about these films I'm going to discuss, and they're ranked in no particular order (except for one, and that will be pretty self-explanatory).

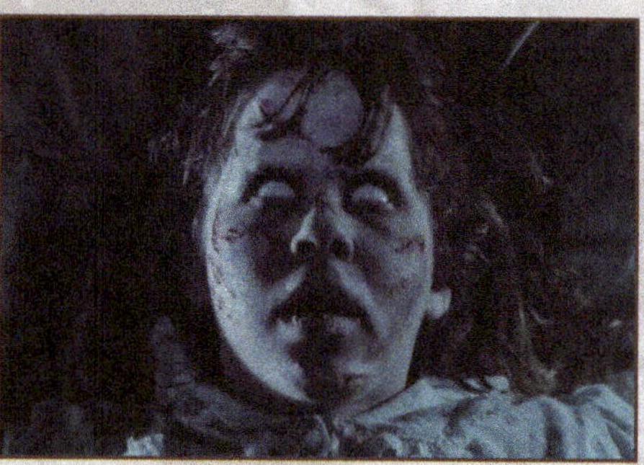

"The Exorcist"

It's odd to think that the late William Peter Blatty started his career as a comedy writer (and in fact co-wrote the screenplay for one of my favorite screwball comedies of all time "A Shot in the Dark") since he is now a legendary contributor to the horror genre having written the novel this film is based on. I'm not going to go heavily into plot, because if you haven't seen "The Exorcist" by now, I don't know what to tell you. There are several disturbing moments within the film (and if you've seen the mini-documentary about the making of the film that's included with special editions of the DVD or Blu-Ray, you'll find more to be disturbed about), but the two moments that stay with me the most are Regan's bloody crucifix masturbation scene and Father Karras' dream sequence. The dream sequence where he's running toward his mother in silence isn't terribly bothersome in and of itself, but the brief flash of the white demonic face haunts my dreams (and some of my waking moments) to this day. I would say that the biggest reason this film tops my list as the most disturbing film I've ever seen is because of my Catholic upbringing. By the time you're confirmed, you're pretty well indoctrinated with the idea of Heaven, Hell, God and Satan. It's pretty damn scary as a kid, and because of how this film changed the horror landscape and the concept of the supernatural horror, it's also pretty damn scary as an adult, even if you're an agnostic like myself.

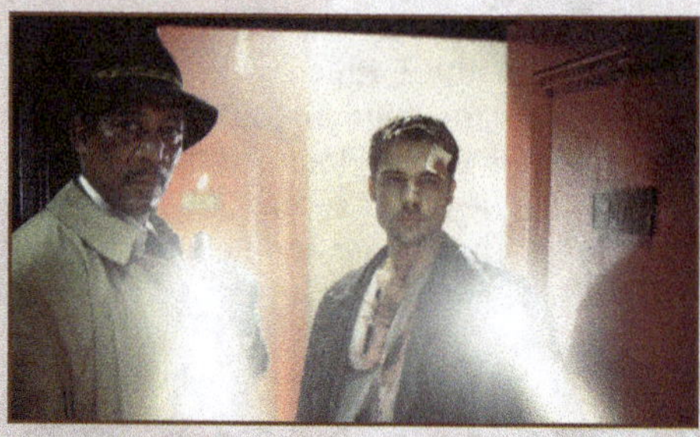

"Se7en"

When David Fincher made his feature film debut with the lackluster "Alien 3", it seemed like this former music video director wasn't going to be one to watch. And when the first trailer for "Se7en" hit the screens, it looked like another traditional mismatched-cops-track-serial-killer thriller. It looked good, but not like the kind of film that would transcend the genre. As it turned out, the film would help a director define a uniquely dark style that would enter the modern filmmaking vernacular (simply calling something "Fincher-esque" has become incredibly evocative) and craft an ending to a film that would leave me so deeply disturbed that I couldn't wait until the end credits rolled so that I could flee the theater. The "What's in the box" finale has three acts to its structure: unrelenting tension (as Somerset pleads with Mills to throw his gun down), horrific reveal ("her pretty head"), and the villain victorious (Mills shooting John Doe). It took me a few days of just sitting with the film to get past the feeling of general hopelessness. I've spoken to people who find the breakdown that Brad Pitt has in those closing moments to be unintentionally funny, and for the life of me, I don't understand people that think that because one of the things that makes those final moments work is the trinity of Pitt, Morgan Freeman and Kevin Spacey working so effectively together.

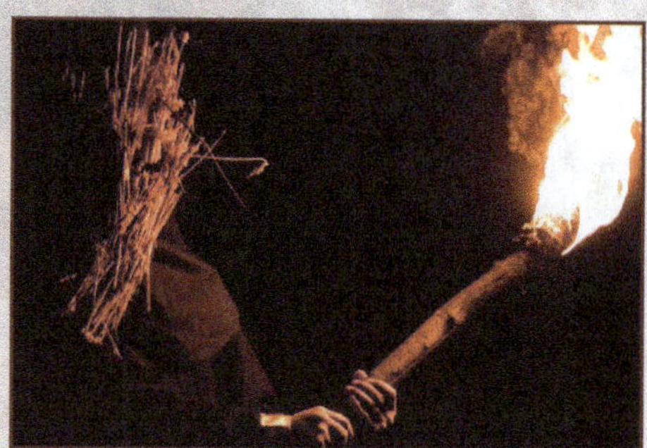

"Kill List"

This is the newest film on this list from one of the most eclectic directors I've come across in recent years. Unlike a director like Fincher, Ben Wheatley seems to be content in not defining his work in any style. He's dabbled in black and white psychedelia ("A Field in England"), social criticism ("High-Rise"), ultraviolent black comedy (the upcoming "Free Fire") and even episodes of "Doctor Who". But if there is a crowning jewel of Wheatley's career, it's this film. It starts out as a workaday look into the lives of professional killers. We follow two men as they make their way through a short list of names, and in its third act, it makes a VERY HARD left turn from crime thriller into nightmarish horror with an ending that will leave you crouched in a fetal position for several hours after viewing it. The finale is hard to describe, but once the reveal of "the Hunchback" is made clear, it was emotionally devastating in much the same way that the ending of "Se7en" affected me.

"Videodrome"

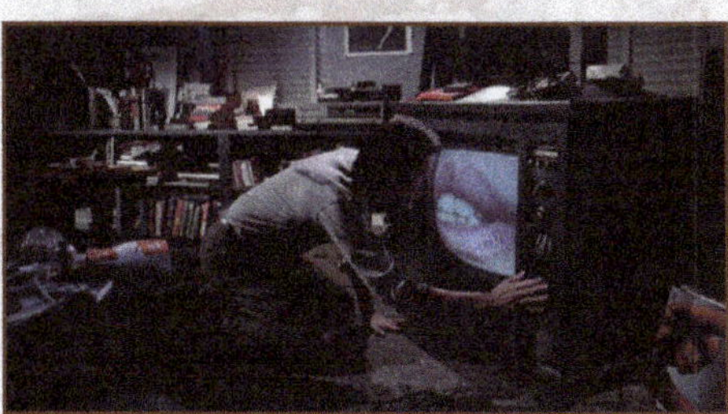

This one was arguably the toughest choice to make because so many of David Cronenberg's films have truly and deeply disturbed me. The nightmarish surrealism of "Naked Lunch", the sexual panic of "Rabid" and the monstrous romance/body-horror of "The Fly"; truthfully, the two I had to choose between were the tragic co-dependence of "Dead Ringers" and this film. Because my first experience with "Videodrome" came earlier in my life than "Dead Ringers", the "body horror" of Cronenberg's filmography edged the other out. If I were to choose one moment among the many disturbing moments of this film, it would have to be the image that stayed with me since I was a child who saw this late one night on an obscure UHF channel. The image of Max Renn alone on the abandoned ship looking at a television, seeing Nicki Brand give him his final instructions, and then showing him turning his gun to his head. The television explodes outwards with fragments of brain and other viscera. No other scene in my film viewing history had left such an intensely disturbing mark on my soul, because it's a moment like no other.

"Jeepers Creepers"

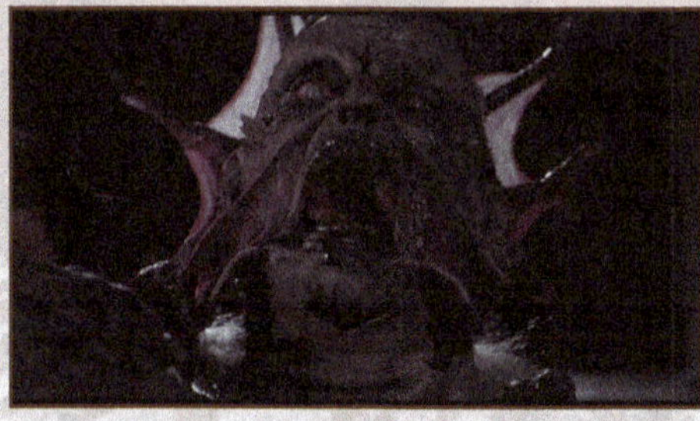

This one might make some people roll their eyes, but when I first saw this film, I was in no way prepared for what was coming. I knew it was a creature feature and it was from the director of "Powder". But once Justin Long fell into The Creeper's lair and there were hundreds of bodies plastered into the walls and ceilings of the cave, I knew that this was going to be a different kind of horror experience. And while, again, there is a multitude of horrific imagery, the moment where The Creeper picks up the head of a decapitated police officer and pulls the cop's tongue out with his teeth, I knew that image was going to stay with me until this very day and well beyond.

Before I get into the next five, I want to talk a little about what I find truly disturbing in these films and why many of the more traditional rankings of these films don't appear here. There are films like "Saw" and "Hostel" and similar films that found themselves on these lists because once the audience is strapped in for the ride, the gore becomes constant and unrelenting. Films like these or films like "Cannibal Holocaust", "The Bunny Game", "The Human Centipede" or "A Serbian Film"; I have no interest in. My reason for this is because

they're all designed to be repulsive and disgusting. You can't form a connection with the people involved because they're just fodder for the next scene of grotesquerie. But then there are films like "Requiem for a Dream" and "Irreversible", where you do form attachments to the characters. In the case of "Requiem", while disturbing, I couldn't truly get past the inevitability of each character's story, and in the case of "Irreversible"... to tell the truth, I haven't seen it and I don't honestly think I could being the spouse of a rape survivor. Each of these films allows me to connect with the characters and wonder at their fates, and in most of these films, they offer respite from the carnage or the shock or the emotional trauma. The more quiet the hush, the louder the noise that comes after, and that's a lesson that many filmmakers, especially in the horror genre, don't seem to take to heart anymore.

"Angel Heart"

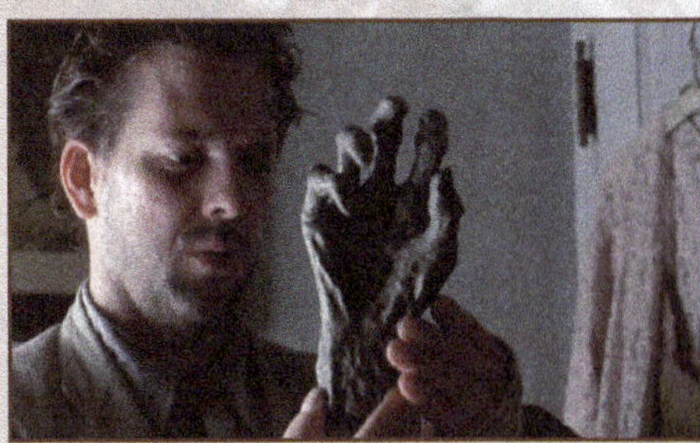

The 1980's were a hell of a decade for Alan Parker, another filmmaker who never seemed satisfied to define himself by making one kind of film or another. From "Pink Floyd's The Wall" to "Birdy" to "Mississippi Burning", he made films that were different and powerful and visually stunning, and none seemed to resemble the other. But "Angel Heart" was a tour de force of story, performance and direction. A blend of 50's hard-luck gumshoe noir and supernatural terror, it was able to transcend the genres of both by infusing the two like a shot of rye in some satanic bar. All of the talk about the film to this day is the highly-controversial blood-soaked sex scene between Mickey Rourke and Lisa Bonet, and while that is truly disturbing, it doesn't hold a candle to the finale. When Harry Angel shatters the vase and sees his dog tags, I mark that as one of the most devastating moments I've ever seen. His wail of anguish at this realization echoes long after the credits have rolled and disturbs more than any amount of copious bloodletting.

"Oldboy" (2003)

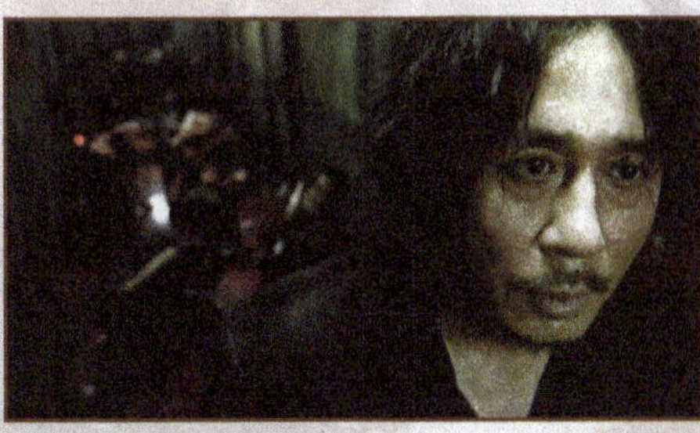

Chan-wook Park loves tales of revenge. From "Sympathy for Mr. Vengeance" to "Lady Vengeance", his unofficial trilogy of revenge stories was often unrelenting but the films had a beating heart to them. With "Oldboy" though, vengeance truly cuts both ways. Min-sik Choi (the only actor that will also appear on another film in this list) plays Oh Dae-su, a character that's already kind of a dick, but once he's kidnapped and held prisoner without explanation in a shabby hotel room for fifteen years, you start to feel a little for the guy. He did have a wife and young daughter, but he had been framed for the murder of his wife during his imprisonment. Now you feel like this guy deserves more consideration. But what starts out as a quest for vengeance and discovery becomes a waking nightmare for Dae-su. When the villain of the piece reveals his revenge on Dae-su (who caught the villain having incestuous relations with his sister back in high school, driving his sister to suicide) as revealing Dae-su's young lover to be his daughter, the moments between Dae-su begging him not to reveal this truth to her and cutting out his own tongue are sheer emotional terror. While the removal of the tongue is indeed as difficult to watch viscerally as anything else I've seen, it's the moments leading up to this that are truly and deeply disturbing.

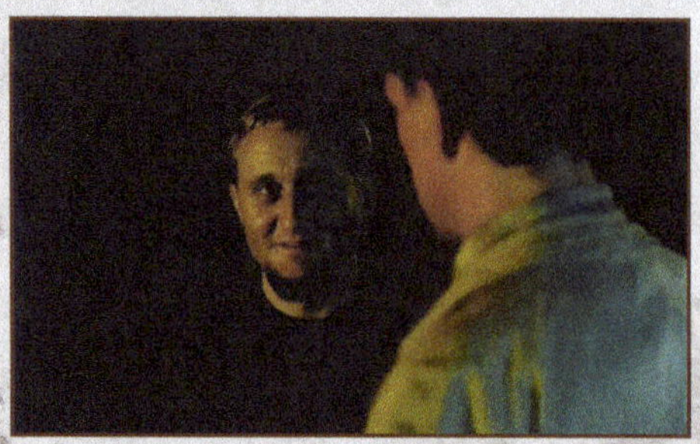

"The Vanishing" (1988)

Not to be confused with the truly awful American remake from 1993, George Sluzier's original Dutch product is truly an amazing, haunting and incredibly troubling experience. Perhaps the most disturbing thing about this film is actually how average everyone seems in it; from the protagonist Rex, searching desperately for his missing fiancée to the kidnapper Raymond who has no conscience and gently taunts our protagonist. Except the kidnapper is no evil genius like John Doe from "Se7en"; he's a relatively normal person with a normal family life. But no moment is quite like when Raymond offers to show Rex what exactly happened to his fiancée. He gives him a cup of drugged coffee and Rex wakes up in a wooden box, buried in the earth. That's bad enough, but when we next see Raymond, he's simply relaxing at his home with his wife and children, completely devoid of any misgivings or conscience about the two people he's killed. It's a horrifying reminder that not all devils wear horns. Speaking of devils…

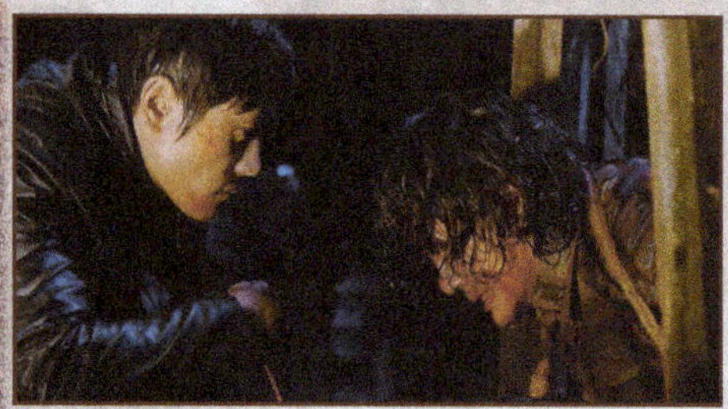

"I Saw the Devil"

Kim Jee-woon's resume, while not as diverse as someone like Alan Parker or Ben Wheatley, is certainly not content to be defined to a single genre. With wild action films like "The Good, The Bad and The Weird" and the Schwarzenegger vehicle "The Last Stand" and with horror like "A Tale of Two Sisters" under his belt, apparently he felt that a hybrid of the two would be a cool idea. And while "I Saw the Devil" is a great film, it's a film I'm in no great rush to watch again. For those unfamiliar, it's a tale of revenge. A sadistic serial killer (played by "Oldboy" himself Min-sik Choi) brutally murders the fiance of an elite Korean intelligence agent (played by Byung-hun Lee). The agent swears revenge by any and all ways and his training has prepared him for it. Knowing the killer's penchant for sadism, the agent swoops in to stop a vicious sexual assault or murder right before it happens and brutally beats the killer, but keeps letting him go. And of all the horrific and disturbing moments of the film, the one that still haunts me is the first of these beatings by the agent, after the killer has beaten and is prepared to sexually assault one of his young victims. It's not the physical aspect of what he does that's so disturbing, but rather that the agent himself is so single-mindedly driven by his revenge that he doesn't care about what the killer was going to do. He takes no time to comfort his would-be victim, but almost completely disregards her. It's a key moment in the transformation of the "hero". They don't cross axis with one another, but rather they end the film meeting in the middle, when the agent has his final revenge. If there was ever a film that reflected Nietzsche's quote, "Battle not with monsters, lest ye become a monster", this is it. Speaking of monsters…

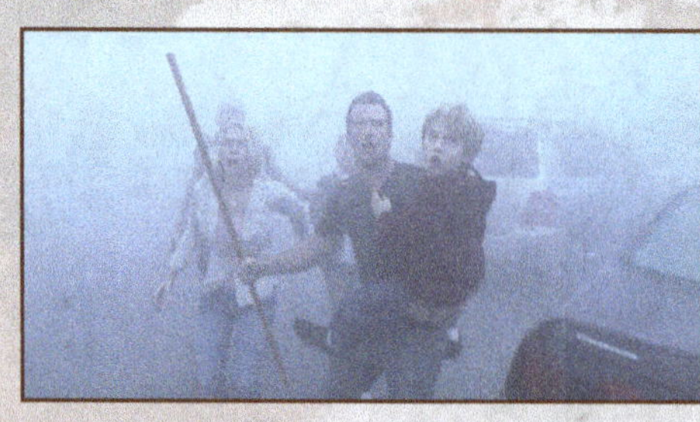

"The Mist"

When I heard that Frank Darabont was adapting a Stephen King horror story, I was pretty excited, considering that his previous adaptations of "The Shawshank Redemption" and "The Green Mile", while being excellent, were more tragic/bittersweet that terrifying. But when you watch "The Mist", it deals with a lot of King's favorite character archetypes (the creative hero, the kindly yet acerbic elderly woman, the town outcast, and the cruel religious zealot) being placed into a throwback to the B-grade monster movies of the 50's and 60's with a modern twist (on home video, you can see the black and white version of the film, which really hits that point home, and is, in my opinion, the superior version). There are moments of real terror as the extra-dimensional monsters threaten a cross-section of humanity as they're trapped in a supermarket, but nothing truly disturbing… at least not until the end. And while the "Twilight Zone"-esque ending furthers the tragedy, there are very few moments in cinema history that affected me the way David's son waking up right before he's killed in the would-be mercy killing that he shares with Jeffrey DeMunn, Frances Sternhagen and Laurie Holden's characters. The question of how can you save people you've sworn to protect from harm when there's no way to save them is only part of the nihilistic questions you end up asking yourself. For a film that employs a B-movie premise, Darabont keeps it grounded in all-too-real human instinct and emotion, making the final moments of the film just soul-crushing.

Wow. Just writing about these films takes a lot out of me because I have to recount these moments so that I can pass them onto you. A truly disturbing film is something that has become something of a rarity. A lot of horror of the modern era tends to lean into more of a parlor of grotesquerie and insisting on being shocking rather than truly horrific. Some of the films on this list wouldn't even really qualify as "horror" as far as genre is concerned, but are more horrifying than what standard horror fare could ever be and that is how these films will continue to stand the test of time and continue to test the mind. ∎

SEATTLE SOUNDS

by Dawn Wood

SKöLD SEATTLE SHOW 2016

Tim Sköld has been appealing to, impressing and delighting us since 1989 with Shotgun Messiah. I still remember Sköld's transition into the industrial realms that shaped his illustrious career. "Violent New Breed" was the divine perfect merging of industrial and metal. The album was released in 1993 and is now considered a cult classic due to the industrial influences. However, at the time of release, it received mixed reviews and unfortunate public indifference, which eventually ended Shotgun Messiah and led Sköld to embark on his solo project. Some of the songs on the solo Sköld album were used in movies like "Disturbing Behavior" ("Hail Mary"), "Universal Soldier": "The Return" ("Chaos") and the PlayStation game "Twisted Metal 4" ("Chaos").

During his solo career, Sköld also provided remixes for bands. He met KMFDM frontman Sascha Konietzko during his solo time in the studio. Sköld performed as fill-in guitarist with Taime Downe's The Newlydeads on December 13, 2000 at the Pretty Ugly Club in Los Angeles. Sköld, on bass, joined Ohgr, a project of Skinny Puppy vocalist Nivek Ogre, for the tour in support of its first album, "Welt." Sköld's involvement with Marilyn Manson began as producer for the single "Tainted Love," and he officially joined Marilyn Manson in 2002 after the departure of bassist Twiggy Ramirez. At this time, not only was Sköld the bassist for the band, but he was also producing, editing, creating artwork, electronics, programming drums and beats, playing guitar, keyboards, accordion and synthesizer bass for the album "The Golden Age of Grotesque." Sköld produced Motionless in White's studio album "Infamous" and also contributed songwriting on 5 songs.

And so here we are, at the long awaited return of Sköld in 2016, when rejoined with Metropolis Records to release the new solo stuff. In support of this album, Sköld began "The Undoing Tour 2016" in May, 2016 with the western United States; the live line up featured Tiffany Lowe on keyboards and Eli James on drums. I was fortunate enough to be playing in the band as direct support to Sköld for the Seattle show. The show was jammed packed full of energy and he performed classic songs from the past (much to the delight of the crowd) in addition to songs off of his latest release "The Undoing."

Prior Carpe Nocturne interviewee Asher Vast of Endless Sunder also (just so happened) to produce Skold's video while Skold was in Seattle. The amazing video was filmed at Satsop Nuclear Power Plant in Elma, Washington. Asher, accompanied by Kevin Preston, Corey Wittenborn and Jesse Orr, captured stunning scenery. The shots were absolutely breathtaking and the video has already skyrocketed on YouTube in popularity. Asher and Kevin's video company is called Tetraknot Production. You can find out more about their work here: http://www.tetraknot.com/

All and all, the Sköld show was absolutely fantastic. We, at Carpe Nocturne, look forward to more shows in 2017!

Catch Sköld on Instagram: https://www.instagram.com/tim_skold/
Facebook: https://www.facebook.com/skoldofficial
His brand new video by Tetraknot Film Production: https://www.youtube.com/watch?v=tcvEF7rSWMk ∎

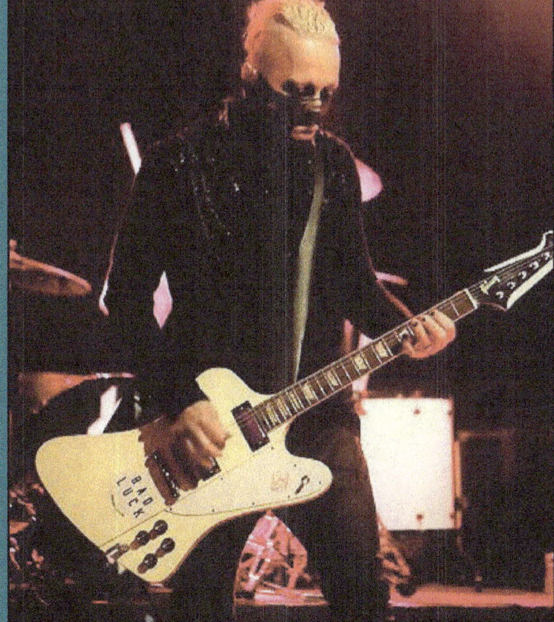

www.ingramcontent.com/pod-product-compliance
Lightning Source LLC
Chambersburg PA
CBHW082249060726
47592CB00021B/3305